100 facts
Arms & Armour

100 *facts*
Arms & Armour

Rupert Matthews

Miles
KeLLY

First published as hardback in 2007 by Miles Kelly Publishing Ltd
Harding's Barn, Bardfield End Green, Thaxted, Essex, CM6 3PX

This edition published 2014

4 6 8 10 9 7 5

Publishing Director: Belinda Gallagher
Creative Director: Jo Cowan
Editor: Rosalind Neave
Editorial Assistant: Carly Blake
Volume Designer: Michelle Cannatella
Image Manager: Lorraine King
Indexer: Jane Parker
Production Manager: Elizabeth Collins
Reprographics: Anthony Cambray, Stephan Davis,
Liberty Newton, Ian Paulyn
Archive Manager: Jennifer Cozens
Assets: Lorraine King

ISBN 978-1-84810-104-3

Printed in China

British Library Cataloguing-in-Publication Data
A catalogue record for this book is available from the British Library

ACKNOWLEDGEMENTS
The publishers would like to thank the following artists who have contributed to this book:
Peter Dennis, Mike Foster, Alan Hancocks, Richard Hook, Angus McBride,
Andrea Morandi, Alex Pang, Carlo Pauletto, Mike Saunders, Mike White
Cover artwork: Mike White
All other artworks from the Miles Kelly Artwork Bank

The publishers would like to thank the following source for the use of its photograph:
Page 43 Ninja Museum, Uemo

All other photographs are from:
Corel, digitalSTOCK, digitalvision, John Foxx, iStockphoto.com, PhotoAlto,
PhotoDisc, PhotoEssentials, PhotoPro, Stockbyte

Made with paper from a sustainable forest

www.mileskelly.net
info@mileskelly.net

Contents

Weapons of war

1 People have used arms and armour to hunt, defend themselves and attack other people for thousands of years. Arms are weapons that are carried by a single person. Armour is something that is worn or carried to protect against injury. Early armour was made from wood or leather, and the first arms were made from wood or stone.

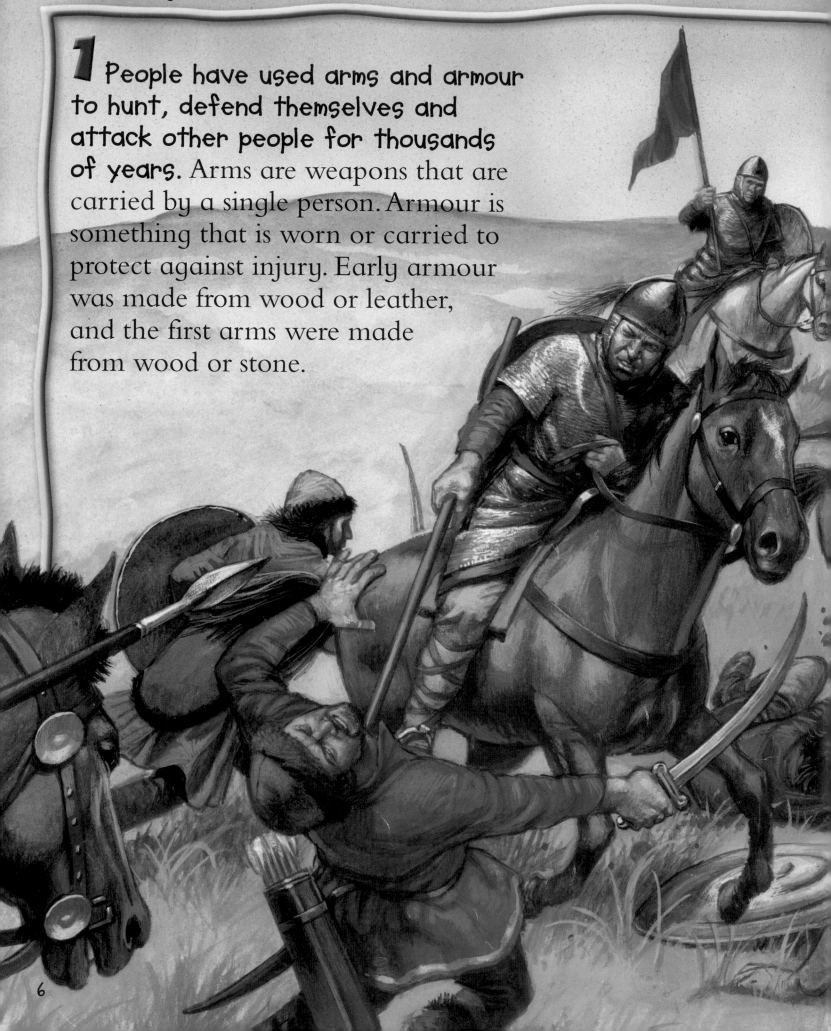

▼ At the battle of Lechfeld in AD 955 the Germans crushed the much larger army of Magyars. The Germans succeeded because they were wearing suits of mail armour and carrying new weapons.

The first arms

2 **Some of the first arms were made from stone.** The earliest humans lived hundreds of thousands of years ago. Archaeologists (scientists who study the remains of ancient humans) have found weapons made of sharpened stone that were made by these ancient people.

▲ This handaxe is made from a single piece of stone. It was held in the hand and used with a chopping motion.

3 **Early weapons were used for both hunting and fighting.** Archaeologists have found bones from cattle, deer and mammoths, and discovered that these animals were hunted and killed by ancient people using stone weapons.

▶ Around 75,000 years ago, spears were made from a stone point, which was attached to a wooden handle with leather straps.

4 **The first warriors did not use armour.** It is thought that early tribes of people fought each other to get control of the best hunting grounds or sources of water. These men may not have used armour, relying instead on dodging out of the way of enemy weapons.

5 Shields were an early form of defence.

A thrust from a spear could be stopped by holding a piece of wood in the way. People soon began to produce shields made of flat pieces of wood with a handle on the back. Over the years, shields came to be produced in many different shapes, and from a wide range of materials including metal, wood and leather.

▲ By about 300 BC, the Celts of Europe were producing beautiful shields decorated with bronze and colourful enamel. Some, like this one found in London, may have been used in ceremonies.

▶ Flint is a hard stone that can be chipped and flaked into a wide variety of shapes to produce different types of weapons, such as these points or tips for arrows.

6 Spears were the first effective weapons.

Many early spears consisted of a stone point mounted on the end of a wooden pole. With a spear, a man could reach his enemy while still out of reach of the opponent's hand-held weapons. The earliest known spears are 400,000 years old and were found in Germany.

I DON'T BELIEVE IT!

The oldest signs of warfare come from Krapina, Croatia. Human bones over 120,000 years old have been found there that show marks caused by stone spearheads.

Ancient civilizations

7 **Early Egyptians may have used their hair as armour.** Some ancient Egyptians grew their hair very long, then plaited it thickly and wrapped it around their heads when going into battle. It is thought that this may have helped protect their heads.

▲ The Egyptian pharaoh Tutankhamun is shown firing a bow while riding in a chariot to attack the enemies of Egypt.

8 **Some Egyptian soldiers had shields that were as big as themselves.** Around 1800 BC, soldiers carried shields that were the height of a man. They hid behind their shields as the enemy attacked, then leapt out to use their spears.

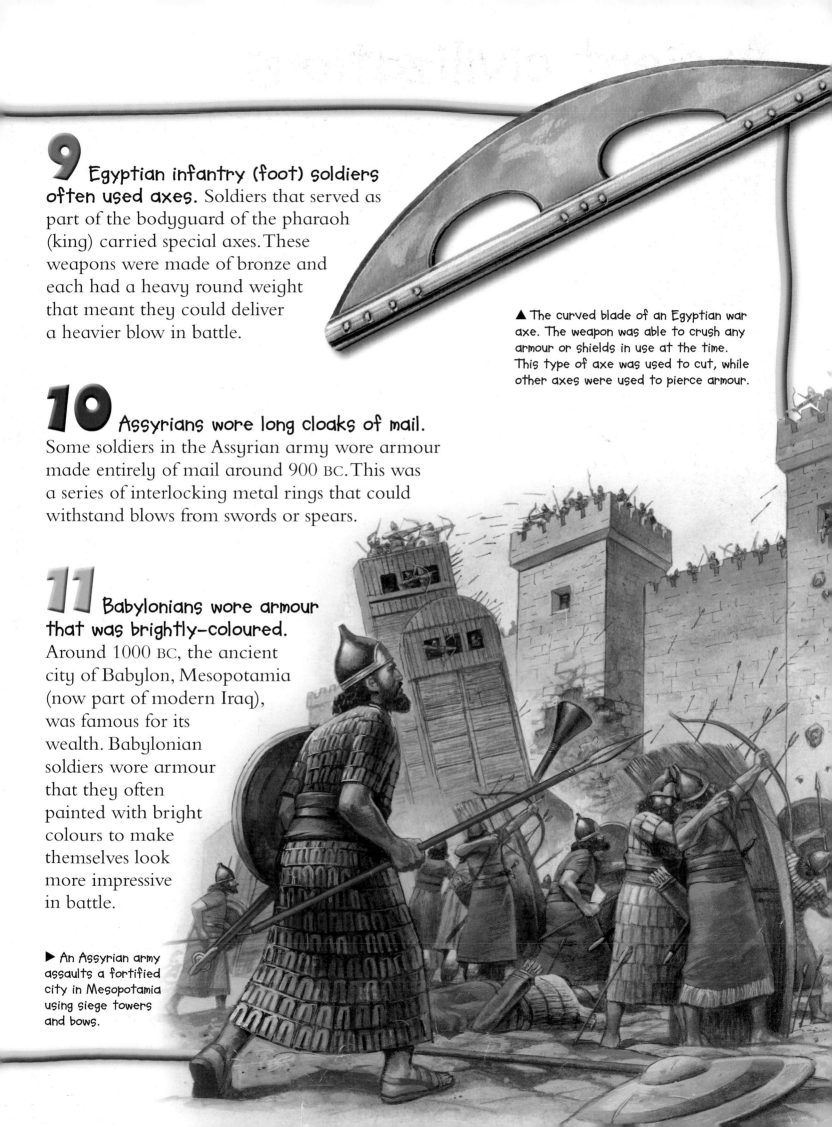

9 Egyptian infantry (foot) soldiers often used axes. Soldiers that served as part of the bodyguard of the pharaoh (king) carried special axes. These weapons were made of bronze and each had a heavy round weight that meant they could deliver a heavier blow in battle.

▲ The curved blade of an Egyptian war axe. The weapon was able to crush any armour or shields in use at the time. This type of axe was used to cut, while other axes were used to pierce armour.

10 Assyrians wore long cloaks of mail. Some soldiers in the Assyrian army wore armour made entirely of mail around 900 BC. This was a series of interlocking metal rings that could withstand blows from swords or spears.

11 Babylonians wore armour that was brightly-coloured. Around 1000 BC, the ancient city of Babylon, Mesopotamia (now part of modern Iraq), was famous for its wealth. Babylonian soldiers wore armour that they often painted with bright colours to make themselves look more impressive in battle.

▶ An Assyrian army assaults a fortified city in Mesopotamia using siege towers and bows.

Hoplites and phalanxes

12 **Hoplites were armoured infantry.** From about 700 BC Greek infantry (foot soldiers) were equipped with a shield, helmet, spear and sword. They were called 'hoplites' ('armoured men'). Each hoplite used his own weapons and armour.

13 **A Greek who lost his shield was a coward.** The shield carried by hoplites was over one metre across and made of wood and bronze. It was very heavy, and anyone trying to run away from an enemy would throw it away, so men who lost their shields in battle were often accused of cowardice.

14 **Hoplites fought in formations called phalanxes.** When going into battle, hoplites stood shoulder to shoulder so that their shields overlapped, and pointed their spears forwards over the shields. A phalanx was made up of six or more ranks of hoplites, one behind the other.

▶ The success of Greek soldiers in battle depended on them keeping tightly in formation so that enemy soldiers could not get past the line of shields.

I DON'T BELIEVE IT!

Spartan hoplites were so tough that they reckoned they could easily win any battle, even if they were outnumbered by as many as five to one!

15 Greek spears had a 'lizard stabber'. Hoplite spears had a bronze spike at the bottom end. This was used to stick the spear upright into the ground and was called a 'sauroter', meaning 'lizard stabber'.

16 The best helmets were made from a single sheet of metal. Skilled metalworkers in the Greek city of Corinth invented a way to make a helmet by beating a single sheet of bronze into shape. This produced a helmet that was much stronger than one made of several pieces of metal. The helmets were called 'Corinthian'.

13

Roman legions

▲ A Roman legion marches out of a border fortress supervised by the legate, who commands the legion.

17 **Armoured infantry formed the legions.** The main fighting formation of the Roman army was the legion, a force of about 6000 men. Most were equipped with body armour, a helmet, a large rectangular shield, a sword and a throwing spear.

▶ The armour of a legionary was made up of several pieces, each of which could be replaced if it was damaged.

18 **Roman armour was made of metal strips.** At the height of the Roman Empire, around AD 50 to AD 250, legionaries wore armour called *lorica segmentata*. It was made up of strips of metal that were bent to fit the body, and held together by straps and buckles.

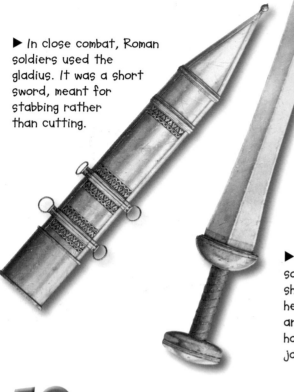

▶ In close combat, Roman soldiers used the gladius. It was a short sword, meant for stabbing rather than cutting.

21 Roman swords were copied from the Spanish.
After 200 BC, Roman soldiers carried swords with straight blades and sharp points. They were copied from swords used by Spanish soldiers who defeated the Romans in battle.

▶ An auxiliary soldier wearing a short mail tunic and helmet, and carrying an oval shield. He has a gladius and javelin as weapons.

19 Roman auxiliaries wore cheaper armour.
Every Roman legion included soldiers called auxiliaries (soldiers from places other than Rome). These units had to provide their own armour, often wearing tunics covered with mail or scale armour, which was made up of lots of small metal plates.

20 Roman shields could form a 'tortoise'.
One tactic used by the Romans was called the 'testudo', or 'tortoise'. Soldiers formed short lines close together, holding their shields so they interlocked on all sides and overhead, just like the shell of a tortoise. In this formation they could advance on an enemy, safe from spears or arrows.

The fall of Rome

22 Later Roman infantry abandoned armour. By around AD 350, Roman legions preferred to fight by moving quickly around the battlefield. They stopped wearing heavy armour and relied upon large shields and metal helmets for protection.

23 Later Roman armies used mercenary archers. Roman commanders found that archers were useful for attacking barbarian tribesmen. Few Romans were skilled at archery, so the Romans hired soldiers (mercenaries) from other countries to fight as archers in the Roman army.

24 Roman shields were brightly coloured. Each unit in the late Roman army had its own design of shield. Some were decorated with pictures of eagles, scorpions or dolphins, while others had lightning bolts or spirals.

◄ Late Roman shields were brightly decorated. Each unit in the army had its own design.

▼ By about AD 350, Roman armies had large numbers of cavalry that were used to fight fast-moving campaigns.

25 **The eagle was a sacred standard.** Each Roman legion had an eagle standard, the *aquila* – a bronze eagle covered in gold leaf mounted on top of a pole about 3 metres long. The *aquila* was thought to be sacred to the gods and it was a great humiliation if it was captured by the enemy.

▶ A Roman *aquilifer* (standard bearer) carrying an eagle standard. Each legion had an eagle standard that was sacred to the gods. Units of cavalry and auxiliaries carried standards of other animals instead of an eagle.

26 **Later Roman cavalry had enormous shields.** One later group of Roman mounted soldiers was the *scutati*. These men wore coats of mail, and carried enormous shields with which they were expected to defend themselves and their horses. They would gallop towards the enemy army, throw javelins and then ride away before the enemy could strike back.

I DON'T BELIEVE IT!

Alaric the Goth and his men looted Rome in AD 410. Alaric was famously known to carry a sword with a handle made of solid gold.

17

Gladiators

27 **Gladiators fought in the arena.** Many Roman cities had a building called an arena, which had banks of seating and an oval area in the centre covered with sand. The arena was used to stage fights between men known as gladiators, who were trained to fight to the death to please the crowd. They used swords, spears, knives and other weapons when fighting.

Samnite

28 **Gladiator helmets were large and decorative.** Fights were staged as part of an impressive show. The armour worn by gladiators was decorated with bright feathers, beautiful designs and may even have been coated with silver or gold leaf.

Thracian

◀ Most gladiator helmets had metal masks to cover and protect the face.

▲ Samnite gladiators used a large shield and short sword, while Thracian gladiators had a small shield and curved sword.

29 Gladiator armour was not designed to save lives.

The purpose of these fights was to put on a show of skill with weapons, and the penalty for defeat was death. If a gladiator was wounded in the arms or legs it was unlikely to kill him, but would mean an end to the fight. Some gladiators wore leg and arm armour so that the show could continue for as long as possible.

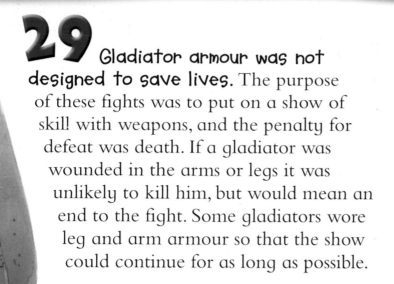

▶ A helmet worn by an andabata gladiator. It had no eyeholes so the wearer had to fight blind.

▲ The Retiarius was a type of gladiator based on a fisherman, so he carried a net and trident.

30 One type of helmet had no eyeholes.

Sometimes gladiator show organizers would make the gladiators wear helmets called andabatae, which covered the eyes, so the gladiators had to rely entirely on their sense of sound.

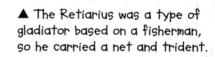

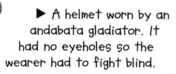

QUIZ

1. Which gladiators fought without being able to see?
2. Which types of gladiator carried a curved sword?
3. What was the name of the building where gladiators fought?

Answers:
1. Andabatae 2. Thracian 3. The arena

The Barbarians

31 **Celts used chariots to intimidate the enemy.** Battles between rival Celt tribes often began with famous warriors riding in chariots and performing tricks to show how skilled they were.

32 **The Huns were lightly equipped.** Around the year AD 370 the Huns swept into Europe from Asia. They fought on horseback with bows and spears, but wore no armour. They moved quickly, and showed no mercy.

33 **The Dacian falx was a terrible weapon.** The Dacians lived in what is now Romania around AD 400–600 and fought mostly on foot. Some Dacian warriors carried a long, curved sword with a broad blade that was called a falx. This weapon was so sharp and heavy that it could slice a person in half.

▶ The speed and accuracy of mounted Hun archers terrified the Romans.

34 **The Franks were named after their favourite weapon.** One tribe of Germans who lived around AD 300-600 were famous for using small throwing axes. These weapons had a short haft and a small, square-shaped head and were called 'francisca'. The men who used them were called franks, and soon the entire tribe took the name. They later gave the name to the country France.

◀ A Dacian warrior carrying a falx. Dacians were a people who lived outside the Roman Empire and often fought the Romans.

QUIZ

1. Did Hun warriors wear armour?
2. What was a 'francisca'?
3. Who did the Romans call 'barbarians'?

Answers:
1. No 2. A small throwing axe 3. Any uncivilized people who lived outside the Roman Empire

▼ A helmet belonging to an Anglo–Saxon king who ruled in East Anglia, England, about AD 625. It was made of iron and decorated with gold and silver.

35 Many barbarians wore armour decorated with gold, silver and precious stones. 'Barbarian' was the Roman name for uncivilized peoples outside the Roman Empire. They loved to show how rich they were and did this to emphasise their status within their tribe.

The Heavenly Kingdom

36 Chinese troops wore armour made of dozens of metal plates. The plates were about 8 centimetres by 6 centimetres and were sewn onto a leather garment or held together by leather thongs. Around 221 BC the various Chinese states were united. The Chinese believed this unity was the basis of their power and wealth.

37 Silk shirts helped protect against arrows. Many Chinese soldiers wore silk shirts under their armour. If an arrow pierced the armour it would drag the silk shirt into the wound without tearing it. By gently pulling on the shirt, the arrow could be extracted cleanly.

▼ A patrol of Chinese soldiers guarding the Great Wall around AD 200.

38 **Crossbows were first used in China.** They were more powerful than the bows used by nomadic tribesmen living north of China, so they were often used by troops manning the northern frontier. Crossbows consist of a short, powerful bow mounted on a wooden shaft and operated by a trigger.

39 **Infantry used pole weapons.** Chinese infantry often carried spears around 2 metres in length. Often an axelike chopping weapon, a slicing blade or a side spike replaced the spearhead. These weapons allowed the infantry to attack their enemies with a variety of actions to get around shields.

40 **Chinese cavalry were heavily armed.** When patrolling border regions, the Chinese cavalry operated in large formations that could defeat any tribal force causing trouble. The men were equipped with iron helmets and body armour, together with wooden shields and long lances tipped with iron.

QUIZ

1. In what year was China first united?
2. What did Chinese soldiers wear as protection against arrows?
3. Did the nomadic tribesmen live north or south of China?

Answers:
1. 221 BC 2. Silk shirts 3. North of China

The Dark Ages

41 The Dark Ages followed the fall of Rome in AD 410. Barbarian peoples took over the Western Roman Empire, and ancient culture and skills were lost. The Eastern Roman Empire lost power and lands to barbarians, but survived to become the Byzantine Empire. The Byzantines continued to use Roman-style arms and armour.

▲ English warriors patrol the great dyke built by King Offa of Mercia to define the border with Wales in AD 784.

42 English cavalry were lightly armed. Britain was invaded and settled by Germanic tribes from around AD 450, and by around AD 700 they ruled most of the island. Only the richest Englishmen wore body armour. Most went into battle armed with a spear and sword and carrying a round shield and a helmet as armour.

43 Berserkers wore animal skins instead of armour. Some Viking warriors were known as 'berserkers', meaning 'bear-shirts', from their habit of wearing bear or wolf skins in battle.

◀ A Viking berserker attacks dressed in a bear skin. These warriors would fall into a terrible rage in battle and seemed to ignore all danger.

QUIZ

1. Which warriors wore animal skins?
2. Who won the Battle of Lechfeld?
3. Who built a dyke between England and Wales?

Answers:
1. Berserkers
2. The Germans 3. Offa

44 **The battleaxe was a terrible weapon.** Many Scandinavian peoples used a battleaxe that had a haft up to 2 metres long and a blade more than 30 centimetres across. It was used with both hands. In the hands of a master, it could kill a horse and rider with a single blow.

◀ A Viking raiding party wielding battleaxes attacks a group of Englishmen.

45 **The heavy cavalrymen ruled the battlefield.** In AD 955 a small army of German knights destroyed the larger Magyar cavalry at the Battle of Lechfeld, in Germany. Knights (mounted men in armour carrying a spear and sword) were recognized as the most effective type of soldier.

25

Early knights

46 **The first knights wore mail armour.** Around the year 1000, most body armour in Europe was made of mail. This was flexible to wear and could stop a sword blow with ease. Such armour was expensive to make so only richer men could afford to wear it.

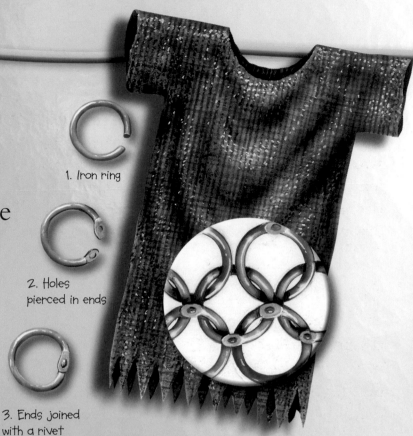

1. Iron ring

2. Holes pierced in ends

3. Ends joined with a rivet

▲ Mail armour was made by linking together hundreds of small iron rings. The rings could be linked in a number of different ways, just like knitting a sweater.

47 **Shields were decorated to identify their owners.** From about 1150, knights wore helmets that covered their faces for extra protection. Around the same time, they began to paint heraldic designs (coats of arms) on their shields so that they could recognize each other in battle.

48 **Early knights sometimes used leather armour.** Mail armour was effective, but heavy and expensive, so some knights wore armour made of boiled, hardened leather. This was lighter and easier to wear, and was still some defence against attack.

◀ A knight in about 1100. He wears a shirt and trousers made of mail and a helmet shaped from a sheet of steel. His shield is made of wood.

49 **Plate armour gave better protection than mail.** By about 1300, new types of arrow and swords had developed to pierce mail armour. This led to the development of plate armour, made of sheets of steel shaped to fit the body, which arrows and swords could not easily penetrate.

50 **The mace could smash armour to pieces.** The most effective of the crushing weapons developed to destroy plate armour, the mace had a big metal head on a long shaft. A blow from a mace crushed plate armour, breaking the bones of the person wearing it.

The armour around the stomach and groin had to be flexible enough to allow bending and twisting movements

The most complicated section of plate armour was the gauntlet that covered the hands. It might contain 30 pieces of metal

The legs and feet were protected by armour that covered the limbs entirely

▶ A suit of plate armour made in Europe in the early 14th century.

Archers and peasants

51 **Infantry were usually poorly armed.** Around 1000 years ago, ordinary farmers or craftsmen would turn out to protect their homes against an enemy army. Such men could not afford armour and usually carried just a spear and a large knife or an axe. They usually guarded castles and towns.

▼ A Welsh spearman in about 1350. He carries a spear and sword, but has no armour at all.

◀ An English archer in about 1400. He wears a metal helmet and has quilted body armour.

52 **The longbow was a deadly weapon.** From about 1320 the English included thousands of archers in their armies. The archers were trained to shoot up to eight arrows each minute, producing a deadly rain of arrows that could slaughter an enemy force at a distance.

53 Some weapons were based on farming tools. Many soldiers used weapons that were simply specialized forms of farming tools. The bill was based on a hedge-trimmer but could be used to pull a knight from his horse, and then smash through his plate armour.

▲ The heads of an English bill (left) and Dutch godendag (right). Both were pole weapons used by infantrymen.

54 Crossbows were used in some countries. Soldiers from Italy, the Low Countries (now Belgium and the Netherlands) and some other areas of Europe preferred to use the crossbow instead of the bow. It could not shoot as quickly, but was easier to learn how to use and much more powerful.

55 Some foot soldiers wore armour. Infantrymen sent to war by wealthy towns or cities were often equipped with armour. They usually formed solid formations with their long spears pointing forward, and could be highly effective in battle.

◄ A crossbowman would hide behind a large shield called a pavise while reloading his weapon.

Make a castle bookmark

You will need:
card • scissors • crayons • sticky tape

1. Draw a tower 12 centimetres tall on card and cut it out.

2. Draw the top half of a soldier holding a shield on card and cut it out.

3. Colour in the tower and soldier.

4. Place the soldier so that his body is behind the tower and his shield in front.

5. Tape the soldier's body to the back of the tower to hold it in place.

Your bookmark is ready to use!

Later knights

56 Armoured knights were the most important troops. Knights had the best arms and armour and were the most experienced men in any army, so they were often put in command.

57 Knights sometimes fought on foot, instead of on horseback. English knights fought on foot after about 1300. This enabled them to hold a position more securely and co-operate more effectively with other soldiers.

▶ The bascinet helmet had a visor that could be lifted so the wearer could see and breathe.

I DON'T BELIEVE IT!

At the Battle of Agincourt in France in 1415, the English killed 10,000 Frenchmen, but only about 100 Englishmen lost their lives.

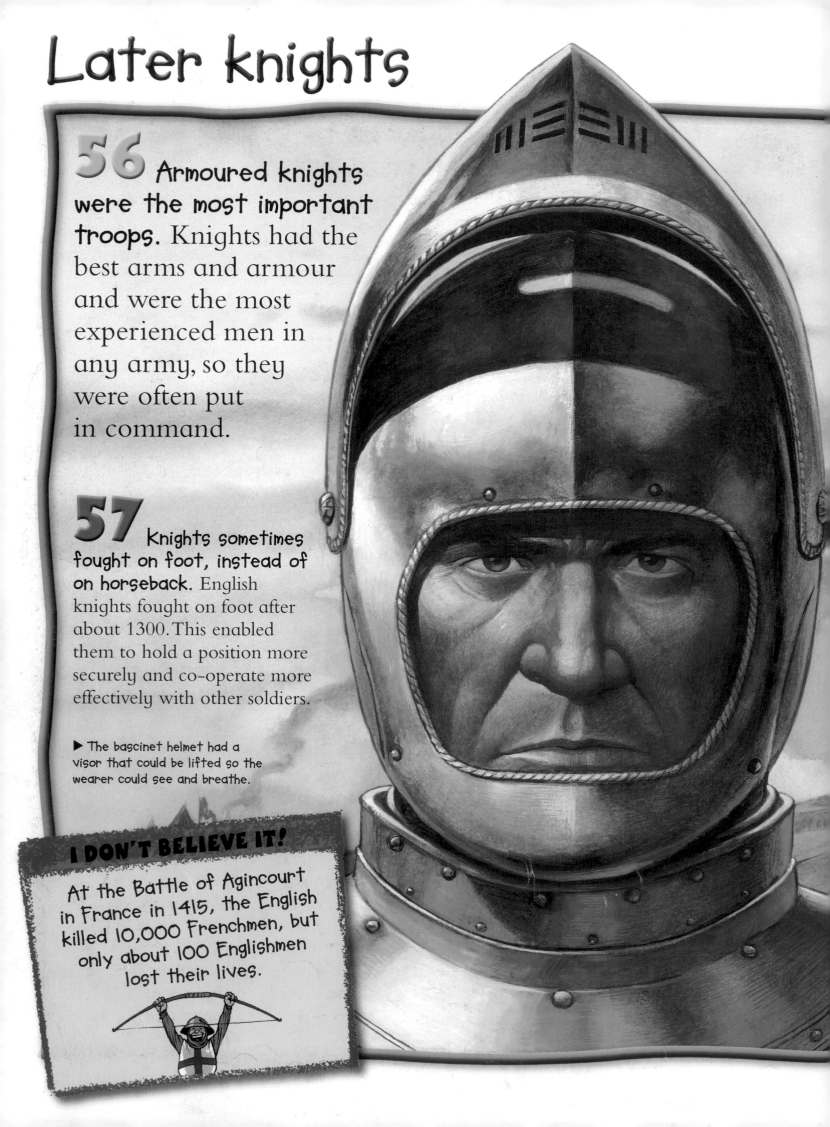

58 Horse armour made of metal and leather was introduced to protect horses. By about 1300, knights began to dress their horses in various sorts of armour. Horses without armour could be killed or injured by enemy arrows or spears, leaving the knight open to attack. Men with armoured horses were put in the front rank during battle.

▶ Horse armour was shaped to fit the horse's head and neck, then was left loose to dangle down over the legs.

59 The flail was a difficult weapon to use. It consisted of a big metal ball studded with spikes and attached to a chain on a wooden handle. It could inflict terrible injuries, but also swing back unexpectedly, so only men who practised with it for hours each day could use it properly.

◀ A knight uses a flail in foot combat.

60 Each man had his place in battle. Before each battle, the commander would position his men to ensure that the abilities of each were put to best use. The men with the best armour were placed where the enemy was expected to attack, while archers were positioned on the flank (left or right side) where they could shoot across the battlefield. Lightly armoured men were held in the rear, ready to chase enemy soldiers if they began to retreat.

Desert warfare

61 **Bows were made of many materials.** In the desert areas of the Middle East, soldiers used bows made from layers of animal horn, bone and sinew that were stuck tightly together and then carved into shape. These were called 'composite bows', and fired arrows with much greater force than longbows.

▲ The recurved bow was short, but powerful.

62 **The Mongols wore light armour.** A tribe from central Asia called the Mongols were led by Genghis Khan (1162–1227). Their armour was light because there was a lack of iron in Central Asia. As a result, they developed tactics based on fast-moving cavalry attacks.

63 Curved swords were known as scimitars. Armourers working in the city of Damascus, Syria, invented a new way to make swords around the year 1100. This involved folding the steel over on itself several times while the metal was white hot. The new type of steel was used to make curved swords that were both light in weight and incredibly sharp, called scimitars.

64 Teneke armour was made up of a mail coat onto which were fixed overlapping pieces of flat metal. These pieces were about 6 centimetres by 2 centimetres. The plates were loosely hinged so that air could pass through easily but blows from a sword could not. The armour was light, comfortable and effective, but it was also expensive.

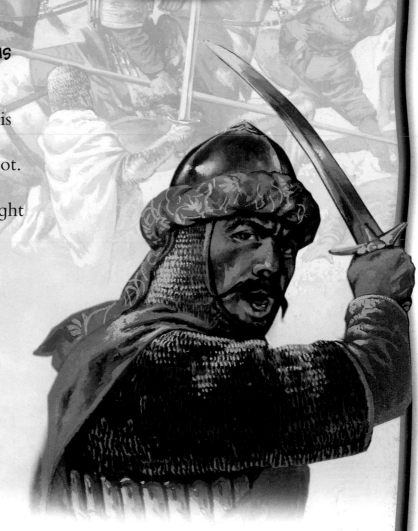

▲ A Saracen wearing teneke armour and wielding a scimitar. The Saracens wore flowing cloaks and turbans to help combat the heat of the desert.

◄ A Mongol army attacks men from the city of Kiev, Ukraine. Although designed for grasslands and deserts, Mongol weaponry was effective in cold forests as well.

65 Armour was light because of the desert heat. The plate armour in use in Europe was not worn in the deserts of the Middle East. The plates of metal stopped air circulating around the body and were very uncomfortable to wear. Instead desert fighters in the 13th to 15th centuries wore loose robes and light pieces of armour.

Indian arms

▼ An Indian soldier who wears no armour, but carries a shield and a pata sword.

▶ Indian shields often had intricate designs to make them look more impressive.

66 India had a unique tradition of arms manufacture. Between 1650 and 1800 the vast lands south of the Himalayas, modern India, Pakistan and Bangladesh, were divided into lots of small states. Each state had its own army, and made great efforts to have impressive weapons.

67 The khanda was a sword with a long, straight blade. These swords had heavy, double-edged blades that often had handles big enough to allow them to be held in both hands. Larger khanda were slung from a belt over the shoulder so that they hung down the user's back.

68 Indian soldiers used the pata. This was an iron glove (gauntlet) that extended almost to the elbow, attached to a sword blade. It was very useful for thrusting, especially when attacking infantry from horseback, but was less effective at cutting.

69 Talwars were curved swords with a single, sharp cutting edge. The handles were often rounded, rather like the butt of a pistol. They were highly decorated with silver, gold and semi-precious stones.

▲ The talwar sword was invented around AD 1000 and was used in battle for over 900 years.

70 Elephants were used in warfare. A small platform, ('howdah'), was strapped to the back of the elephant. Men armed with bows, or later with guns, sat in the howdah and shot at the enemy over the elephant's head.

▶ War elephants were often covered in armour, while the howdah, in which the soldiers sat, could be covered with iron.

Island wars

71 **Polynesians fought without armour or shields.** The islands in the Pacific Ocean were home to people of the Polynesian culture. Before contact with Europeans around 1750, the Polynesians made their weapons from natural materials. They preferred to rely on skill and movement in battle rather than armour, though some men wore thick shirts of plaited coconut fibres as protection.

72 **Shark teeth were made into swords.** In western Polynesia, shark teeth were added to the sides of long clubs to produce a weapon called the tebutje. This was used to cut as well as smash and was a vicious close-combat weapon.

▼ A Polynesian war canoe on its way to a raid on another island. The warriors paddling the canoe kept their weapons beside them.

▲ Boomerangs often had decorative carvings or were brightly painted.

73 The boomerang didn't always come back.

Native Australian people used spears and bows and arrows, as well as the boomerang. This heavy throwing stick was shaped so that it spun round in the air and could be thrown with accuracy. Only the lighter boomerangs, used for hunting birds, were designed to come back to the thrower.

74 War clubs were favoured weapons.

Wooden clubs were carved from single pieces of wood and were over one metre in length. They had wide, heavy heads that were often elaborately carved with shapes and patterns.

▶ A Maori mere, or short club. These weapons were made from very hard woods.

75 The Maori used wooden weapons.

The Polynesian people who live in New Zealand are known as the Maori. They produced unique types of club. One type was the mere, which had a short handle and a wide curved blade that could be used for slashing at the enemy.

I DON'T BELIEVE IT!

In the Fiji islands warriors would often use a wooden club shaped like a pineapple to attack their victims.

African arms

76 **The iklwa was a deadly weapon.** The Zulu nation of southern Africa was ruled by King Shaka from 1816–1828, who built up an empire covering thousands of square kilometres. Shaka introduced a new weapon, the iklwa, a short spear with a broad blade used for stabbing. It proved more deadly than the traditional throwing spears used by other peoples in the area.

77 **Assegai were throwing spears.** They had smaller and lighter heads than the iklwa. Zulu warriors would begin a battle by throwing their two or three assegai. Then they would run quickly forward to attack with their iklwa.

78 **Helmets were for show, not defence.** Zulu warriors wore headdresses to make them look tall and impressive. They were made of wickerwork with tall ostrich feathers, flowing crane feathers and strips of coloured fur or woollen tufts attached.

79 **Knobkerries could crush skulls.** Many Zulu warriors carried a heavy wooden club, or knobkerrie, as well as the iklwa. If the iklwa was lost, the knobkerrie could be used for close fighting.

80 **Shields were made of cowhide.** Zulu shields were nearly 2 metres in length, and were cut from cowhide, which was laced onto a central wooden pole with strips of leather.

Make Zulu puppets

You will need:
card • ice-lolly sticks
crayons • glue

1. Draw some Zulu warriors onto card.
2. Cut out each of the warriors and colour them in.
3. Glue an ice-lolly stick to the back of each warrior.
4. If you make enough Zulus, glue the lolly sticks to a straight piece of wood so that the warriors form a rank.

◀ A Zulu impi, or army, on the march. Boys followed the warriors carrying bedding, food and spare weapons.

The Americas

81 **In South America, spears were thrown at the start of a battle.** The Aztec people built up a large empire in what is now Mexico between 1400 and 1510. Their warriors won a series of battles against other American peoples. Each battle began with men on both sides throwing light javelins at the enemy. Then the men would charge at each other to fight at close quarters.

◄ In battle, some Aztec warriors dressed as eagles, jaguars and other fierce animals.

82 **Obsidian stone was razor sharp.** The Aztec, Maya and other peoples of South America did not know how to make iron or bronze, so they made their weapons from natural materials. The most effective weapons were edged with slivers of obsidian, a hard, glasslike stone that has a very sharp edge when first broken.

83 **Clubs were used to knock enemies unconscious.** One of the main purposes of warfare among the Maya and Aztec people was to capture prisoners. The prisoners were then taken to temples to be sacrificed to gods such as Huitzilopochtli, the god of war, by having their hearts cut out while still beating.

84 **Shields were highly decorated.** The shields used by Aztec and Maya warriors were made of wood, and covered with brightly coloured animal skins and feathers. They often had strings of feathers or fur dangling down underneath to deflect javelins.

◄ The Maya tried to capture enemy noblemen and rulers to use as sacrifices to the gods.

85 **The tomahawk was a famous weapon of the North American tribes.** This was a short-handled axe with a heavy head. The first tomahawks were made with stone heads, but after Europeans reached North America, the tribes began buying steel-headed tomahawks.

▶ The native peoples of the eastern areas of North America used spears and special axes, known as tomahawks.

41

The code of Bushido

86 Samurai wore elaborate armour. From around 800–1860, warriors known as the samurai ruled the islands of Japan. Samurai wore suits of armour made from hundreds of small plates of metal laced together with silk. Each group of samurai had a badge, or sashimono, which was often a picture of a plant or animal.

87 The swords of the samurai took weeks to make. The samurai sword was produced by blending strips of different types of steel, and shaping them to produce a smooth blade. Each sword was made by a master craftsman in a process that involved prayers and religious rituals as well as metalwork.

88 Bushido was the way of the warrior. By around 1500 the samurai were expected to follow a code of behaviour known as Bushido, which demanded loyalty and honour as well as bravery and skill with weapons.

▲ The samurai practised with weapons and armour for long periods. They sometimes exercised with elaborate displays.

▲ All samurai were trained in mounted combat and were expected to use their bows as well as their swords when riding at a gallop.

89 Archery was a great skill.

Around AD 800, the earliest samurai called their profession 'the path of the arrow'. This was because skill at archery was thought to be the most important for a warrior. Swords later became more important, but archery remained a key skill until the end of the samurai period in the 1860s.

90 Most samurai carried two

swords. The katana was most often used in combat, while the shorter wakizashi was used in an emergency or for ritual suicide. Some samurai preferred the much longer two-handed nodachi sword when going into battle.

▶ A print of a samurai warrior showing the brightly patterned clothes that the warriors liked to wear.

The end of an era

◀ A wheel-lock pistol from about 1650. The wheel-lock was the first reliable firing mechanism.

91 **The first guns could not penetrate heavy armour.** Early forms of gunpowder were not powerful enough to shoot a bullet from a hand-held gun with much force. By 1600, armourers were producing helmets and breastplates that were bulletproof.

93 **Cavalry continued to wear body armour.** Until 1914, cavalry engaged in fast-moving fights could often not reload their guns once they had been fired. As a result cavalrymen often fought using swords and lances, so armour was still useful.

92 **Cannons could destroy armour.** Large cannons fired iron or stone balls that weighed up to 25 kilograms. They were designed to knock down stone walls, but were also used in battle. No armour could survive being hit by such a weapon.

◀ A musketeer in about 1660. Each cartridge on his belt holds a bullet and powder to fire it.

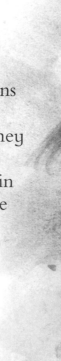

▼ A French cavalryman in 1810. He wears an iron helmet and iron body armour.

94 Infantry officers wore gorget armour. This was one of the last kinds of armour to be worn. It was a small piece of armour that fitted under the front of the helmet and protected the neck. Gorgets were often used to show the rank of the man wearing them, so they continued to be worn long after helmets were abandoned. They were used until 1914 in some countries.

▶ A musketeer in about 1770. He is using a ramrod to push the bullet and gunpowder down the barrel of a gun before firing it.

95 By 1850 most soldiers no longer wore armour. As guns became more effective, they were able to fire bullets with greater accuracy over longer distances and with more power. By 1850 most infantry were armed with guns that could shoot through any type of armour, so most soldiers stopped wearing armour.

I DON'T BELIEVE IT!

As late as 1914 some French cavalry went to war wearing armour, despite the fact that they had to face artillery and machine guns.

Modern arms and armour

96 The first modern use of chemical weapons was in World War I. In April 1915, the Germans used poison gas against French soldiers. It worked by irritating the lining of the lungs and throat. Soldiers then began to wear anti-gas uniforms as protection.

▶ A British infantryman in 1944. He wears a steel helmet and carries a Sten gun – a light machine gun.

▲ A British cavalryman charges in 1916. Both the man and horse wear gasmasks to protect them against poison gas.

QUIZ

1. Was poisoned gas first used in World War II?
2. What does APC stand for?
3. Do bomb disposal men wear special anti-blast armour?

Answers:
1. No. It was first used in World War I 2. Armoured Personnel Carrier 3. Yes

97 Modern soldiers always wear helmets. Exploding shells and rockets often throw out sharp splinters of metal called shrapnel. Soldiers take cover in trenches or holes. Metal helmets protect the head, the most likely part of the body to be hit by shrapnel.

► A Main Battle Tank (MBT) advances through the desert. The arrival of tanks and other armoured vehicles has transformed modern warfare.

98 Modern armoured warfare involves tanks. The armour needed to stop modern shells and rockets is too heavy for a person to carry, but it can be mounted on a vehicle, such as a tank or an armoured personnel carrier (APC). These vehicles are the key feature of a modern army, as the armoured knights were in the middle ages.

99 The best armour makes you disappear. Camouflage conceals soldiers by using colours that blend into the background of plants, sky or sand. Helmets often have a strap that can be used to attach vegetation for extra camouflage.

▼ An American soldier in Iraq. He wears bulletproof body armour as well as a helmet.

100 Bomb disposal soldiers use special armour. Designed to give protection against blast waves, the armour covers as much of the body as possible while still allowing the soldier to use his hands to defuse the bomb.

Index

ABC OF
OCCUPATIONAL AND
ENVIRONMENTAL MEDICINE

Second Edition

Edited by

DAVID SNASHALL

Head of Occupational Health Services, Guy's and St Thomas's Hospital NHS Trust, London
Chief Medical Adviser, Health and Safety Executive, London

DIPTI PATEL
Consultant Occupational Physician, British Broadcasting Corporation, London

© BMJ Publishing Group 1997, 2003

First published in 1997 as *ABC of Work Related Disorders*
This edition published as *ABC of Occupational and Environmental Medicine—Second edition* 2003
by BMJ Publishing Group, BMA House, Tavistock Square,
London WC1H 9JR
www.bmjbooks.com

British Library Cataloguing in Publication Data
A catalogue record for this book is available from the British Library

The cover shows an scanning electron micrograph of asbestos fibres. With permission from
Manfred Kage/Science photo Library

ISBN 0 7279 1611 4

Typeset by Newgen Imaging Systems (P) Ltd, Chennai, India
Printed and bound in Malaysia by Times Offset

Contents

Contributors

Anil Adisesh
Consultant in Occupational Medicine,
Trafford Healthcare and Salford Royal
Hospitals NHS Trusts, and Honorary
Clinical Lecturer in Occupational and
Environmental Medicine, Centre for
Occupational and Environmental Health,
University of Manchester, Manchester

Nicola Cherry
Chair, Department of Public Health Sciences,
University of Alberta, Canada

David Coggon
Professor of Occupational and
Environmental Medicine, MRC
Environmental Epidemiology Unit,
Community Clinical Sciences, University of
Southampton, Southampton

Tom Cox
Professor of Organisational Psychology,
Institute of Work, Health and Organisation,
University of Nottingham, Nottingham

Martyn Davidson
Chief Medical Adviser, John
Lewis Partnership, London

William Davies
Consultant Occupational Physician,
Occupational Health Unit,
South Wales Fire and Local Authorities, Pontyclun, Wales

Tony Fletcher
Senior Lecturer, Department of Public
Health and Policy, London School of Hygiene and
Tropical Medicine, London

Mats Hagberg
Professor, Chief Physician, and Director,
Department of Occupational and Environmental
Medicine, Sahlgrenska Academy at Gothenburg
University and Sahlgrenska University Hospital,
Gothenburg, Sweden

John Hobson
Consultant Occupational Physician,
MPCG Ltd, Stoke on Trent

Malcolm IV Jayson
Emetrius Professor of Rheumatology and
Professorial Fellow, University of
Manchester, Manchester

Rachel Jenkins
Director of WHO collaborating Centre,
Institute of Psychiatry,
King's College, Denmark Hill, London

Paul Litchfield
BT Group Chief Medical Officer,
London

Deborah Lucas
Head of Human Factors Team,
Hazardous Installations Directorate
Health and Safety Executive,
Bootle, Merseyside

Ron McCaig
Head of Human Factors Unit,
Better Working Environment Division Policy Group,
Health and Safety Executive, Bootle,
Merseyside

Ira Madan
Consultant Occupational Physician,
East Kent Hospitals NHS Trust,
Canterbury

Robert Maynard
Senior Medical Officer, Department of
Health, Skipton House, London

Keith T Palmer
MRC Clinical Scientist and Consultant,
Occupational Physician,
MRC Environmental Epidemiology Unit,
Community Clinical Sciences,
University of Southampton, Southampton

Dipti Patel
Consultant Occupational Physician,
British Broadcasting Corporation,
London

Andy Slovak
Company Chief Medical Officer,
British Nuclear Fuels plc, Warrington,
Cheshire

David Snashall
Senior Lecturer in Occupational
Medicine, Guy's, King's and St Thomas's
School of Medicine, London; Honorary
Consultant and Head of Service,
Occupational Health Department, Guys'
and St Thomas's Hospitals NHS Trust,
London; Chief Medical Advisor, Health
and Safety Executive, London

Ian R White
Consultant Dermatologist,
St John's Institute of Dermatology,
London

Preface

Although work is generally considered to be good for your health and a healthy working population is essential to a country's economic and social development, certain kinds of work can be damaging. Occupational health is the study of the effect—good and bad—of work on peoples' health and, conversely, the effect of peoples' health on their work: fitness for work in other words.

Work places are specialised environments, capable of being closely controlled. Generally, it is the lack of control imposed by employers that is the cause of ill health because of exposure to hazardous materials and agents at work, and of injury caused by workplace accidents.

Working life does not, however, begin and end at the factory gate or the revolving office door: many people walk, cycle, or drive to work—a journey that often constitutes the major hazard of the day. Others have to drive or travel by other means as part of their job, live away from home, be exposed to other food, other people, other parasites. Even work from home, increasing in some countries, can have its problems. Occupational health practitioners deal with all these aspects of working life.

A working population consists of people mainly between 15 and 70 years (disregarding for the moment the ongoing scandal that is child labour), who may be exposed for 8-12 hours a day to a relatively high concentration of toxic substances or agents, physical or psychological. At least that population is likely to be reasonably fit—unlike those who cannot work because of illness or disabilities, the young, and the very old, who are more vulnerable and spend a lifetime exposed to many of the same agents in the general environment at lower concentration. This enters the realm of environmental medicine of such concern to those who monitor the degradation of our planet, track pollution and climate change, and note the effect of natural disasters and man made ones, especially wars.

This book was first published in 1997 as the *ABC of Work Related Disorders*. It is a much expanded and updated version that attempts, in a compressed and easy to assimilate fashion, to describe those problems of health relating to work in its widest sense and to the environment.

The pattern of work is changing fast. There is pretty full employment in most economically developed countries now. Manufacturing industry is now mainly concentrated in developing countries where traditional occupational disease such as pesticide poisoning and asbestosis are still depressingly common. Occupational accidents are particularly common in places where industrialisation is occurring rapidly as was once the case during the industrial revolution in 19th century Britain. Work is also more varied, more intense, more service oriented, more regulated, and more spread around the clock in order to serve the 24 hour international economy. There are more women at work, more disabled people, and a range of new illnesses perhaps better described as symptom complexes which represent interactive states between peoples' attitudes and feeling towards their work, their domestic environment, and the way in which their illness behaviour is expressed.

All occupational disease is preventable—even the more "modern" conditions such as stress and upper limb disorders can be reduced to low level by good management and fair treatment of individuals who do develop these kinds of problems and who may need rehabilitation back into working life after a period of disability. These areas are covered in the chapters on musculoskeletal disorders, stress, and mental health at work. There are chapters also on the traditional concerns of the occupational health practitioner such as dermatoses, respiratory disorders and infections, and other chapters reflecting occupational health practice covering workplace surveys, fitness for work, sickness absence control issues, and, unfortunately increasing in prevalence, legal considerations. Genetics and its application to work and the effects of work on reproduction are described in chapter 17.

Concerns beyond the workplace are covered in the chapter on global issues and on pollution. The control of hazards in the general environment presents issues of problem solving at a different level. Ascertainment of exposure is more difficult than in workplaces, and to find solutions needs transnational political will and commitment as well as science to succeed. Many believe that the rash of "new" illnesses attributed to environmental causes are manifestations of a risk-averse public's response to poorly understood threats in the modern world and an unconscious wish to blame "industry," or some state institution—agencies that represent irresponsible emitters of toxins, inadvertent releasers of radiation, regardless sprayers of pesticides, or unwitting providers of vaccinations. Chapter 20 addresses this important subject.

In common with the previous edition, this new edition of *ABC of Occupational and Environmental Medicine* will still appeal to non-specialists who wish to practise some occupational medicine; but will also provide all that students of occupational and environmental medicine and nursing will need as a basis for their studies. Each chapter has an annotated further reading list. Most, but not all, of the book is written with an international audience in mind.

David Snashall

1 Hazards of work

David Snashall

Most readers of this book will consider themselves lucky to have a job, probably an interesting one. However tedious it might be, work defines a person, which is one reason why most people who lack the opportunity to work feel disenfranchised. As well as determining our standard of living, work takes up about a third of our waking time, widens our social networks, constrains where we can live, and conditions our personalities. "Good" work is life enhancing, but bad working conditions can damage your health.

Global burden of occupational and environmental ill health

According to the International Labour Organisation (ILO), between 1.9 and 2.3 million people are killed by their work every year—including 12 000 children—and 25 million people have workplace injuries, causing them to take time off. Two million workplace associated deaths per year outnumber people killed in road accidents, war, violence, and through AIDS, and cost 4% of the world's gross domestic product in terms of absence from work, treatment, and disability and survivor benefits.

The burden is particularly heavy in developing countries where the death rate in construction—for example, is 10 times that in industrialised countries, and where workers are concentrated in the most dangerous industries—fishing, mining, logging, and agriculture.

In the United States some 60 000 deaths from occupational disease and 860 000 cases of work related injury occur each year.

Environmental disease is more difficult to quantify because the populations at risk are much larger than the working population. As an example, the US Centers for Disease Control and Prevention reckons that one million children in the world have lead poisoning.

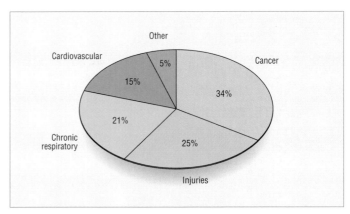

Estimated global work related mortality (1.1 million every year, based on 1990-5 data). Other diseases include pneumoconioses, nervous system, and renal disorders

Reporting occupational ill health

Occupational diseases are reportable in most countries, but are usually grossly underreported. Even in countries like Finland (where reporting is assiduous), surveys have shown rates of occupational disease to be underestimated by three to five times.

Classifications of occupational diseases have been developed for two main purposes: for *notification*, usually to a health and safety agency to provide national statistics and subsequent preventive action, and for *compensation* paid to individuals affected by such diseases. There are no universally accepted diagnostic criteria, coding systems, or classifications worldwide. Modifications of ICD-10 (international classification of diseases, 10th revision) are used in many countries to classify occupational diseases, along with a system devised by the World Health Organization for classifying by exposure or industry. It is the association of these two sets of information that defines a disease as being probably occupational in origin. A number of reporting systems exist in the United Kingdom but these are not comprehensive, nor coordinated. After all, they arose at different times and for different purposes.

Children are more vulnerable to occupational disease—they are smaller, have the potential to be exposed for many years, and their tissues are more sensitive. They are also more likely to be exploited and, being less aware, more accident prone

1

Classification and notification of occupational diseases

The World Health Organization gives the following classification:

1. Diseases caused by agents
   1.1 Diseases caused by chemical agents
   1.2 Diseases caused by physical agents
   1.3 Diseases caused by biological agents
2. Diseases by target organ
   2.1 Occupational respiratory diseases
   2.2 Occupational skin diseases
   2.3 Occupational musculoskeletal diseases
3. Occupational cancer
4. Others

Notification

In addition to the diagnosis of occupational disease, additional information should be included in the notification. The ILO has defined the minimum information to be included:

(a) Enterprise, establishment, and employer
   (i) Name and address of employer
   (ii) Name and address of enterprise
   (iii) Name and address of the establishment
   (iv) Economic activity of the establishment
   (v) Number of workers (size of the establishment)
(b) Person affected by the occupational disease
   (i) Name, address, sex, and date of birth
   (ii) Employment status
   (iii) Occupation at the time when the disease was diagnosed
   (iv) Length of service with the present employer

Classification for labour statistics

- International Standard Classification of Occupations (ISCO)
- International Classification of Status in Employment (ICSE)
- International Standard Industrial Classification of all Economic Activities (ISIC)
- International Standard Classification of Education (a UNESCO classification) (ISCED)
- Classifications of occupational injuries

Occupational injuries are also reportable in Great Britain under the Reporting of Injuries, Diseases and Dangerous Occurrences Regulations 1995 and, for purposes of compensation, to the Department of Work and Pensions' Industrial Injuries Scheme. The recording of injuries is generally more reliable because the injuries are immediately obvious and occur at a definable point in time. By contrast, cause and effect in occupational disease can be far from obvious, and exposure to the hazardous material may have occurred many years beforehand. Given that, worldwide, industrial injuries and, in particular, occupational ill health are poorly recorded and reported, the economic losses to the countries concerned are massive.

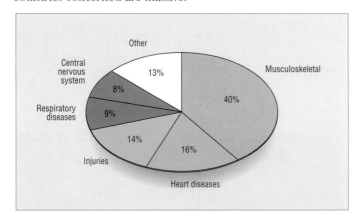

Breakdown of costs for work related injuries and diseases. Other diseases include cancer, skin diseases, and mental disorders

Occupational or work related?

Some conditions, such as asbestosis in laggers, and lead poisoning in industrial painters, are hardly likely to be anything other than purely occupational in origin. (About 70 of these "prescribed" occupational diseases are listed by the Department for Work and Pensions.) However, mesothelioma can be the result of environmental exposure to fibrous minerals (as in the case of cave dwellers in Turkey), and lead poisoning can be a result of ingesting lead salts from—for example, low

---

The cost of disease and injury at work

- **1992: European countries**
  Direct costs for compensation of work related diseases and injuries:
  27 000 million ECUs
- **1995-1996: United Kingdom**
  Overall costs to society for workplace injuries and ill health (including net present value of costs in future years): £14-18 billion (2-2.5% of gross domestic product). Ratio of illnesses/injuries about 3:1
- **1992: United States**
  Total direct and indirect costs associated with work related injuries and diseases: US $171 000 million. This is more than AIDS and on a par with cancer and heart disease

---

United Kingdom occupational ill health statistics

No single source of information is available in the United Kingdom on the nature and full extent of occupational ill health. The statistics in the 2000-1 report by the Health and Safety Executive are based on the following sources:

- Household surveys of self reported work related illness (SWI): these have been held in 1990 and 1995, linked to the Labour Force Survey (LFS). Health and safety questions were also included in the Europewide LFS in 1999
- Voluntary reporting of occupational diseases by specialist doctors in The Health and Occupation Reporting (THOR) network (which succeeded the Occupational Disease Intelligence Network (ODIN) in 2002). THOR and ODIN comprise the Occupational Physicians Reporting Activities (OPRA) scheme, and six other schemes covering mental illness and stress, musculoskeletal disorders, skin diseases, respiratory disorders, hearing loss, and infectious diseases
- New cases of assessed disablement under the Department of Work and Pensions' Industrial Injuries Scheme (IIS): the most longstanding source, based on a list of prescribed diseases and associated occupations, again giving annual figures
- Statutory reports under the Reporting of Injuries, Diseases and Dangerous Occurrences Regulations (RIDDOR): these were expanded when RIDDOR 1995 replaced RIDDOR 1985 and are similar to the IIS list
- Deaths from occupational lung diseases recorded on death certificates (principally mesothelioma and other asbestos related diseases)

temperature, lead glazed ceramics used as drinking vessels, mainly in developing countries. In these situations the history and main occupation will differentiate the causes. The situation may be far less clear in conditions such as back pain in a construction worker or an upper limb disorder in a keyboard operator when activities outside work may contribute, as might psychological factors, symptom thresholds, etc. A lifetime working in a dusty atmosphere may not lead to chronic bronchitis and emphysema, but when it is combined with cigarette smoking this outcome is much more likely. Common conditions for which occupational exposures are important but are not the sole reason or the major cause can more reasonably be termed "work related disease" rather than occupational disease.

Some important prescribed diseases such as chronic bronchitis, emphysema, and lung cancer are work related in the individual case only on the "balance of probabilities." Certain occupations carry a substantial risk of premature death, whereas others are associated with the likelihood of living a long and healthy life. This is reflected in very different standardised (or proportional) mortality ratios for different jobs, but not all the differences are the result of the various hazards of different occupations. Selection factors are important, and social class has an effect (although in the United Kingdom this is defined by occupation). Non-occupational causes related to behaviour and lifestyle may also be important.

Presentation of work related illnesses

Diseases and conditions of occupational origin usually present in an identical form to the same diseases and conditions caused by other factors. Bronchial carcinoma—for example, has the same histological appearance and follows the same course whether it results from working with asbestos, uranium mining, or cigarette smoking.

The possibility that a condition is work induced may become apparent only when specific questions are asked, because the occupational origin of a disease is usually discovered (and it is discovered only if suspected) by the presence of an unusual pattern. For example, in occupational dermatitis, the distribution of the lesions may be characteristic. A particular history may be another clue: asthma of late onset is more commonly occupational in origin than asthma that starts early in life. Indeed, some 40% of adult onset asthma is probably occupational. Daytime drowsiness in a fit young factory worker may be caused not by late nights and heavy alcohol consumption but by unsuspected exposure to solvents at work.

The occupational connection with a condition may not be immediately obvious because patients may give vague answers when asked what their job is. Answers such as "driver," "fitter," or "model" are not very useful, and the closer a health professional can get to extracting a precise job description, the better. For example, an engineer may work directly with machinery and risk damage to limbs, skin, and hearing, or may spend all day working at a computer and risk back pain, upper limb disorders, and sedentary stress. Sometimes patients will have been told (or should have been told) their job is associated with specific hazards, or they may know that fellow workers have experienced similar symptoms.

Timing of events
The timing of symptoms is important because the symptoms may be related to exposure events during work. Asthma provides a good example of this: many people with occupational asthma develop symptoms only after a delay of

Proportional mortality ratios (PMR) in selected occupations

Occupation	High PMR	Low PMR
Teachers	Multiple sclerosis Leukaemia Aplastic anaemia Parkinson disease Bicycle accidents	Lung cancer Bronchitis Alcohol related disease
Doctors, dentists and nurses	Suicide Alcohol-related disease Hepatitis (doctors) Prostatic cancer (dentists)	Ischaemic heart disease
Farmers	Allergic pneumonitis Influenza Hernia Poisoning Accidents Epilepsy Suicide Haemolytic anaemia	Cancer Heart disease Alcohol related disorders
Construction workers	Cancer of pleura and peritoneum Asbestosis Nasal cancer Falls	Suicide

Exposure to solvents at work can be the cause of erratic behaviour at home

How to take an occupational history
Question 1
What is your job? or What do you do for a living?

Question 2
What do you work with? or What is a typical working day for you? or What do you actually do at work?

Question 3
How long have you been doing this kind of work? Have you done any different kind of work in the past?

Question 4
Have you been told that anything you use at work may make you ill? Has anybody at work had the same symptoms?

Question 5
Do you have any hobbies, like do-it-yourself or gardening, which may bring you into contact with chemicals?

Question 6
Is there an occupational health doctor or nurse at your workplace who I could speak to?

some hours and the condition may present as nocturnal wheeze. It is essential to ask whether symptoms occur during the performance of a specific task and if they occur solely on workdays, improving during weekends and holidays. Sometimes the only way to elucidate the pattern is for the person to keep a graphic diary of the time sequence of events.

Working conditions

Patients should be asked specifically about their working conditions. Common problems are dim lighting, noisy machinery, bad office layout, dusty atmosphere, draconian management, and bad morale. Such questioning not only investigates possibilities, but also gives the questioner a good idea of the general state of a working environment and how the patient reacts to it. A visit to the workplace may be a revelation, and just as valuable as a home visit if one wants to understand how a patient's health is conditioned by their environment and how it might be improved. Knowing about somebody's work can help to provide a context and to gain insight. Patients are often happy to talk about the details of their work: this may be less threatening than talking about details of their home life and can promote a better relationship between patients and health professionals.

The causes of occupational disease can extend beyond the workplace and can affect local populations through water or soil pollution. Overalls soiled with toxic materials such as lead or asbestos can affect members of workers' families when the overalls are taken home to be washed.

Trends in work related illnesses

Changes in working practices in the industrialised world are giving rise to work that is more demanding in a psychosocial sense but less so in terms of hard physical activity. Jobs are also safer (although this may not be true in those countries where extremely rapid industrialisation is occurring)—the result of a shift in many countries from agricultural and extractive industry via heavy factory industry to technology intensive manufacturing and services, which are inherently safer. Also, most countries have a labour inspectorate that can orchestrate a risk based strategy of hazard control with varying degrees of efficiency. Life outside work has also become safer, although rapid industrialisation and growing prosperity in some countries have meant huge increases in road traffic, with an accompanying increase in accidents. Traditional occupational diseases such as pneumoconiosis and noise induced deafness can be adequately controlled by the same strategies of hazard control used to limit accidental injury. However, the long latent period between exposure and appearance of occupational diseases makes attribution and control more problematic. Thus, the modern epidemic of musculoskeletal disorders and complaints of work induced stress may reflect a new kind of working population with different characteristics from its forebearers, as well as changes in the work environment itself.

Completely new jobs have appeared, with new hazards—for example, salad composers (dermatitis), aromatherapists (allergies), and semiconductor assemblers (exposure to multiple toxins).

Although working conditions are undoubtedly cleaner, safer, and in many ways better than before, work itself has changed. In the economically developed world there has been a shift from unskilled work to more highly skilled or multiskilled work in largely sedentary occupations. There is greater self employment and a remarkable shift towards employment in small and medium sized enterprises. The percentage of women in employment has been growing for

---

An example of the interface between occupational and environmental disease was the pollution of Minamata Bay in Japan by discharges of mercury from industrial sources and the severe neurological consequences on those who consumed the resulting contaminated fish

---

Annual death risks: some examples from the United Kingdom

Cause of death	Annual risk
Whole population	
Cancer	1 in 387
All forms of road accidents	1 in 16 800
Lung cancer caused by radon in dwellings	1 in 29 000
Lightning	1 in 1 870 000
Workers	
Fatalities to employees	1 in 125 000
Fatalities to the self employed	1 in 50 000
Construction	1 in 17 000
Agriculture, hunting, forestry, and fishing (not sea fishing)	1 in 17 200
Service industry	1 in 333 000
Activities	
Surgical anaesthesia	1 in 185 000 operations
Scuba diving	1 in 200 000 dives
Fairground rides	1 in 834 000 000 rides
Rock climbing	1 in 320 000 climbs
Rail travel accidents journeys	1 in 43 000 000 passenger
Aircraft accidents	1 in 125 000 000 passenger journeys

Antidiscrimination legislation in many countries has provided more working opportunities for disabled and older workers, and has provided their employers with some challenges. Occupational health professionals need to understand organisational development as well as occupational disease

---

Useful websites

WHO http://www.who.int/home-page
ILO http://www.ilo.org/public/English
ICOH http://www.icoh.org.sg/eng/index.html

Africa
http://www.sheafrica.info

Australia
http://www/nohsc.gov.au

Europe
http://europe.osha.eu.int

Finland
http://www.occuphealth.fi

Sweden
http://www.arbetslivsinstitutet.se

United Kingdom
http://www.hse.gov.uk
http://www.facoccmed.ac.uk

United States
http://www.cdc.gov/niosh/homepage.html
http://www.epa.gov/
http://www.acoem.org

decades. Not everyone can cope with the newer, more flexible, less stable, intensively managed work style demanded by modern clients and contractors.

Public perceptions and an expectation of good physical health and associated happiness, allied to improved sanitation and housing, availability of good food, and good medical services, have highlighted those non-fatal conditions which might hitherto have been regarded as trivial but which have large effects on social functioning (such as deafness), work (such as backache), and happiness (such as psychological illness), contributing in turn disproportionately and adversely to disability-free years of life. The public is also more environmentally aware and concerned that some of the determinants of ill health are rooted in modern life and working conditions, giving rise to allergies, fatigue states, and various forms of chemical sensitisation. The estimation, perception, and communication of risk—a social construct— may still, however, be quite primitive even in the most sophisticated of populations. The media definition of risk remains "hazard plus outrage," and life as a threat has become a reality for many.

The figures showing global work related mortality and the breakdown of costs for work related injuries and diseases use data from ILO, 1999 and ILO, 1995.

2 Occupational health practice

Anil Adisesh

Occupational health is a multidisciplinary activity that draws on a wide base of sciences for its implementation. The range of practitioners employed in any one organisation will tend to reflect the resources allocated, hazards identified, and the prevailing regulatory requirements of the host country. Occupational health is practised by physicians, nurses, safety and risk assessors, and occupational hygienists, sometimes with support from ergonomists, psychologists, toxicologists, and epidemiologists. The competent occupational health practitioner will have some understanding in all these fields but will have an area of special knowledge—for example, the physician will be primarily expert in occupational medicine.

The work of occupational health teams may contribute directly or indirectly to the intrinsic health values of the product (or service). For example, a cement manufacturer might add ferrous sulphate to reduce the likelihood of occupational allergic contact dermatitis in the product users; a hospital may screen and immunise healthcare workers for hepatitis B to prevent occupational acquisition but thereby also prevent iatrogenic disease in patients.

In the course of making recommendations to the UK government on improving access to occupational health support services, the Occupational Health Advisory Committee formed the view that occupational health embraced a range of functions.

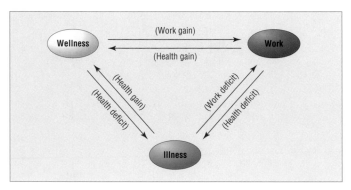

The occupational health paradigm

The integration of safety and occupational health is common and many units are described as "occupational health and safety services." In private industry, in particular, environmental responsibilities have also been incorporated, to form a "safety, health, and environment" function, with management board level representation. The amalgamation of these activities can provide a global focus for occupational health, which then needs to engage with a wider public and political agenda.

The interaction between health and work has been a long held paradigm for occupational health that tends to emphasise the adverse effects of work on health and of ill health on capacity for work. It is perhaps time to add a third factor— "wellness"—to acknowledge that in favourable circumstances work contributes to good health (health gain), and healthier workers to better performance (work gain).

The Finnish concept of "maintenance of work ability" refers to a set of measures designed to assist workers to achieve a high level of work capacity in a changing job market over a working

Aims of occupational health services, formulated by the World Health Organization (WHO) and International Labour Organisation (ILO)

Occupational health should aim at: the promotion and maintenance of the highest degree of physical, mental, and social wellbeing of workers in all occupations; the prevention among workers of departures from health caused by their working conditions; the protection of workers in their employment from risks resulting from factors adverse to health; the placing and maintenance of the worker in an occupational environment adapted to his physiological and psychological capabilities; and, to summarise, the adaptation of work to man and of each man to his job

Joint ILO/WHO Committee on Occupational Health First Session (1950) and revised 12th Session (1995)

Mission statement for an occupational health department

"To support and ensure that the company health and safety community assists company management fulfil its responsibilities for employees' health and safety by promoting their physical, mental and social wellbeing, a safe, healthy environment and safe and healthy products"

Macdonald EB. Audit and quality in occupational health. *Occup Med* 1992;42:7-11

Occupational health functions

(a) Evaluating the effect of work on health, whether through sudden injury or through long term exposure to agents with latent effects on health, and the prevention of occupational disease through techniques that include health surveillance, ergonomics, and effective human resource management systems

(b) Assessing the effect of health on work, bearing in mind that good occupational health practice should address the fitness of the task for the worker, not the fitness of the worker for the task alone

(c) Rehabilitation and recovery programmes

(d) Helping the disabled to secure and retain work

(e) Managing work related aspects of illness with potentially multifactorial causes (for example, musculoskeletal disorders, coronary heart disease) and helping workers to make informed choices regarding lifestyle issues

Occupational Health Advisory Committee, 2000

Occupational health services can help an employer

- Comply with legal responsibilities
- Identify hazards and quantify health risks at work
- Implement controls for health risks at work
- Confirm the adequacy of controls through health surveillance
- Select and place workers according to health criteria for particular jobs
- Support employees with a disability
- Ensure fitness for work
- Manage work related disorders
- Control sickness absence and advise on ill-health retirement
- Develop policies relating to health and safety
- Promote health among workers
- Provide training and education in health aspects of employment
- Organise adequate first aid arrangements
- Reduce legal liability
- Design new work processes
- Provide travel health services for work related travel or postings overseas

lifetime. Its application has been found to reduce sickness absence rates and early ill-health retirement.

Occupational health services are in a good position to promote work ability maintenance by:

- Actions directed towards the improvement of employees' physical and mental health, and social wellbeing (by advising the client)
- Actions directed towards competence building, better control of work, encouragement, and motivation (by advising the managers)
- Actions directed to developing the work environment, work processes, and work community that are safe and healthy (by advising the employer).

A work ability index (WAI) has been developed consisting of a questionnaire (translated into many languages) which allows workers to rate their own work ability, track it over the years, and use the score distribution to act as an early warning of decline and guide interventions to improve matters.

The function of occupational health services is to minimise both work and health deficits while maximising health and work gains. To achieve these aims an occupational health service needs:

- to perform a health protection role
- to liaise with treating health professionals
- to undertake active work rehabilitation
- to engage in workplace health promotion and support national health screening programmes
- to provide advisory function to management and workers anticipating the benefits and losses that may arise from changes to work or work practices
- importantly, to monitor its own activities so that meaningful data accrue.

Provision of occupational health

Statutory provision of occupational health is the norm in many European countries, including France, Spain, the Netherlands, Belgium, Portugal, Germany, Denmark, and Greece. Italy provides occupational and environmental health services within the national health service. In the United Kingdom there is no regulation that requires the provision of occupational health services by employers, although all NHS employees should have access to an accredited specialist in occupational medicine.

The NHS is now being encouraged to make its occupational health services available on a commercial basis to small and medium sized enterprises that may not otherwise have access to occupational health. It is, however, more usual for firms to contract private occupational health provision, or to employ occupational health staff.

Employers can seek advice from the Employment Medical Advisory Service of the HSE, but they will usually be directed towards suitable sources of occupational health provision. To implement health and safety legislation effectively, an employer may need the support of a health professional—for example, to perform health surveillance under the Management of Health and Safety at Work Regulations 1999. It might also be prudent to take the advice of an independent health professional at several stages of the employment process, to ensure compliance with disability discrimination legislation and to support other risk management initiatives for the organisation.

The fact that so few private companies use occupational health services is perhaps indicative of their failure to manage certain risks. The HSE promotes a five step process of risk assessment for hazard identification and risk reduction.

Use of health professionals at work

- The following information is contained in research* carried out in 1992†
- In total, 8% of private sector establishments use health professionals to treat or advise about health problems at work. "Health professionals" includes physicians, nurses, and other professions allied to medicine (whether or not they have specialist occupational health (OH) qualification), occupational hygienists, health and safety consultants, and other practitioners with specific OH knowledge or qualifications
- The use of health professionals varies substantially by size of company, with over two thirds (68%) of large employers using professionals, compared with 5% of employers with less than 25 employees. In the private sector, use is highest in manufacturing (14%). The high level of use of health professionals in the public sector means that overall almost half the total workforce are employed by organisations using health professionals

*HSE Contract Research Report 57/1993 on Occupational Health Provision at Work
†There is no more recent data of a comparable nature available

A 2002 survey of UK occupational health provision commissioned by the Health and Safety Executive (HSE) found that among a sample of private companies:

- 15% received services comprising hazard indentification, risk management, and provsion of occupational health and safety information
- 3% received the above plus modification of workplace activities, training, measurement of workplace hazards, and monitoring of trends (mainly larger companies)
- Health was secondary to safety
- Services were mainly provided by private doctors and nurses
- There was rarely a health and safety budget
- Small and medium sized enterprises (SMEs) were generally happy with the occupational health and safety situation within their company

The Health and Safety Executive's five steps to risk assessment

Step 1: Look for the hazards
Step 2: Decide who might be harmed and how
Step 3: Evaluate the risks and decide whether the existing precautions are adequate or whether more should be done
Step 4: Record your findings
Step 5: Review your assessment and revise it if necessary

Access to Medical Reports Act 1988

The Act established a right of access by individuals to reports relating to themselves provided by medical practitioners for employment or insurance purposes and to make provision for related matters. The Act gives patients certain rights. The patient may:

- Refuse to allow a medical report from their treating doctor
- Allow the report to be sent unseen
- See the report during the six month period after it was written
- See the report before it is sent to the employer (a 21 day period is allowed)
- Ask their doctor to change any part of the report which they consider to be wrong or misleading before consenting to its release
- Append their own comments
- Refuse to let the doctor send the report

Health and safety risk management has tended to focus on accidents, yet the cost to employers of workplace injuries and work related illness is estimated (based on the UK Labour Force 1995-6 Survey) to be about £2.5 billion a year (at 1995-6 prices)—about £0.9 billion for injuries and £1.6 billion for illness. Figures from the US Bureau of Labor Statistics report 5 650 100 cases of non-fatal injury or illness in private industry in 2000, with 1 664 000 cases involving days away from work.

Communication

Before any important employment decisions are made, it is in the interests of all parties to gain a full understanding of the facts pertaining to an employee's medical situation. In these circumstances it may be necessary for the occupational health service to request information from the employee's treating doctor. Sometimes information that is not known to the treating doctor is available to the occupational health service. For example, screening procedures may have found a healthcare worker to be infected with hepatitis B virus; health surveillance may have found that a paint sprayer may develop occupational asthma. In such circumstances it is important for the treating doctor to be made aware of these diagnoses with the agreement of the employee.

Communication between an employer and an employee's treating doctor is usually initiated by the occupational health service requesting information from the doctor. Occasionally a request may come directly from a manager or personnel department. The request should be accompanied by appropriate authorisation to disclose medical details to an employer or their medical representative. In the United Kingdom this is under the provisions of the Access to Medical Reports Act 1988.

When asked to provide a report, the corresponding doctor must establish whether the report is intended to go to a doctor retained by the company or to a lay person, such as the employee's manager. A lay person may not fully understand medical jargon, and misinterpretation could give rise to unnecessary concern, to the detriment of the employee.

Reports received by an occupational health department are held in medical confidence, unless the employee has disclosed these or specifically requested that they are disclosed to the employer. The work related implications can be explained to management with advice based on a knowledge of the working environment. It is in everyone's interest (patients, family doctors, hospital doctors, employers, occupational physicians, society as a whole) to get patients back to work as safely and quickly as possible but to prevent their premature return. Rapid and accurate communication is the answer, but the biggest delay occurs when treating doctors fail to answer requests for information from the occupational health service. Delays often cause difficulty to patients, sometimes including financial loss resulting from the inability to work or perform overtime, pending decisions on fitness for work.

Opinions on the part of the treating doctor regarding fitness to work may be unhelpful when these have not been specifically asked for, particularly if the patient is aware of the opinion. For example, a family doctor may consider a "process worker" who is undergoing investigation for syncope as fit to work. The safety of the individual and others in the workplace may be at risk if the doctor is not aware of the duties entailed—for example, working alone in a control room, wearing breathing apparatus, and so on. Doctors may create legal liabilities for themselves in providing opinions when they are

---

Occupational health reports (The Association of National Health Occupational Physicians, 1996—see Further reading)

Occupational health reports to management must be in writing and include the following:

(a) Details (not clinical details, but information on functional limitations) of any disabilities which may temporarily or permanently affect the ability of the employee to undertake his or her full range of contracted work duties
(b) An estimate of the likely duration of absence or disability
(c) Fitness to undertake the full range of duties, or a limited range of his or her contracted work
(d) Whether and when any further review would be appropriate
(e) Whether an application for retirement on grounds of ill health could be supported (this requires an understanding of the criteria applicable to the scheme)

It is essential that an employee is fully aware of the advice that is being sent to management and the implications of this advice. The employee should be provided with a copy of the advice.

This letter to a manager from a doctor acting as medical adviser to the company contains too many medical terms

Dear Harry,

I saw Mr .... He was well until 19 ..., when he had a coronary thrombosis. He made a good recovery from that until about 19 ..., when he began to complain of constant ache in his legs, which was worse on exercise. He now has persistent ache in both legs and an exercise limitation of about 200 yards. He recently had an episode of right-sided hemianopia, in which the outside half of the vision in the right eye disappears due to vascular disease of the eye. This is related to his generalised vascular disease as instanced by his coronary thrombosis and by his leg pains. He also complained recently of some shortness of breath and when I examined him I noticed that his heart beat was irregular. This man has quite severe generalised vascular disease and his life expectancy is not good. However, the only problem affecting his ability to work presently is the difficulty in focusing, due to his recent eye problem. This will hopefully improve sufficiently for him to be able to undertake his work in the office, provided no further disaster occurs. I would hope that he can resume employment in three to four weeks. However, as I said previously, the prognosis here is extremely poor. I hope this is of some assistance to you in organising your plans.

Yours sincerely,

Letter is written by a specialist to support a patient's application for a job in a remote tropical location. Knowledge of the medical facilities and the risks of disease in an immunosuppressed person must be considered

Dear Dr ...

I am writing in support of Ms J's application to work abroad. In 19 ... Ms J had a right leg DVT which was treated with warfarin but one month later she had a pulmonary embolus. Eight months after this, in January, she had an acute illness with fever and a vasculitic rash. A diagnosis of SLE was made and she was treated with prednisolone. In June she had an epileptiform seizure due to cerebral SLE. Glomerulonephritis was diagnosed on renal biopsy in July. The changes were consistent with SLE. She was treated with azathioprine in addition to the prednisolone. She then developed hypertension.

The current situation is that she has heavy proteinuria, indicating active glomerulonephritis; however, she seems clinically well. Her treatment is prednisolone 10 mg daily, azathioprine 100 mg daily, bendrofluazide 5 mg daily, propranolol 320 mg daily, and prazosin, 10 mg twice daily. She will need to continue on long term immunosuppressants but the short term outlook is good, although her renal function is likely to deteriorate in the longer term. Given her fortitude with illness I am sure she would make an excellent field worker for the ... project.

not aware of all relevant information and are without sufficient expertise.

The issue of payment for reports can also cause difficulties, and, ideally, fees should be agreed beforehand. Generally speaking, a higher fee is appropriate if the reporting doctor has been asked for an opinion on matters such as fitness for work; simply reporting on a previous diagnosis, and current and proposed treatment does not require exercising of specific judgement. As a matter of good practice and professional courtesy, payments to medical colleagues should be made promptly on the receipt of a report.

Having assessed the individual, the occupational physician may advise restriction of specific duties—for example, for a nursing care assistant with resolving back strain—that they can return to work under the restriction that no manual handling of patients nor of loads greater than 10 kg is undertaken. This still allows the nursing care assistant to perform a wide range of useful functions: assisting with food preparation and feeding, personal care tasks, checking supplies, and social interaction with clients. It is the skill of the manager to accommodate such advice.

A telephone conversation between the treating doctor and the occupational health department may help clarify the options in managing a return to work. Also, under disability discrimination legislation, there may be a duty on the employer to make a "reasonable accommodation" to facilitate work.

In the rare event of a complete disagreement between the occupational physician and the family doctor or specialist on an individual's fitness for work, legal authorities tend towards the occupational physician's opinion. They regard the occupational physician as being in fuller possession of all the facts, both clinical and relating to the actual work to be done, and therefore in a better position to make a balanced and independent judgement.

Ethics and confidentiality

Some doctors are wary of releasing medical details to occupational health professionals, believing that medical confidentiality may be compromised and information given to the employer. This should never happen. All communication between occupational health services and other doctors is held in strict medical confidence. Communication by occupational health services to managers is generally made in broad terms without revealing specific medical details. From a medical report indicating that an employee has angina on exertion, the occupational physician may inform the manager that "Mr. X has a medical condition that prevents him from working in the loading bay and performing other heavy manual work. He should be fit for his other duties as a senior storesman and will be kept under regular review."

It is unnecessary for a manager to be aware of specific medical details, but sometimes it is helpful, with the patient's agreement, for fellow workers to be aware of a medical condition such as epilepsy so that appropriate help can be given (or unhelpful actions avoided).

Some doctors also believe that occupational health services usually act in the interests of the employer, rather than the employee/patient. To behave in such a way is contrary to the ethics of occupational health practice, but this misconception still inhibits useful communication between the specialties. In fact, occupational health physicians and nurses act as independent and objective advisors to the individual *and* to the organisation, hopefully to their mutual benefit.

A "Mushroom worker"— without specific details the circumstances of work may not be obvious from the job title alone

General practitioners and hospital specialists may not be aware of the hazards associated with certain jobs: "blowing down" equipment with an air line, a poor practice that creates airborne dust and its attendant hazards

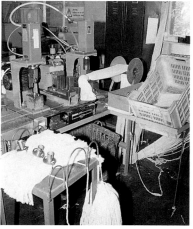

Cramped working conditions with ergonomic difficulties

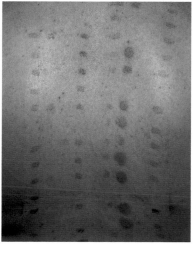

Positive patch tests to acrylates in a worker who glued lead flashing onto window units. She had developed an allergic contact dermatitis affecting the hands. In such a situation, two way communication can be beneficial to the patient— a patient may see their general practitioner for hand dermatitis, and liaison with the occupational health department may help identify the cause

Ill-health retirement

Sometimes medical conditions will preclude a return to work because of permanent incapacity for a particular job. Information will often be requested in order to support ill-health retirement, or it may be necessary to explain why an employee's job is to be terminated because of incapacity (where a person has not attended work for an excessive period because of sickness absence, but recovery of fitness is envisaged), the latter being a managerial decision. The pension fund's grounds for ill-health retirement may be explicit and leave little room for clinical opinion, or may be quite open. There is potential for disagreement between the occupational physician and other medical advisers, particularly if restricted duties or redeployment are viable propositions. Ideally, views should be discussed openly and an equitable decision made.

The interface between occupational health and other healthcare providers should therefore be open and two way, initiated either by primary care and hospital services or by occupational health services whenever discussion of patient care in relation to employment could be advantageous.

Audit and monitoring

It is important that occupational health practitioners critically evaluate their practice and, through application of the iterative audit cycle, improve the quality, effectiveness, and efficiency of their service. Audit is conventionally divided into structure (resources), process (procedures), and outcome (results). The use of audit should not be confined to clinical matters, and the inclusion of occupational health practitioners from other disciplines—for example, occupational hygiene or safety, will contribute to better services for all.

For a service to report on its activities in a meaningful way there needs to be in place a basic dataset that allows comparison between time periods, different employee groups, or operational divisions. Data that may be appropriate include new appointments, review appointments, health surveillance activity, immunisations, referral reason, type of clinician (doctor or nurse), and diagnosis. This information is invaluable for presentation to management to show changes in activity or areas for which increased funding is needed when making a business case. It will also be useful when discussing issues from the perspective of occupational health in organisational meetings such as health and safety meetings, risk management, and when compiling an annual report or business plan. These data are ideally compiled in a computerised database, either bespoke or a commercially available occupational health software package.

Research

Research is an essential occupational health function. It is only through testing hypotheses that we can advance our knowledge of occupational disease causation, the effectiveness of screening programmes, the benefits of workplace health promotion, quantification of occupational risk, establishment of exposure levels, and the economic impact of occupational injuries and ill health.

Occupational health practitioners may also be faced with ethical difficulties in this field. For example, an organisation may not wish to publicise adverse information about its products or activities. If private companies or national bodies

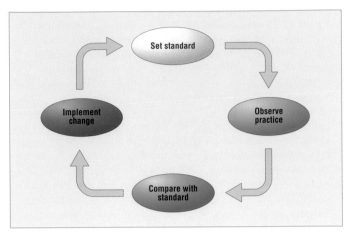

The audit cycle

Information technology and occupational health

When implementing an occupational health computer system consider:

- The information required from the system and therefore the data entry fields that will be needed
- Data security, in the context of confidentiality and back up in the event of system failure (there are advantages of having the computer server in the organisation's IT department)
- Whether the system is to be "stand alone," networked within a department, or over multiple sites
- Compatability with other organisational systems—for example, personnel or payroll for downloads of starters and leavers, incident reporting systems, sickness absence recording
- Production of reports and database queries
- Maintenance of data quality—that is, that the information recorded accurately represents the information presented
- The use of coding systems if comparisons with other occupational health services may be useful in the future, perhaps for audit, benchmarking, or research.

Practitioners also need to ensure that they meet professional requirements for continuing development. These responsibilities are usually set by professional bodies and it is important that employers recognise that continuing professional development is a necessary component of ongoing competence

An exposure chamber for respiratory challenge studies. The subject is seated inside the metal chamber and gas or vapour is passed through a laminar flow wall into the chamber, inside which spirometry can be performed

are concerned with or participate in research, their influence on what is finally published and intellectual property rights should be formally agreed at the outset. Too often there is reluctance for employers, unions, charities, and government bodies to fund occupational health research. Each seems to feel that the responsibility belongs to one of the other parties. It therefore behoves occupational health practitioners to participate in or act as advocates for occupational health research activities.

The box showing the use of health professionals at work is adapted from the report and recommendations on improving access to Occupational Health Support, Occupational Health Advisory Committee, 2000.

Further reading

- International Labour Organisation. *Technical and ethical guidelines for workers' health surveillance.* Geneva: ILO, 1997. *A discussion of the principles and purpose of health surveillance, including consideration of the ethical implications involved*
- World Health Organization. *Health and Environment in Sustainable Development: Five Years after the Earth Summit: Executive Summary.* Geneva: WHO, 1997. Http://www.who.int/ environmental_information/Information_resources/htmdocs/ execsum.htm. *This is an executive summary of the WHO report* Health and environment in sustainable development: five years after the earth summit. *It contains extracts from the report, selected figures and tables, and the conclusions in full*
- Macdonald EB. Audit and quality in occupational health. *Occup Med* 1992;42:7-11
- US Bureau of Labor Statistics. http://www.bls.gov/home.htm. *A website providing statistical information and reports relating to the United States*
- Occupational Health Advisory Committee. *Report and Recommendations on Improving Access to Occupational Health Support.* London: HMSO, 2001. *A comprehensive review of occupational health provision and functions, with proposals for improving access for small and medium size employers in the United Kingdom*
- Health and Safety Executive. *Five Steps to Risk Assessment.* Sudbury: HSE Books 1998. (INDG163 (Rev1)). *A short guide to risk assessment, aimed at employers*
- MacDonald E, ed. *Quality and audit in occupational health, Report of the Faculty of Occupational Medicine.* London: Royal College of Physicians, 1995. *This publication describes the essential principles and practical requirements for audit in occupational health practice*
- *The role of occupational health in the process of managing sickness absence.* Association of National Health Occupational Physicians, 1996. *The Association of National Health Occupational Physicians provides a forum for clinical networking, education, and audit and produces guidance for members*
- *Occupational safety and health and employability programmes, practices and experiences.* Luxembourg: European Agency for Safety and Health at Work, 2001. *This report gives an overview of the different types of initiatives in the Member States that aim to increase the employability of workers by using interventions deriving from the field of occupational safety and health*

3 Investigating the workplace

Keith T Palmer, David Coggon

Investigation of the workplace is as central to the practice of occupational medicine as clinical assessment is of the individual patient. It is an essential step in the control of occupational hazards to health. Moreover, by visiting a place of work, a doctor can understand better the demands of a job, and thus give better advice on fitness for employment. Investigations may be prompted in various circumstances.

Direct inspection and the walk through survey

One method of investigation is direct inspection of the workplace. Inspections often take the form of a structured "walk through" survey, although more narrowly targeted approaches may sometimes be appropriate.

Planning

Industrial processes are often complex, and hazards are plentiful. How should a walk through survey be conducted? The arrangements and context are important. The initial visit should be by appointment. Arrangements should be checked before visiting, as a planned visit saves time.

The survey should be structured, but the precise way it is organised is less important and at least three approaches are commonly adopted.

- *Following a process from start to finish*—from raw materials coming in to finished goods going out. What hazards occur at each stage? How should they be controlled? Do the controls actually work? Focusing the assessment on the process helps with basic understanding of the work and its requirements.
- *Auditing a single category of activity or hazard* (such as dusty or noisy procedures or manual handling) wherever it occurs within the organisation. Does the control policy work everywhere, or are there special problems or poor compliance in certain groups of workers or sites? This approach is useful for introducing and monitoring new policies.
- *Detailed inspection site by site*—What are the hazards in this particular site? How are they handled? The inspection moves on only when the geographical unit of interest has been thoroughly inspected. This site focused approach is often appreciated by shop stewards and workers' representatives with local ownership of the problem. They may accompany the inspection and often give insight into working practices and problems not apparent during the visit.

When planning a walk through survey an unannounced snap inspection may be revealing, but is practicable only for a health and safety professional who has an established relationship of trust with the employer

Arranging a walk through survey

- Visit by appointment (at least to begin with)
- Check whether you will:
  - be accompanied by someone with responsibilities for safety
  - see someone who can explain the process
  - have a chance to see representative activities
- Look at documentation on health and safety, such as data sheets, risk assessments, safety policy, accident book
- Do some preliminary research: identify sorts of hazard likely to be encountered and legal standards that are likely to apply
- If visiting because of an individual's complaint, discuss it first with complainant

A hazard represents a potential to cause harm. A risk represents the likelihood of harm. In risk assessment the hazard is put in its correct context

What to cover in a walk through survey

After listing the hazards, it is important to consider who might be exposed and in which jobs, how likely this is under the prevailing circumstances of the work (including any precautions followed), the magnitude of the expected exposures, and their likely impact on health (that is, the risks to health). The aim is to determine whether risks are acceptable, taking into account both the likelihood of an adverse outcome and its seriousness, or whether further control measures are required and, if so, what these should be.

As prevention is better than cure, can the hazard be avoided altogether, or can a safer alternative be used instead? Otherwise, can the process or materials be modified to minimise the problem at source? Can the process be enclosed, or operated remotely? Can fumes be extracted close to the point at which they are generated (local exhaust ventilation)?

Have these ideas been considered before issuing ear defenders, facemasks or other control measures that rely on workers' compliance ("Do not smoke," "Do not chew your fingernails," "Lift as I tell you to")? A realistic strategy should always place more reliance on control of risk at source than on employees' personal behaviour and discipline.

> Health and safety professionals use checklists to ensure that all the major types of hazard are considered and to ensure that the control options are fully explored. They seek to verify that these options have been considered in an orderly hierarchy

Simple checklist of control measures

Option	Key questions to ask	Possible controls*
Avoidance or substitution	Does the material have to be used or will a less noxious material do the job?	Try using a safer material if one exists
Material modification	Can the physical or chemical nature of the material be altered?	Is it supplied as granules or paste rather than powder? Can it be used wet?
Process modification	Can equipment, layout, or procedure be adapted to reduce risk?	Can it be enclosed? Can the dust be extracted? If material is poured, tipped, or sieved, can the drop height be lowered?
Work methods	Can safer ways be found to conduct the work? Can it be supervised or monitored? Do workers comply with methods?	Avoid dry sweeping (it creates dust clouds). Be careful with spills. Segregate the work; conduct it out of hours
Personal protective equipment	Have all other options been considered first? Is equipment adequate for purpose? Will workers wear it?	Provision of mask, visor, respirator, or breathing apparatus suitable for intended use

*A dust hazard is used as an example. See also Verma DK, et al. *Occup Environ Med* 2002;59:205-13.

What the survey may find

The purpose of the walk through survey is to be constructively critical. When good practices are discovered these should be warmly acknowledged. Faulty ones arise from ignorance as often as from cutting corners.

In certain workplaces that we have visited, expensive equipment provided to extract noxious fumes from the workers' breathing zone was switched off because of the draught, or directed over an ashtray to extract cigarette smoke rather than the fumes, or obstructed by bags of components and Christmas decorations.

Local exhaust ventilation may be visibly ineffective: the fan may be broken, the tubing disconnected, the direction of air flow across rather than away from the workers' breathing zone. Protective gloves may have holes or be internally contaminated; the rubber seals of ear defenders may be perished with age; and so on. Poor housekeeping may cause health hazards. There may be no system of audit to check that items of control equipment are maintained and effective. Simple commonsense observations, made and recorded systematically, will go a long way towards preventing ill health at work.

The walk through survey may prompt improvements directly or highlight a need for further investigation, such as workplace measurements or a health survey.

Workplace inspection aids understanding of the job demands and risks. This stonemason is exposed to hand transmitted vibration, noise, and silicaceous dust

This industrial process (scabbling) generates a lot of dust. Formal measurements showed that respirable dust and silica levels were several times in excess of those advocated in British standards. The highest exposure arose during sweeping up

Formal assessment of exposures

More formal measurement of exposure may be required if an important hazard exists and the risk is not clearly trivial. Often a specialised technique or sampling strategy will be needed, directed by an occupational hygienist. The UK Health and Safety Executive publishes guidance on methods of measurement and acceptable exposure levels for some physical hazards, such as noise and vibration, and many airborne chemical hazards. In some cases legal standards exist. For some chemicals absorbed through the skin or lungs, exposure can also be assessed by blood or urine tests, and biological action levels have been proposed.

Action after a workplace assessment

The aim in assessing a workplace should be to draw conclusions about the prevailing risks and the adequacy of the controls. But if this is to have a lasting benefit the results must be communicated to senior managers who have the authority to set, fund, and oversee policies in the workplace. A written report is advisable, but a verbal presentation, perhaps at a meeting of the organisation's safety committee, may have more impact, as may a short illustrated slide show. Feedback on the findings of a workplace health survey can make important contributions to the promotion of change and a safer working environment.

Some exposure standards for airborne chemicals

- The UK Health and Safety Executive publishes an annual list of exposure standards (EH40) and also advice on measuring strategies (EH42) and techniques (various EH publications)
- The listed chemicals generally fall into one of two categories. Occupational exposure standards (OES) are prescribed when a level can be specified below which long term exposure is thought not to present a risk to health. In other cases, where the safe level is less certain, a maximum exposure limit (MEL) is specified. This must not be exceeded, and there is a requirement to minimise exposure as far below the MEL as is reasonably practicable
- Other international exposure limits include the threshold limit values (TLVs) published by the American Conference of Governmental Industrial Hygienists (ACGIH) (see http://www.acgih.org)

The worker is exposed to noise during grinding. He should be wearing ear defenders

Frayed electrical cable and homemade plug discovered at a work site

Investigating new occupational hazards

As well as inspecting workplaces to identify and control known hazards, health and safety professionals should be alert to the possibility of previously unrecognised occupational hazards. Suspicions may be aroused in various circumstances. The demonstration and characterisation of new hazards requires scientific research, often using epidemiological methods. The most frequent types of investigation include cohort studies, case-control studies, and cross sectional surveys.

An advantage of epidemiology is that it provides direct information about patterns of disease and levels of risk in humans. However, because of the practical and ethical constraints on research in people, it also has limitations that must be taken into account when results are interpreted. Epidemiological findings should therefore be evaluated in the context of knowledge from other relevant scientific disciplines such as experimental toxicology, biomechanics, and psychology.

Reasons for suspecting an occupational hazard

- Parallels with known hazards—for example, use of a substance that has a similar chemical structure to a known toxin
- Demonstration that a substance or agent has potentially adverse biological activity *in vitro*—for example, mutagenicity in bacteria
- Demonstration that a substance or agent causes toxicity in experimental animals
- Observation of sentinel cases or clusters of disease

Commonly used epidemiological methods

Cohort studies
People exposed to a known or suspected hazard are identified, and their subsequent disease experience is compared with that of a control group who have not been exposed or have been exposed at a lower level. Cohort studies generally provide the most reliable estimates of risk from occupational hazards, but need to be large if the health outcome of interest is rare

Case-control studies
People who have developed a disease are identified, and their earlier exposure to known or suspected causes is compared with that of controls who do not have the disease. Case-control studies are often quicker and more economical to conduct than cohort studies, especially for the investigation of rarer diseases. However, risk estimates tend to be less accurate, particularly if exposures are ascertained from subjects' recall

Cross sectional surveys
A sample of people are assessed over a short period of time to establish their disease experience and exposures. The prevalence of disease is then compared in people with different patterns of exposure. This method is best suited to the investigation of disorders that do not lead people to modify their exposures (which might occur because associated disability makes them unfit for certain types of work). Where a disease causes people to leave a workforce, cross sectional surveys may seriously underestimate the risks associated with exposure

Interpretation of epidemiological findings

In evaluating epidemiological results, consideration must be given to the following factors:

Bias
A systematic tendency to overestimate or underestimate an outcome measure because of a deficiency in the design or execution of a study. For example, in a case-control study assessing exposures by questioning participants, affected persons might tend to recall exposures better than controls (because they are more motivated). The effect would be to spuriously exaggerate any association between exposure and disease

Chance
The people included in a study may be unrepresentative simply by chance, leading to errors in outcome measures. The scope for such errors can be quantified statistically through calculation of confidence intervals. Generally, the larger the sample of people studied, the lower the potential for chance error

Confounding
This occurs when a hazard under study is associated with another factor that independently influences the risk of disease. For example, an occupational group might have high rates of lung cancer not because of the chemical with which they worked, but because they smoked more heavily than the average person (that is, exposure to the chemical was associated with heavier smoking)

Assessment of disease clusters

One starting point for investigation of a workplace may be the observation of a disease cluster. A disease cluster is an excess incidence in a defined population, such as a workforce, over a relatively short period (less than a day for acute complaints such as diarrhoea to several years for cancer).

Apparent clusters are not uncommon in occupational populations, and investigation sometimes leads to the recognition of new hazards. For example, on the one hand, the link between nickel refining and nasal cancer was first discovered when two cases occurred at the same factory within a year. On the other hand, excessive investigation of random clusters wastes resources. The extent to which a cluster is investigated depends on the level of suspicion of an underlying hazard and the anxiety that it is generating in the workforce. A staged approach is recommended.

A cluster of wheezing and rhinitis occurred on this prawn processing line. High pressure hoses (used to free the prawns from the shells) had created aerosols containing crustacean protein

Is there a true cluster?

The first step is to specify the disease and time period of interest and to confirm the diagnoses of the index cases that prompted concern. Sometimes no further action is needed. Of three cases of brain cancer, two might turn out to be secondary tumours from different primary sites. If suspicion remains, it is worth searching for further cases. Often, the number of identified cases is clearly excessive, but if there is doubt, crude comparison with routinely collected statistics such as of cancer registration or mortality should establish whether the cluster really is remarkable.

Further steps

If a raised incidence is confirmed, the next step is to find out what the affected workers have in common. Do they work in the same job or building, and do they share exposure to the same substances? If so, what is known about the risks associated with their shared activities and exposures? This information may come from published reports or manufacturers' data sheets. Scientific articles should also be searched to identify known and suspected causes of the disease of interest. Could any of these be responsible for the cluster?

Getting help

At this stage the cause of the cluster may have been identified, or suspicions sufficiently allayed to rule out further investigation. If concerns remain it may be necessary to carry out a more formal epidemiological investigation to assess more precisely the size of the cluster and its relation to work. Help with such studies can often be obtained from academic departments of occupational medicine. Also, patients may need to be referred to specialist centres for investigations such as dermatological patch testing or bronchial challenge.

Hazards controlled

Over the years, investigation of workplaces has made a major contribution to public health through the identification and control of occupational hazards, and improved placement and rehabilitation of workers with illness or disability. Although some types of investigation need special technical expertise, all health and safety professionals should be familiar with the principles, and capable of inspecting and forming a preliminary assessment of working environments.

Stages in investigating occupational clusters of disease

1. Specify disease and time period of interest. Confirm diagnoses of index cases
2. Search for further cases. Is the observed number of cases excessive?
3. What do affected workers have in common? Do their shared exposures carry known or suspected risks?
4. What is known about the causes of the disease?
5. Further investigation: epidemiology and clinical investigation

---

Some important occupational hazards that have been identified and controlled through investigation of workplaces

Hazard	Control measures
• Bladder cancer from aromatic amines in dyestuffs and rubber industries	• Substitution of the chemicals with non-carcinogenic alternatives
• Lung cancer and mesothelioma from asbestos	• Substitution by less hazardous materials such as manmade mineral fibres; dust control and personal protective equipment in asbestos removal
• Coal workers' pneumoconiosis from dust in mines	• Dust suppression by water spraying
• Occupational deafness from exposure to noise	• Substitution or enclosure of noisy processes; exclusion zones; personal protective equipment

---

Further reading

- Olsen J, Merletti F, Snashall D, Vuylsteek K. *Searching for causes of work-related disease: an introduction to epidemiology at the worksite.* Oxford: Oxford University Press, 1991
- Pittom A. Principles of workplace inspection. In: Howard JK, Tyrer FH, eds. *Textbook of occupational medicine.* Edinburgh: Churchill Livingstone, 1987:91-106. *These two references describe in greater detail the process of workplace inspection*
- Health and Safety Executive. *Five steps to risk assessment.* Sudbury: HSE Books, 1998. (INDG163 (Rev 1)). *This free leaflet suggests a simple five point plan for assessing the risks in a workplace*
- Health and Safety Executive. *Occupational exposure limits.* Sudbury: HSE Books, 2000. (Guidance Note EH40/00). *This HSE publication, which is updated annually, provides guidance on the permissible limits for exposure to a number of chemicals*
- Health and Safety Executive. *Monitoring strategies for toxic substances.* Sudbury: HSE Books, 1999. *Assessment of exposure requires a strategy of representative sampling: this booklet explains the required approach*
- Coggon D, Rose G, Barker DJP. *Epidemiology for the uninitiated,* 4th ed. London: BMJ Publishing Group, 2003. *This short primer provides a useful introduction to epidemiological methods and principles*
- Harrington JM, Gill FS, Aw TC, Gardner K. *Occupational health pocket consultant,* 4th ed. Oxford: Blackwell Science, 1998. *This concise textbook explains how to make and interpret measurements of the working environment. It also provides a very good overview of other topics in occupational medicine*
- Verma DK, Purdham JT, Roels HA. Translating evidence of occupational conditions into strategies for prevention. *Occup Environ Med* 2002;59:205-13. *This review illustrates how evidence on risks and control measures can be used to develop effective preventive strategies in the workplace*

4 Fitness for work

William Davies

Assessments of fitness for work can be important for job applicants, employees, and employers. Unfitness because of an acute illness is normally self evident and uncontentious, but assessing other cases may not be straightforward and can have serious financial and legal implications for those concerned. Commercial viability, efficiency, and legal responsibilities lie behind the fitness standards required by employers, and it may be legitimate to discriminate against people with medical conditions on these grounds. Unnecessary discrimination, however, is counterproductive and may be costly if legislation is breached. The Disability Discrimination Act 1995 makes it unlawful for employers of 15 or more staff (all employers from 2004) to discriminate without justification against those with disability as defined by the Act. The Employment Rights Act 1996 requires procedural standards and fairness before any decision to dismiss an employee. Fortunately, balancing these often complex socioeconomic and legal issues to achieve a sustainable decision on fitness is not primarily a medical responsibility. Doctors do, however, have responsibilities to assess the relevant facts competently and to assist with the decision making process.

Basic principles and responsibilities

Staying on track
This chapter deals with assessing fitness for "identified employment." To avoid confusion with related issues, the following points should be noted at the outset:

- Fitness for work in relation to ill health retirement benefits will depend on the specific provisions of the pension scheme. Pivotal issues that frequently arise are the interpretations that should be given to incapacity and to permanence, and whether fitness relates to current employment or all work. General guidance has been issued and specific guidelines for all UK public sector schemes should now be available following the recommendations of a HM Treasury report in 2000
- The Disability Discrimination Act 1995 has encouraged good medical practice in assessing and deciding on fitness for work by requiring individual and competent assessments, and by obliging employers to be more accommodating to those covered by the legislation
- Key health and safety concepts—hazard, risk, negligible risk, and competence—apply to assessing fitness for work and should be clearly understood
- Rehabilitation back to work and an emphasis on capability rather than limitations are now central themes of legislation, guidance, and government policies on health and safety and occupational health.

Medical responsibilities
Doctors' responsibilities vary according to their role. General practitioners and hospital doctors acting as certifying medical practitioners have direct responsibilities to their patients to provide statutory evidence of advice given about fitness for the patient's regular occupation. Such doctors also have an obligation to provide related information to a medical officer working for the Department for Work and Pensions.

Implications of fitness assessments
- Security of employment
- Rejection at recruitment
- Justifiable or unfair discrimination
- Retirement because of ill health
- Termination of contract
- Claim for disability discrimination
- Claim for unfair dismissal
- Employment tribunals
- Medical appeal
- Civil litigation for personal injury
- Criminal prosecution for breach of health and safety legislation
- Professional liability
- Pension entitlements
- Benefit claims

Basic principles and responsibilities—when fitness assessments may be required
- Before employment, placement, or redeployment
- Routine surveillance in safety critical jobs
- During or after sickness absence
- To identify adjustment needs
- When attendance or performance issues arise
- If health and safety concerns arise
- To examine ill health retirement issues
- If required by statute
- Benefit assessment—for example, the "own occupation test" administered by the Department for Work and Pensions (DWP)

The personal capability assessment is the medical assessment used to determine if a person is eligible for state incapacity benefit. It does not consider fitness for a specific type of employment but assesses general functional ability in relation to everyday physical and mental activities. Decision makers within the Department for Work and Pensions who apply the test will take advice from a specially trained doctor approved for the purpose by the Secretary of State

17

Medical responsibilities

General and hospital practitioners

To patient
- Act in patient's best health interests
- Provide advice on fitness for regular occupation
- Consider clinical management that would support employment wherever clinically reasonable
- Provide patient with statutory forms (for example, Med 3) recording the advice given

To Department for Work and Pensions (DWP)
- Supply on request relevant clinical information to a medical officer

Occupational health practitioners

To patient
- Act in patient's best health interests
- Consider clinical management that would support employment wherever clinically reasonable

To employer
- Assess functional ability and occupational risks
- Make recommendations on fitness in accordance with valid predetermined standards
- Provide information and advice that enables management to make an informed decision on compatibility of subject with employer's requirements and legal responsibilities

To society and the general public
- In certain circumstances public interest will override any duty to the individual patient or employer—for example, a surgeon infected with hepatitis B who continues to work in a way that puts patients at risk

Detailed advice for general and hospital practitioners on DWP issues is available in the guide IB204 (March 2000) and from regional Medical Services Centres

Detailed advice on medical responsibilities of occupational health practitioners is available in *Fitness for Work. The Medical Aspects* or from accredited specialists in occupational medicine

---

Occupational health practitioners have direct responsibilities to the employee or job applicant and the employer. Both groups have a responsibility to society.

These groups may take different approaches but have important common ground. If patients, employees, and job applicants are to be treated fairly, every medical opinion on their fitness for a job should be based on a competent assessment of relevant factors, and should satisfy the same basic criteria. Patients' interests will be best served when there is clear understanding, due consultation, and, as far as possible, agreement between doctors.

Key principles in practice

The first principle in the table opposite establishes three basic criteria for fitness: attendance and performance, health and safety risk to others, and health and safety risk to self. In this context, "without risk" reflects a fundamental ethical concept of occupational medicine that limits medical discretion. Doctors should not presume to decide for others that risks are acceptable; employers must take this responsibility, and they require medical advice and information on the nature and extent of risk to make informed decisions.

The second principle means that an appraisal of the subject's medical condition and functional ability, together with a review of the relevant occupational considerations, should provide an empirical assessment of ability and risk. This assessment may be judged against the required fitness criteria to determine what the outcome should be.

The third, fourth, and fifth principles point to the potential there may be for preventing or controlling risk, and for accommodating the needs of people with disabilities or medical conditions. Such measures may justify a conditional recommendation of fitness.

The sixth principle means that technically all decisions on fitness rest with the employer. This is because the employer determines what is required of the employment and ultimately carries responsibility for the risks.

Framework for assessing fitness for work

The terms fitness and incapacity are open to interpretation, and responsibilities for assessing and deciding on fitness issues span medical and management disciplines. A systematic

Key principles of assessing fitness for work

1. The primary purpose of the medical assessment of fitness to work is to ensure that the subject is fit to perform the task required effectively and without risk to the subject's or others' health and safety
2. The subject's fitness should be interpreted in functional terms and in the context of the job requirements
3. Employers have a duty to ensure, so far as is reasonably practicable, the health, safety, and welfare of all their employees and others who may be affected (Health and Safety at Work etc. Act 1974)
4. Legal duties of reasonable adjustment and non-discrimination in employment are imposed by the Disability Discrimination Act 1995
5. Good employment practice involves due consideration of the needs of all job applicants and employees with disabilities or medical conditions (Employment Rights Act 1996)
6. It is ultimately the employer's responsibility to set the objectives for attendance and performance, and to ensure compliance with the law on health and safety and employment

Framework for assessing fitness for work

Stage 1—Workplace assessment of ability and risk
Step 1: Assess medical condition and functional capacity
Step 2: Consider occupational factors
Step 3: Explore enabling options

Stage 2—Relate Stage 1 findings to fitness criteria
Step 4: Identify any attendance or performance limitations
Step 5: Identify nature and extent of any risks to others
Step 6: Identify nature and extent of any risks to self

Stage 3—Report on outcome in suitable terms
Step 7: Confirm fitness or unfitness
Step 8: Present assessment conclusions if 7 not possible
Step 9: Provide supplementary advice to 8 if appropriate

approach is required to ensure consistency and to avoid confusion of roles.

The framework is based on the key principles and relevant legal provisions. There are three stages and up to nine logical steps. In simple cases where no medical conditions apply, steps 1, 2, and 7 should suffice. In other cases, seven, eight, or all nine steps may be required.

Reporting the outcome

When the parameters of the fitness criteria are defined and the assessment clearly satisfies or fails to satisfy the employer's requirements and responsibilities, a confirmation of fitness or unfitness can be made (see green columns in the desktop aid on page 23).

When the parameters of the fitness criteria are uncertain (when the employer's requirements and responsibilities cannot be predetermined or presumed) the conclusions of the assessment should be made clear to the employer. In addition, an opinion on the reasonableness of any enabling options identified or the case for employment or continued employment may be given as supplementary advice (see red columns in desktop aid).

It should be noted, however, that supplementary advice offered under step 9 above relates to management rather than medical issues, and should be qualified accordingly. All reports should comply with professional standards on disclosure and consent.

Assessment of ability and risk

Medical functional appraisal

Doctors should always have a basic knowledge of the job's demands and working environment before undertaking a medical functional appraisal so that the extent and emphasis of the appraisal may be tailored accordingly. Any medical conditions that could pose a risk to the subject's or others' health and safety, or that could affect attendance and performance, should be identified and evaluated.

A suitably constructed questionnaire is the simplest form of assessment; for pre-employment screening, a questionnaire or health declaration will be sufficient to permit medical clearance in many categories of employment. Some occupations have statutory standards (for example, in the United Kingdom, there are statutory medical standards for seafarers), and appraisals must include measuring necessary factors. Others have standards set by authoritative recommendations or guidance (for example, the Health Advisory Committee of the UK Offshore Operators Association has drawn up guidelines on the medical standards for offshore work).

If no guidance exists, doctors must judge how extensive the assessment should be by taking account of the nature of any medical conditions identified, the type of work, and the reasons for management's request for medical advice.

Occupational considerations

In straightforward cases a medical functional appraisal and the doctor's existing knowledge of the job demands and working environment may be sufficient for a confirmation of fitness. However, a closer look at occupational factors is often needed to determine the precise requirements of the job, the subject's real abilities in a working environment, the nature of any hazards, and the probability of harm occurring (the actual risk in the workplace).

Medical functional appraisal

History and examination
- Pre-employment questionnaire or health declaration
- Health interview, occupationally relevant direct questions
- Physical examination focusing on job requirements

Functionally specific questionnaires
- Respiratory (MRC questionnaire)
- Pre-audiometry

Consultation and research
- Details from general practitioner and medical specialist, under Access to Medical Reports Act 1988 or non-UK equivalent
- Details from other specialists such as psychologists or audiologists
- Advice or second opinion from specialist occupational physician
- Advice or second opinion from independent specialists such as cardiologists or neurologists
- Clinical guidelines and evidenced based reviews
- Texts, journals, and research

Work related tests and investigations
Perceptual tests
- Snellen chart: special visual standards may be required for certain occupations such as aircraft pilots, seafarers, and vocational drivers
- Colour vision tests such as Ishihara plates or City University test, or matching tests, may be necessary if normal colour vision is essential—for example, for some jobs in transport, navigation, and the armed services
- Voice tests
- Audiometry: occupations such as the armed services, police, and fire service may have specific standards

Functional tests
- Lung function tests (for example, UK regulations require fire service employees to have their respiratory parameters measured before employment
- Dynamic or static strength tests
- Physical endurance and aerobic capacity (for example, the fire service or commercial divers)
- Step test
- Bicycle ergometer

Diagnostic (health on work)
- Exercise electrocardiography: needed—for example, for vocational drivers and offshore workers
- Drug and alcohol tests may be a requirement in certain safety critical industries

Diagnostic (work on health)
- Haematology, biochemistry, and urine analysis: UK commercial divers will have full blood count and haemoglobin S assessed before employment
- Radiographs: long bone radiographs are a requirement before employment for saturation diving in the United Kingdom

- A subject may be able to show satisfactory ability in a job simulation exercise despite a physical impairment that might have affected fitness—for example, a work related test of manual dexterity for an assembly line worker with some functional loss resulting from a hand injury
- In teaching, health care, and many other occupations, the perceived hazards of epilepsy are often found to be negligible when the potential for harm to others is properly assessed
- If diabetes is well controlled, the risk of injury from hypoglycaemia may be found to be very remote when the true frequency and duration of hazardous situations are taken into account.

Enabling options

A subject's potential fitness often depends on intervention. There may be unexplored treatments that can be provided. Rehabilitative support may be needed to achieve or speed recovery. Employers can make reasonable adjustments, temporary or permanent, to meet the needs of people with medical conditions. Prevention and control measures can reduce or eliminate health and safety risks that would otherwise prohibit a recommendation of fitness.

- Unexplored treatments that are often identified during assessments include physiotherapy, anxiety management, and psychotherapy
- A tailored, stepwise rehabilitative programme can make the prospect of returning to work after serious illness less daunting and may be vital for recovery from anxiety, depression, occupational stress, and other demotivating conditions
- Modifying a job specification may allow a recommendation of fitness with minimal inconvenience to the employer (for example, removing the requirement to undertake occasional lifting for an arthritic subject)
- Substituting a sensitising or irritant product may, with other sensible precautions, enable an employee with asthma or eczema to continue working as—for example, a paint sprayer or cleaner.

These measures may be applicable under the Health and Safety at Work etc. Act 1974. The Disability Discrimination Act 1995 may also require reasonable adjustments to be made. Even if intervention is not obligatory, employers may recognise the benefits of positive action. Doctors should therefore always bear these options in mind, as it may be possible to give a conditional recommendation of fitness that the employer would be willing to accommodate.

Fitness criteria in difficult cases

This approach should produce a reliable opinion in most cases, but further steps may be needed if the criteria for fitness for work are uncertain. In a fitness assessment this may occur with one, two, or all three of the criteria. Dealing with the issues in turn is advisable.

Attendance and performance

The possible impact of a medical condition on a subject's ability to meet required levels of attendance and performance is a major source of employers' requests for medical opinion. When asked by an employer about an employee's performance and attendance capabilities, the doctor's responsibility is to give the most accurate opinion that the circumstances allow. Conclusions and advice should be as positive as possible but without misrepresenting the facts, and should be discussed with the subject. This should help motivation and may improve recovery.

Occupational considerations

Ability in the workplace—consider actual effect of physical or medical condition on performance
- Confirm job requirements such as perception, mobility, strength, and endurance
- Ask employee what the work entails
- Review job description or inspect worksite
- Perform field tests of specific abilities or structured job simulation exercises
- Consider trial of employment with feedback from management

Nature of hazards—consider interaction of occupational factors and medical condition
- Harm from:
  - demands (heart attack, back strain, prolapsed disc, repetitive strain injury)
  - exposures (asthma, dermatitis, hearing loss)
  - situations (seizure, trauma, accidents)
  - infections (food handling, surgical procedures)
- How much harm is likely (temporary, permanent, minor, major, fatal)?
- Who may be affected (self, colleagues, clients, public)?

Extent of risk—focus on facts and avoid presumption
- Question employee on relevant details
- Obtain management report on material facts
- Examine documentation such as exposure records, accident reports, etc.
- Observe work, workplace, and working practices
- Identify frequencies and duration of hazardous exposures or situations
- Request technical data from hygienist, ergonomist, etc. if required
- Review relevant literature, journals, and research

Enabling options

Unexplored treatments
- Drug treatment or surgery
- Physiotherapy or occupational therapy
- Counselling or psychotherapy

Rehabilitative measures
- Graded resumption of responsibilities
- Refamiliarisation training
- Temporary reduction of workload
- Management appraisal or progress reports
- Scheduled or self requested medical reviews

Reasonable adjustments
- Modification of duties or working hours
- Redeployment to existing vacancy
- Modifying or providing equipment
- Time off for rehabilitation or treatment
- Providing supervision

Risk prevention and control
- Elimination or substitution of hazard
- Implementation of methods to reduce worker exposure to hazards
- Personal protection or immunisation
- Information, instruction, and training
- Health and medical surveillance

- Employers do not like open ended statements such as "Unfit; review in three months;" they prefer uncertainties to be expressed as probabilities: "Mr Smith has been incapacitated but is progressing well and is likely to become fit to return to work within four weeks"
- The doctor should may need to ask management for an appraisal of capabilities before making definitive conclusions on the relevance of medical factors: "I will therefore require a management report on her progress after week 6 of the rehabilitation programme"
- In cases of prolonged sickness absence, the doctor should not be pressured into recommending ill health retirement for doubtful reasons: "Mr Green is likely to remain unfit for the foreseeable future, but there are not sufficient grounds for ill health retirement under the pensions scheme."

If social or motivational factors are evident, discuss these with the subject, and advise management accordingly: "Mrs Jones' incapacitation is due to family commitments that are likely to continue for the foreseeable future. She realises that her employment could be at risk and would welcome an opportunity to discuss her situation with management."

Health and safety risk to others

Employers have a legal duty to ensure the health and safety of employees and the public. In principle, the doctor identifies hazards and quantifies any risks; management decides on a subject's fitness on the basis of the medical conclusions and advice. In practice, however, doctors confirm fitness when there is no risk, and unfitness if there are clearly unacceptable risks. For the many cases that lie in between, there may be confusion as to whether it is a management or medical responsibility to decide on fitness. A pragmatic approach is suggested.

For negligible risk, the doctor may advise that the subject be considered fit provided that the judgement of negligible risk is made objectively, is based on a competent risk assessment, and that the employer applies all reasonably practicable precautions.

For greater than negligible risk, the doctor should define the type of hazard and extent of risk as clearly as possible to enable management to make an informed decision.

Advice from a specialist occupational physician may be required to confirm the competence of the risk assessment or to assist management on acceptability.

Health and safety risk to self

The principles of assessing risk to others applies here, but medical advice can go further. In some cases employment may pose a risk of ill health but the employer is satisfied that everything possible has been done to prevent or reduce risks (for example, the risk of relapse in a teacher with a history of work related anxiety depressive disorder). To advise that in such cases the subject should always be deemed unfit because of a risk of work related illness is unrealistic. The benefits of employment for the subject, and possibly their employer, may considerably outweigh the risks. On the other hand, there could be issues of liability for both employer and doctor if the risks are overlooked.

The parameters of the fitness criteria may be uncertain when:

- Attendance or performance limitations resulting from a medical condition are identified, but the employer's willingness to accommodate them cannot be prejudged
- Health and safety risks to others exist, but they seem remote enough to ignore
- Health and safety risks to self are identified, but they do not seem to justify a recommendation of unfitness.

Reasonable adjustments under the Disability Discrimination Act (DDA) 1995 (see chapter 5)

- Reasonable adjustments are essentially any steps relating to arrangements and premises that are reasonable for an employer to take in all the circumstances to prevent the disabled person being at a disadvantage. Many of the enabling options listed above fall within this definition
- The DDA Code of Practice expands on examples given in the Act and provides guidance on the reasonableness of adjustments (Paragraphs 4.12-4.48)
- A comprehensive series of practical briefing guides on the DDA is published by the Employers Forum on Disability, Nutmeg House, 60 Gainsford Street, London SE1 2NY

Data sources for standards of fitness (see Further reading)

Key publications
For drivers, pilots, food handlers, and many other occupations: Cox et al., DVLA

General guidance
Health and Safety Executive

Professional associations
ALAMA (Association of Local Authority Medical Advisors) for firefighters, police, teachers, etc.
ANHOPS (Association of National Health Occupational Physicians) for healthcare professions

Government departments
Department for Education and Skills for teachers

Statute
Seafarers: Merchant Navy Shipping (Medical examination) Regulations 1983. Revised in 1998 [Merchant shipping notice MSN 1712(M)]

The autonomy of the subject must be reconciled with the needs and responsibilities of the employer. Legal precedent does not provide clear guidance on how this should be done; the issues are complex and the implications serious. A rational basis for providing helpful medical advice includes a full discussion of the prognosis with the subject to determine where the balance of benefits and risks lies

- If the subject thinks the benefits outweigh the risks and the doctor agrees, advice should be given in support of employment, provided that the assessment and the judgement of balance between benefit and risk have been competently undertaken
- If the subject thinks the benefits outweigh the risks but the doctor cannot agree, consider seeking a second opinion from a specialist occupational physician before providing management with definitive advice
- If the subject thinks the risks outweigh the benefits and the doctor agrees, early retirement should be considered
- If the subject thinks the risks outweigh the benefits when the hazard and risk seem disproportionately low, then motivational factors (such as a common law claim or ill health retirement incentives) may be relevant. If so, the doctor should proceed cautiously and consider obtaining a second opinion from a specialist occupational physician.

The conclusions should be presented to management in context, indicating the nature of the hazard, the extent of risk, and strength of medical consensus. This will enable the employer to discharge his or her responsibility in a complex area with the benefit of such medical support as the circumstances allow.

Definitive opinion

The conclusions, recommendations, and advice outlined above are valid only for the specific fitness criterion considered. In each case, the outcomes of all three criteria should be consolidated to provide an all embracing definitive report. The desktop aid includes a synopsis of the outcomes commonly encountered and may be adapted as a classification guide for audit purposes.

Further reading

- Cox RAF, Edwards FC, Palmer K. *Fitness for work. The medical aspects*, 3rd ed. Oxford: Oxford Medical Publications, 2000. *A comprehensive text on medical issues covering background issues, all medical systems and specific occupations*
- Benefits Agency, Department of Social Security. *A guide for registered medical practitioners*. Revised with effect from April 2000. (IB204) *Medical evidence for statutory sick pay, statutory maternity pay, and social security incapacity benefit purposes.* Supplemented in April 2002 by chief Medical Officer's Bulletin and Desk aid. Publications available on www.dwa.gov.uk/medical. *Detailed practical reference, related website has evidenced based information and guidance*
- Drivers Medical Unit, DVLA. *At a glance guide to current medical standards of fitness to drive. March 2001.* Available on www.dvla.gov.uk/ataglance/content.htm. *Regularly updated prescriptive standards for wide range of medical conditions*
- Royal College of General Practitioners. *Clinical guidelines for the management of acute back pain.* 1997, updated 1999. Faculty of Occupational Medicine. *Occupational heath guidelines for the management of low back pain evidence review and recommendations,* March 2000. *Two complementary guides providing a positive practical approach to medical management and rehabilitation*
- Health and Safety Executive. *Your patients and their work, an introduction to occupational health for family doctors.* Bootle: HSE Books, 1992. *Simple general guide*
- Health and Safety Executive. *Pre-employment screening.* London: HMSO, 1982. (Guidance note MS20.) *Reviews main principles; would benefit from updating*
- ALAMA, ANHOPS, at Society of Occupational Medicine, 6 St Andrews Place Regents Park London. *Membership gives access to website facilities and current guidance and on firefighters, police, and healthcare professionals*
- DfEE. *Fitness to teach. Occupational health guidance for the training and employment of teachers. The physical and mental fitness to teach of teachers and of entrants to initial teacher training.* London: HMSO, 2000. *Focused, up to date, working guidance supported by well balanced complementary guide for employers and managers*

Desktop aid—Framework for assessing fitness for work

Assessment of ability and risk		Fitness criteria		Outcome
• Medical-functional appraisal		• Attendance and performance		• Confirm fit or unfit
• Occupational considerations	+	• Health and safety risk to others	=	• Report conclusions
• Enabling options		• Health and safety risk to self		• Offer advice

Applying fitness criteria—Synopsis of outcomes

Attendance and performance

A	B	C	D	E
Subject's condition compatible with required levels of attendance and performance	Attendance or performance limitations due to medical conditions or disabilities identified but likely to resolve	Attendance or performance limitations due to medical conditions or disabilities identified and likely to remain for foreseeable future	Subject's performance and capabilities cannot be determined by medical assessment alone	Subject's condition clearly incompatible with requirements of post and likely to remain so
	(a) in foreseeable future because of anticipated recovery or (b) if certain enabling options can be accommodated (such as treatment, rehabilitation, reasonable adjustments, or risk prevention)	Do not overlook social or motivational factors that may be relevant. Discuss implications with subject. If necessary seek advice*	Feedback on performance is required to identify possible impact of medical conditions	Help subject come to terms with implications such as ill health retirement, termination of contract, redeployment (if available), or rejection (at pre-employment stage)
Confirm fit	*Report conclusions indicating (a) likely timescale and/or (b) relevance of enabling options Reviews as necessary*	*Report conclusions Review as necessary*	*Report on medical issues and identify need for management appraisal/ feedback. Review as necessary*	*Confirm likely to remain unfit*

Health and safety risk to others

F	G	H	I	J
No risk to others	Risk identified but preventable	Negligible risk	Risk greater than negligible but may be acceptable	Risk to others clearly unacceptable and likely to remain so
	Identify and pursue relevant enabling options such as treatment, rehabilitation, reasonable adjustment, or risk prevention	Ensure judgment of negligible risk is made objectively and based on competent assessment (if unsure seek advice*) and that management applies all reasonably practicable precautions	Inform management of nature and extent of risk as clearly as possible. Specialist occupational physician may be able to help management in deciding on acceptability*	Help subject come to terms with implications such as ill health retirement, termination of contract, redeployment (if available), or rejection (at pre-employment stage)
Confirm fit	*Report conclusions and advise fit (subject to specified conditions)*	*Report conclusions and advise fit (subject to specified conditions) Review if circumstances change*	*Report conclusions advise risk cannot be dismissed as negligible and that acceptability is for management to consider*	*Confirm likely to remain unfit*

Health and safety risk to self

K	L	M	N	O
No risk to self	Risk identified but preventable	Risks identified which subject thinks are outweighed by benefits	Risks identified which subject thinks outweigh benefits	Risk to self clearly unacceptable and likely to remain so
	Identify and pursue relevant enabling options such as treatment, rehabilitation, reasonable adjustment, or risk prevention	*If doctor agrees*—Ensure assessment and judgment of balance between risk and benefit have been competently undertaken (if unsure seek advice*) *If doctor disagrees*—Consider obtaining second opinion before advising	*If doctor agrees*—Consider early retirement *If doctor disagrees*—If risks seem disproportionately low consider relevance of motivational factors (such as common law claim or ill health retirement incentives) If present proceed cautiously and consider obtaining second opinion*	Help subject come to terms with implications such as ill health retirement, termination of contract, redeployment (if available), or rejection (at pre-employment stage)
Confirm fit	*Report conclusions and advise fit (subject to specified conditions)*	*Report conclusions with supplementary advice as appropriate*	*Report conclusions with supplementary advice as appropriate*	*Confirm likely to remain unfit*

Definitive opinion
The confirmations, conclusions, and advice outlined abvoe are valid only for the specific fitness criterion addressed.
In each case the outcomes of all three criteria should be consolidated to provide an all embracing definitive report

*Advice and second opinions should be obtained from doctors with training and expertise to provide proper assistance.
Specialist qualifications for occupational physicians in the UK (MFOM, FFOM) are awarded by the Faculty of Occupational Medicine of the Royal College of Physicians.

5 Legal aspects

Martyn Davidson

Society has become increasingly litigious in recent years, and the modern "blame culture" has encouraged a tendency to look for fault whenever there is harm. In all areas of medicine this has led to increased awareness of the legal process, and occasionally defensive medicine. Employment law and rights based legislation following European Union initiatives have expanded as a result of enlightened social policies, extension of a single European market, and environmental protection. Because employment and rights based legislation affect the worker and the workplace, the occupational health (OH) practitioner needs to understand the legal provisions and the framework in which they operate.

Health and safety legislation aims to prevent the workforce being injured or made ill by their work. Employers have considerable duties, including duties relating to the general public, and the role of the OH practitioner is to advise on steps to achieve compliance. An understanding of the principles is essential, and these are covered here with reference predominantly to English law. Employees also have corresponding duties to take "reasonable care" for their own safety and that of others, and to cooperate with appropriate procedures.

The OH practitioner will become involved in employment law when medical advice is needed, and it is essential that the basics are understood.

The legal framework defining the duty towards the health of the workforce was established in the 19th century. Although prompted by humanitarian concerns, these legal developments were the pragmatic result of the concerns of industry—the toll of premature death and disability threatened the supply of healthy workers required to increase productivity. Reproduced with permission from Hulton Deutsch

Ethics

The position of the OH professional

Physicians are primarily bound by the codes of their profession and in the United Kingdom they are accountable to the General Medical Council for their behaviour. For OH nurses the corresponding body is the Nursing and Midwifery Council. Difficulties sometimes arise because the OH practitioner is often an employee of the company requesting advice. The company may feel that the practitioner's contract of employment overrides professional codes. This is not so, and employers cannot insist on contractual terms that would require a physician or nurse to breach professional codes. If such terms existed, they would be difficult, if not impossible, to enforce.

Confidentiality

The duty of confidentiality applies as it does to any physician or nurse. This includes the safeguarding of all medical information, records, and results. The legal basis of the duty of confidentiality remains unclear, however, and the duty is ultimately relative rather than absolute. Material should be regarded as confidential if it has been obtained in circumstances which would indicate that this was the intention. Circumstances can arise in any medical specialty in which disclosure may be necessary; in such cases the clinician will be expected to justify his or her action, before a court if necessary.

OH practitioners may sometimes feel that they are not in a traditional nurse/doctor-patient relationship when they are acting on behalf of a third party. This might be the case with respect to a job applicant whom an OH practitioner sees in order to advise the employing company. Offers of employment are usually conditional upon "medical clearance"—is the

---

Major responsibilities of occupational health physicians

Professional ethical obligations
- Provide a good standard of practice and care
- Keep up to date and maintain performance
- Respect confidentiality and maintain trust
- Maintain good communications

General Medical Council. *Good medical practice.* London: GMC, 2001
See also: Faculty of Occupational Medicine. *Good medical practice for occupational physicians.* 2001

Guidance
- Health assessments
- Advice on absence
- Confidentiality
- Health records
- Relationships with others

See: The Occupational Health Committee. *The occupational physician.* London: BMA, 2001

The OH physician must exercise professional skill and judgement in giving advice, and there is an ethical duty to inform the applicant of any abnormality uncovered by the process; however, the contractual duty lies with the prospective employer

applicant fit, in medical terms, for the duties of the post? The degree and extent of the duty upon the OH physician has been explored in two leading English cases.

Medical reports

When the OH practitioner is asked to provide advice on an individual's health for employment purposes, they should obtain written consent before releasing their opinion. This is correct ethical practice.

Because the OH practitioner is not usually the clinician caring for that individual, the Access to Medical Reports Act 1988 will not generally apply. It will apply, however, if the OH practitioner seeks further information from any other specialist or general practitioner who has been providing such care. The provisions of the Data Protection Act 1998 apply to obtaining, use, and retention of any personal information, including OH records.

Health and safety law

Statutory duties upon the employer

Health and safety

The Health and Safety at Work etc. Act (HSWA) 1974 is the main statute covering the general responsibilities of the employer. It covers others who might be affected by workplace activities—contractors, visitors, and the general public. The workplace must be safe and well maintained, with safe systems and organisation of work. Equipment and tools must be suitable and well maintained. Ensuring that employees behave safely is also down to the employer, who has the responsibility for supervision. Supervisory staff must be demonstrably competent. This duty is only limited when the employee might be considered to be "on a frolic of his own," as the courts have termed it.

The underlying principle of the statutory framework is that those who generate risk as a consequence of work activities have a duty to protect the health and safety of anyone who might be affected by those risks. Occasionally the duty is absolute but more commonly the extent of the duty is "as far as reasonably practicable." This allows the employer to balance the degree of risk against the difficulty and cost of reducing it. A small employer with modest resources may therefore argue that it could not go so far in risk reduction as a multinational company, for instance.

A great deal of more recent legislation, driven largely by directives from the European Commission, has focused on particular areas.

The general move has been away from the prescriptive approach and towards a duty on the employer (and the self employed) to assess risks arising from work activities. The employer must then identify and institute preventive actions on the basis of their assessment.

Reporting injuries and disease

Fatal and major injuries, those resulting in three or more days lost from work, and certain occupational diseases must be reported to the Health and Safety Executive (HSE), as per the Reporting of Injuries, Diseases and Dangerous Occurrences Regulations 1995 (RIDDOR). For a disease to be reported, the disease must be listed in the regulations, the affected employee must be involved in a relevant task or activity, and there must be a written diagnosis from a doctor. Under-reporting is considerable—the patient or treating doctor may not realise that the condition is work related, employers have little incentive to report, or the patient may fear for their job and therefore not wish to agree to disclosure.

Duty of care at pre-employment

Baker v Kaye (1997)

Mr Baker, applying for a job as International Sales Director, attended for pre-employment assessment by Dr Kaye. During the assessment, Dr Kaye elicited a history of significant alcohol consumption, supported subsequently by abnormal liver enzymes. Mr Baker had already resigned from his existing post, and when Dr Kaye advised the new employer that he did not consider Mr Baker fit for employment, Mr Baker sued for loss of the new post. The court in this case held that the OH physician owed a duty of care to the prospective employee, as well as to the employer, but as Dr Kaye had taken reasonable care in making the assessment, he was found not to be negligent

Kapfunde v Abbey National plc (1998)

However, the Court of Appeal, in *Kapfunde v Abbey National plc* (1998), disagreed with the decision in the case above.

Mrs Kapfunde, who suffered from sickle cell disease, applied for a job at the Abbey National. Dr Daniel, advising Abbey National, reported that the applicant's medical history and previous absence record indicated that she was likely to have an above average sickness record. Mrs Kapfunde was not considered for the job, and subsequently sued Abbey National, arguing that Dr Daniel had been negligent. The Court, in judging Dr Daniel not negligent (because she had exercised reasonable skill and care in reaching her decision), added that neither did she owe a duty of care to Mrs Kapfunde

---

Modern domestic legislation since 1988 based on risk assessment

More than 20 European directives have produced a large number of specific regulations, notably the "Framework" Directive for the Introduction of Measures to Encourage Improvements in Safety of Health of Workers, which was enacted into UK law by the Management of Health and Safety at Work Regulations 1992 (updated in 1999), and together with its five "daughter" directives forms the "six pack" (marked *).

- Management of Health and Safety at Work Regulations 1992 (now MHSWR 1999)*
- Workplace (Health, Safety, and Welfare) Regulations 1992*
- Provision and Use of Work Equipment Regulations 1992*
- Personal Protective Equipment Regulations 1992*
- Display Screen Equipment Regulations 1992*
- Manual Handling Operations Regulations 1992*
- Working Time Regulations 1998

Many of these are accompanied by an approved code of practice or guidance notes. These are not legally binding in their own right. However, they bring detail to the statute, and guidance on how compliance may be achieved. An employer would have to justify a diversion from their recommendations

---

Information on potential health risks must be given to the workforce, with suitable instruction and training on control measures. Sometimes medical surveillance may also be specified

Failure to comply

Despite the extensive legislation to prevent them, work related injuries and illness still occur. In these cases, the legal system has two distinct roles: to punish the negligent employer, and to compensate the injured employee.

Prosecution
The enforcing authorities. The HSE is responsible for enforcement activities in most workplaces, including factories, farms, hospitals, schools, railways, mines, nuclear installations, and also driving as part of work. The exceptions are—for example, retail and finance, where responsibility lies with local authorities. The Health and Safety Commission and the HSE were established by the HSWA 1974. The HSE includes the Employment Medical Advisory Service, which comprises doctors and nurses who are OH specialists and who have the full powers of inspectors.
The law. Breach of the HSWA is subject to criminal sanctions. Prosecutions (most are undertaken by the HSE in the Magistrates' and Crown Courts) will generally result in a fine.
Manslaughter. After a fatal accident, the HSE will defer to the police. The Crown Prosecution Service may then bring a case for manslaughter. However, prosecution is rarely successful. The difficulty is that a "company" is not an individual and therefore not capable of a crime of this nature.

Manslaughter

An unsuccessful case
A total of 188 people died when the Herald of Free Enterprise capsized at Zeebrugge in 1987. The case against P&O showed failures within the management and with several individuals on the vessel. However, no single person was found sufficiently at fault for the charge to apply

A successful case
Peter Kite, the managing director of OII Ltd, received a custodial sentence after four teenagers drowned during a canoeing trip in Lyme Bay in 1993. Kite ran the small company and was found to be the "controlling mind." There was a history of his ignoring warnings about safety and he clearly failed to adhere to accepted standards. The company was also found guilty of manslaughter and fined £60 000

Current thinking
Reform of this area has been considered since the 1996 Law Commission Report. This recommended new offences of corporate killing and individual offences of reckless killing and killing by gross carelessness. However, legislation has not been forthcoming. In May 1998 Simon Jones, aged 24, died on his first day at work at Shoreham Dockyard; the resulting unsuccessful action provoked further outcry. In 2000-1, 26 cases were referred by the Health and Safety Executive to the Crown Prosecution Service for consideration of manslaughter charges; six are proceeding. Since 1992, 162 referrals have led to 45 prosecutions and 10 convictions. Five individuals have received prison sentences

Compensation
An employee who suffers from a work related illness or injury has two possible routes to seek compensation. Firstly, they may claim from the government if they have a "prescribed disease" via the Industrial Injuries Benefit Scheme. Secondly, and entirely separately, they may claim against the employer via a personal injury claim in the civil court.
Prescribed diseases. The Industrial Injuries Scheme administered by the Department of Work and Pensions "prescribes" a number of occupational illnesses for compensation. To qualify for compensation, the applicant must have the prescribed

---

Main powers of enforcement authorities

Health and Safety Executive
- Enters and inspects workplaces
- Issues improvement or prohibition notices (immediate or deferred)
- Prosecutes

Employment Medical Advisory Service
- Gives advice on health and safety issues to employers and employees
- Investigates complaints or concerns about health, or after a report under Reporting of Injuries, Diseases, and Dangerous Occurrences Regulations 1995
- Has the same legal powers as inspectors (where the Health and Safety Executive is the reporting authority)
- Appoints doctors for health surveillance required by regulations (Ionizing Radiation Regulations 2000, Control of Lead at Work Regulations 1998, Diving at Work Regulations 1997)

Criminal law and enforcement activities

UK criminal law
- Arises from statute and is a punitive system for offences against society as a whole
- Acts of parliament and regulations made thereunder provide the "rules" by which employers are expected to abide
- Case law—the court's decisions in specific cases—provides guidance on the interpretation of these rules
- Decisions made in higher courts are binding upon lower courts
- The burden of proof in criminal cases is "beyond reasonable doubt;" a higher standard than that applying in civil claims "on the balance of probabilities"

Health and Safety Executive (2000-1) Activities
- 11,058 enforcement notices (70% in manufacturing and construction)
- 6673 improvement notices
- 2077 prosecutions, resulting in 1493 convictions (72%)
- Average penalty £6250

Local authorities (1999-2000)
- 4850 improvement notices
- 1250 prohibition notices
- 412 prosecutions, resulting in 358 convictions (87%)
- Average fine £4595

Zebrugge ferry disaster. Reproduced with permission from Rex Features

disease, and must also have worked in an occupation recognised to carry a risk of that particular disease. The amount of the payment depends on the degree of disability, as assessed by an adjudication officer.

Civil claims. A claim through the civil courts is a means of compensating one person for damage arising from another's action or inaction. Most claims are brought under the tort of negligence. The employer is held to have a broad, general duty of care to avoid harm to its employees. This is part of the common law (where there is no guiding statute law, but is developed over time by decisions of the judiciary).

The employee must argue that the employer failed in their duty of care to safeguard the worker's health. The applicant employee must show that:

(a) The employer owed the worker a duty of care
(b) The employer negligently breached that duty
(c) The employee suffered damage as a result of that breach.

The level of proof is the "balance of probabilities."

Employees with illnesses that may be occupationally related but are not prescribed can only pursue this route.

Large damages paid in compensation may seem impressive when reported in the media, but the adversarial system as presently practised has its problems, and the impact of new civil procedure rules introduced in 1999 in an attempt to improve the present system (on the basis of the Woolf reports on access to justice) is not yet clear. Furthermore, if state compensation is paid for an industrial disease before the personal injury claim, this may be clawed back from awarded damages in excess of £2500.

Another option in the civil courts is an action for breach of statutory duty. The HSWA expressly excludes any such civil action in sections 2-8, although some regulations made under the HSWA do support such an action. Current plans are to remove the existing civil liability exclusion from the Management of Health and Safety at Work Regulations 1999.

Employment law

Legislation
A considerable body of both European and domestic legislation exists in this area. The Employment Rights Act 1996 (ERA) consolidated employees' rights into a single statute. Other primary and subordinate legislation relates to issues of discrimination, pay, and sick pay and are supported by various influential codes of practice, such as those produced by the Advisory, Conciliation and Arbitration Service.

Complaints in this area are heard by employment tribunals, which were established so that employment disputes can be settled rapidly and without the expense of going to court. The employment tribunal comprises three members, including an experienced lawyer as the chair. Appeals are referred first to the Employment Appeal Tribunal, and ultimately to the Appeal Court.

Dismissal
The Employment Rights Act gives employees the right not to be unfairly dismissed. In general, one year's continuous employment is required before a complaint for unfair dismissal can be brought. Some types of unfair dismissal, notably certain grounds relating to discrimination or health and safety, require no such qualifying period—this might be the case if an employee were dismissed because he or she raised the issue of hazardous working conditions.

How diseases become prescribed
Thirty-nine conditions are listed in four categories; those caused by:

A Physical agents (for example, occupational deafness)
B Biological agents (for example, viral hepatitis)
C Chemical agents (for example, angiosarcoma of the liver)
D Those of a miscellaneous nature (for example, occupational dermatitis)

The list is similar to those diseases reportable under the Reporting of Injuries, Diseases and Dangerous Occurrences Regulations 1995

The Industrial Injuries Advisory Council advises on the addition of new prescribed diseases. Its criteria are narrow: the disease must be a recognised risk in a particular occupation and not to the general population, and the causal link between exposure and disease must be well established. This process may take some time

- Vibration white finger (now hand arm vibration syndrome) was considered four times between 1954 and 1985, when it was prescribed
- Occupational deafness was considered in 1961 and prescribed in 1975

Common law duty of care
The depth and breadth of the employer's duty of care has been developed over the years by landmark cases. The concept of the *"reasonable and prudent employer, taking positive thought for the safety of his workers in the light of what he knows or ought to know"* was clarified by Judge Swanwick in 1968

The duty is greater if the employee has a known vulnerability. This is known as the "eggshell skull" rule, after a 1901 case. A better example is that of *Paris* v *Stepney Borough Council* (1951). Mr Paris, a bus fitter with sight in only one eye, lost the sight in the other eye after entry of a metallic foreign body. The Council was negligent in not providing Mr Paris with eye protection, though, given that the risk of an accident was slight, they were not obliged to provide this for others in their workforce

Exactly when an employer should be aware of a particular health risk in the workplace is inevitably contentious, particularly in relation to claims for occupational illness. Courts may decide on a "date of knowledge," after which no employer could reasonably claim ignorance. This date will often relate to government guidance or other influential advice. For instance, in the case of noise induced hearing loss, the year 1963 became the watershed, after a Ministry of Labour pamphlet in that year

Areas of interest in civil litigation
Work related stress (WRS)
The 1995 case of *Walker* v *Northumberland County Council* attracted considerable attention. Mr Walker was an area social services officer. He had a heavy caseload, and frequently requested help. After five months' absence for a "nervous breakdown," he returned to a backlog of work, and the promised assistance did not materialise. After a second breakdown, he sued his employer. The Council was held not to be liable for his first breakdown as they were not aware that he was susceptible to stress. However, it was liable for the second breakdown. The risk was foreseeable and preventable, and there was a duty not to cause Mr Walker psychiatric injury. Damages were £175 000

However, successful actions for WRS are few and far between, and the burden of proof on the employee remains considerable. In February 2002 the Court of Appeal overturned three awards (*Hatton* v *Sutherland and others*) of almost £200 000. It set down 16 guidelines that it considered relevant, and which will aid both courts and employers. These include the following:

- The employer is entitled to assume that the employee can deal with the normal pressures of the job unless there is a known vulnerability
- No occupations should be regarded as intrinsically dangerous
- If the only alternative would be to dismiss or demote the employee, the employer would not be in breach of duty if the employee willingly continues in the job

The hurdle for applicants under this heading remains high and, if anything, this judgement will make a claim for WRS more difficult

Dismissal occurs when the contract of employment is terminated by the employer, when a fixed term contract expires and is not renewed, or when an employee terminates the contract as a result of the employers' conduct. The five potentially fair reasons for dismissal are given in the box.

Absence from work may generate grounds for dismissal and, if absence is attributed to ill health, OH advice will be required. It is important to differentiate between long term absence and recurrent short term absenteeism.

Long term absence—This may give rise to fair dismissal on the grounds of capability, which includes both ill health and incompetence. The employer is expected to gather enough information to assess the situation fully and to decide on a reasonable course of action. This should include consultation with the employee and will often include a medical opinion. The employer might consider alternative work, although it is under no statutory duty to do so (unless the case falls under the disability discrimination legislation, vide infra). The employer cannot know details of the illness because of confidentiality, but is entitled to ask when the employee might recover, whether the employee will be capable of returning to their former job and, if not, the likely restrictions on capability.

The final decision on employment is a management rather than a medical decision, with the physician in an advisory role. It is important to appreciate that the cause of ill health is irrelevant to the fairness of the dismissal, even if the current employment is likely to have been the cause.

Attendance—The problem of recurrent short term absenteeism may be approached rather differently. Employers may view this as an attendance issue and are entitled to expect a certain level of reliability from employees. The genuineness of the illness is not relevant, as an employer may ultimately fairly dismiss on the grounds of either capability or "some other substantial reason." However, the employer should investigate fully and act in line with its absence policy, giving due warning to the employee that attendance is expected to improve. It is good practice (although not essential, depending on the case) to take medical advice as to whether poor attendance is because of an important underlying medical condition. (If there is, the case might more properly be dealt with as a capability problem.)

Disability discrimination

The employment provisions of the Disability Discrimination Act 1995 came into force on 2 December 1996, with duties on the employer to accommodate disabled people, whether existing employees or job applicants. It is unlawful to discriminate—that is, to treat anyone with a disability less favourably for reasons relating to the disability. There is a duty to make "reasonable adjustments" to allow the disabled person to work. However, the Act can allow the employer to justify discriminatory treatment.

Awards for complaints under the Disability Discrimination Act have no upper limit; the stakes are therefore potentially high. Employment tribunals have sometimes had difficulty dealing with the medical issues, as they do not normally use medical experts. Experience of this legislation has clarified and confused in almost equal measure.

Reasons for fair dismissal

1. Relating to capability ("skill, aptitude, health, or any other physical or mental quality") or qualifications ("any degree, diploma, or other academic, technical, or professional qualification")
2. Relating to conduct (behaviour at, or sometimes outside, the workplace)
3. Redundancy
4. If employee cannot continue to work without breach of statutory duty (such as after loss of driving licence)
5. Some other substantial reason (SOSR) sufficient to justify dismissal

In February 2002 the compensatory award for unfair dismissal was limited to £52 600. The burden of proof is said to be neutral, although the employer is required to show that the dismissal was not unfair. An employment tribunal will judge the circumstances of the case—including elements such as the size, resources, consistency of behaviour, and procedural correctness of the employer—in deciding reasonableness

---

The Disability Discrimination Act (DDA) and some definitions

Disability—"a physical or mental impairment causing a substantial and long term adverse effect on the ability to carry out normal day to day activities"

- A physical impairment is not defined in the legislation, but is likely to encompass any "organic or bodily detriment," including severe disfigurements (facial scars or burns), but excluding deliberately acquired disfigurements (tattoos or body piercings)
- A mental impairment is any clinically well recognised condition (that is, one recognised by a responsible body of medical opinion), and must be beyond a reaction that could be described as a normal human reaction
- A substantial adverse effect is defined as one that is more than minor or trivial
- Normal day to day activities are:
  - Mobility
  - Manual dexterity
  - Physical co-ordination
  - Continence
  - Ability to lift, carry, or otherwise move everyday objects
  - Speech, hearing, or eyesight
  - Memory or ability to concentrate, learn, or understand
  - Perception of the risk of physical danger
- Long term implies an impairment that has lasted 12 months or more, is likely to last 12 months or more, or is terminal

Certain specific conditions (for instance, nicotine or alcohol dependence) are excluded from the Disability Discrimination Act. Controlled or corrected, progressive, and recurring conditions may be included

Reasonable adjustments to allow the disabled to work

- Accessible and equitable recruitment processes
- Modifications to equipment
- Changes to job design and work environment
- Resources and cost are relevant

Justification

- The failure to adjust must be both material to the circumstances of the case and substantial
- Stricter than "reasonable"
- Requires hard evidence

The Disability Discrimination Act does not currently apply to organisations with fewer than 15 employees, but this exemption will be removed from October 2004. The provisions of the Act are also likely to be extended to include the emergency services, and other medical conditions. The justification provision will be removed

Outcomes of the Disability Discrimination Act

5662 cases brought up to March 2000 (England and Wales)—23% successful

Medical conditions
- 21% back or neck conditions
- 16% hand or arm conditions
- 14% depression or anxiety

Legal issues
- 34% concerned failure to transfer to suitable alternative work
- 26% sought to justify on the basis of the amount of sick leave
- 51% required medical evidence

Awards
Total compensation in 1999: £369 297
Average: £9981 per award
Maximum award in 2001: £278 800

Disabled person at work with appropriate aids such as a voice recognition dictation system linked to a laptop computer for an employee no longer able to type rapidly. The photograph was produced by Mr D Griffiths, with the subject's permission

Future developments

Many other areas may come to have relevance to the work of the OH practitioner, two of which are considered below.

Human rights

The Human Rights Act 1998 came into force in October 2000, bringing the European Convention on Human Rights into UK law. It makes no explicit reference to HSWA. However, under the right to privacy it may forseeably impinge on areas such as drug testing and surveillance. The lack of legal aid for employment tribunals (in England and Wales) and the fairness of the employment tribunal system may generate debate under the provisions for the right to a fair trial.

Rehabilitation

In contrast to the numerous duties to prevent ill health or injury, there is currently no requirement to rehabilitate back to the workplace. This has a huge cost: in 2000, 2.29 million people claimed incapacity benefit, and employers paid out £750 million in compensation under employer's liability insurance schemes. The United Kingdom has a poor record; a Swedish worker has an almost 50% chance of returning to work after an injury, whereas in the United Kingdom the figure is only 15%. Employers may have to develop a policy in this area as in all other health and safety fields. The Departments of Health, and of Work and Pensions are working on a pilot initiative to encourage early return to work, with its effectiveness evaluated by the National Centre for Social Research.

Frequent questions for the OH practitioner in relation to the Disability Discrimination Act

- **Is the condition covered?** In practice, employment tribunals have been hesitant to exclude a condition even when there is considerable scientific debate about the exact nature of the diagnosis (for example, chronic fatigue syndrome)
- **Does the Act apply?** This is a legal decision, and judgement rests with the employment tribunals. The OH practitioner can advise, and the employer make its own judgement, but the employment tribunal is the final arbiter
- **Is treatment unequal?** The "comparator" against which the disabled person should be considered must be an able bodied individual; not one who has another condition but does not fall under the Act
- **Have accommodations been considered?** The employer must make genuine efforts to accommodate the disabled individual. The guidance that accompanies the Act must be followed closely
- **Is unequal treatment justified?** Less favourable treatment may currently be justified, but the employer must make a properly constructed argument with evidence to support its case
- **What happens if health and safety may be compromised?** The employer has a difficult balancing act under these circumstances. However, provided the employer has undertaken a proper risk assessment and subsequently generated a rational policy, then the tribunal cannot disregard the policy on the basis of a differing medical view. It is vital, though, that the employer acts on competent advice backed up by good evidence
- **May the disabled person assume a risk to their own health?** In other words, at what threshold does paternalism on the part of the employer take over from the well informed view of the individual? Current case law suggests that when there is a significant risk to health, the employer has the right (or even duty) to exclude the employee from that work activity

Further reading

- General Medical Council. *Good medical practice.* London: GMC, May 2001 (www.gmc-uk.org). *Covers expectations of the regulatory body and duties as a member of the medical profession*
- Faculty of Occupational Medicine. *Good medical practice for occupational physicians.* London: FOM, Dec 2001 (www.facoccmed.ac.uk). *More specific advice applied to occupational medical practice, based on the GMC guidance*
- Faculty of Occupational Medicine. *Guidance on ethics for occupational physicians.* London: FOM, May 1999. *Occupational physicians undertake roles outside the traditional doctor-patient relationship. Guidance on the ethics of commonly encountered situations that differ from clinical medical practice is valuable*
- British Medical Association. *The occupational physician.* London: BMA, June 2001 (www.bma.org.uk). *More detailed consideration of the role of the OH physician, relationships with employing organisations, and terms and conditions of service*
- Kloss D. *Occupational health law.* Oxford: Blackwell Science, 1998. *Widely acknowledged as the "bible" in this area*
- Lewis D, Sargeant M. *Essentials of employment law.* City: IPD 2000. *All the basics from a legal perspective*

- Berlins M, Dyer C. *The law machine.* London: Penguin 2000. *Brief, accessible description of the judicial system and explanation of how it all works*
- Branthwaite M. *Law for doctors.* City: RSM 2001. *Concise and physician orientated, aimed primarily at clinical practice*
- Monitoring the Disability Discrimination Act 1995. First Interim Report March 2000. City: Income Data Services Ltd (www.incomesdata.co.uk). *Analysis of caseload and decisions concerning the employment provisions of the Act*
- Health and Safety Executive Annual Report 2000/1 (www.hse.gov.uk). *Information on the activities of the HSE, and the data collected on occupational ill health and accidents*
- Data Protection Commissioner. www.dataprotection.gov.uk. *How data must be managed, applied to all personal information, including health records*
- www.courtservice.gov.uk. *Employment appeal tribunal and high court decisions*
- www.lawreports.co.uk. *Judgements from the House of Lords downwards*

6 Back pain

Malcolm IV Jayson

The number of working days lost as a result of back problems has increased dramatically in recent years. Over 80 million days were lost because of registered disability in 1994, but the total estimate, including short spells, is probably in the order of 150 million—four times more than 30 years ago. This increase does not reflect an increased incidence of back problems, which has changed little over the period, but it is probably because of an altered reaction to the problem, with increases in sick certification and state benefit, perhaps reflecting patients' and doctors' expectations, concerns by employers, and social and medicolegal pressures. There is, however, recent UK evidence to suggest that the peak in this rise of back pain incapacity is now past and claims for benefit are now falling. Whether the disability has simply been reclassified as "stress" (which is rising) is uncertain.

The costs of back pain are huge. Recent estimates suggest that the overall cost to the UK economy is about £6 billion a year. Improved management and better outcomes would lead to major financial and medical benefits.

Who gets back pain?

The problem affects workers of all ages. It usually starts between the late teens and the 40s, with the peak prevalence in 45-60 year olds and little difference between the sexes. The prevalence of back disability is increased in people performing heavy manual work, smokers, and those in non-managerial positions. Clearly these factors interact in many patients. It is often difficult to determine whether heavy manual work has caused or aggravated a back problem or whether a worker cannot do the job because of back pain. Obesity and tallness are also associated with back problems. Postural abnormalities do not predict back problems, except possibly gross discrepancies in leg length.

Psychological factors are important. Psychological distress in a population without back pain predicts the development of back pain. In the Boeing aircraft factory, workers who did not enjoy their jobs had a greatly increased risk of reporting back injury.

Causes of back pain

The major causes of back pain are mechanical strains and sprains, lumbar spondylosis, herniated intervertebral disc, and spinal stenosis. In many cases it is not possible to make a specific mechanical diagnosis. Such problems are commonly called non-specific back pain. Non-mechanical causes of back pain include inflammatory disorders such as ankylosing spondylitis and infections, primary and secondary neoplasms, and metabolic bone disorders such as osteoporosis. The patient's clinical characteristics and a general health screen will exclude systemic disease.

Pre-employment screening

There is no evidence that physical build, flexibility of spine movements, or other physical characteristics are of any value in predicting the development of back problems, and they should not be used for screening purposes. In particular, lumbar radiographs are not helpful in identifying people liable to develop back pain at work.

A detailed medical and occupational history is required for all employees, and an assessment of their fitness to do the job.

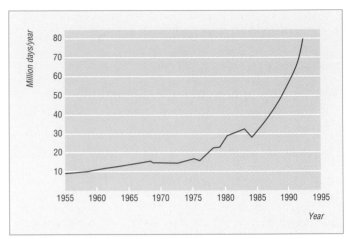

Changes in sickness and invalidity benefit for back pain since 1955

Heavy repetitive manual work increases the risk of back problems

The physical state of the spine determines how well it functions, and use and injury of the back will alter its structure. This interrelation between structure and function is central to understanding many back problems related to work

The principal risk factor for back pain is a history of back pain. Those who have had back problems in the past are likely to experience further episodes in the future

The most useful single item of information in predicting potential back problems is a history of back pain, particularly if it is recent and severe enough to cause absence from work.

Preventing back injuries

Manual handling is commonly associated with strains and sprains of the back and resultant disability. *Manual handling. Guidance on regulations* lists measures that employers should take to reduce the risk of problems. These include:

- Avoiding hazardous manual handling operations as far as is reasonably possible (lifting aids may be appropriate)
- Making an appropriate assessment of any hazardous manual handling operations that cannot be avoided
- Reducing the risks of injuries from these operations as far as is reasonably possible.

Weight limits

In Britain no limits for weights that may be lifted have been stated. This is because setting a weight limit is a fallacious approach as so much depends on the individual and the circumstances of any procedure. When a load is moved away from the trunk the level of stress on the lower back increases. As a rough guide, holding a load at arms' length imposes five times the stress experienced with the same load held close to the trunk. Moreover, the further away the load is from the trunk the less easy it is to control, adding to the problems.

Guidelines to loads that may be lifted are necessarily crude, given the wide range of individual physical capabilities even among fit and healthy people. There are no truly safe loads. Present guidelines do no more than identify when manual lifting and lowering operations may not need a detailed risk assessment. If the handler's hands enter more than one of the box zones during the operation, the smallest weight figures apply. Where the handler's hands are close to a boundary an intermediate weight may be chosen. Where lifting or lowering with the hands beyond the box zones is unavoidable, a more detailed assessment should always be made.

Lifting techniques

The technique for lifting is important. Simple ergonomic principles will protect the back against excessive strains. A poor posture increases the risk of injury. Examples include stooping and twisting while weight bearing, carrying loads in an asymmetric fashion, moving loads excessive distances, and excessive pushing and pulling. Repeated or prolonged physical effort may carry additional risk. Many episodes of back pain develop after sudden or unanticipated movements such as a stumble on the stairs or an unexpected twist.

Wherever manual handling occurs employers should consider the risks of injury and how to reduce them by reviewing the task required, the load carried, the working environment, and individual capability. Redesigning the job and providing mechanical assistance may be appropriate, and individual workers should be trained in safe manual handling.

Diagnosis and prognosis

Diagnostic triage

On simple clinical grounds, patients with acute back problems can be triaged into simple backache, nerve root pain, and possible serious spinal conditions. Simple back pain will be managed by an occupational health physician or general practitioner. Nerve root pain will initially be dealt with by a general practitioner in a similar way to simple backache, although at a slower pace, providing there is no major or

Excessive loading—simple mechanical aids can eliminate this

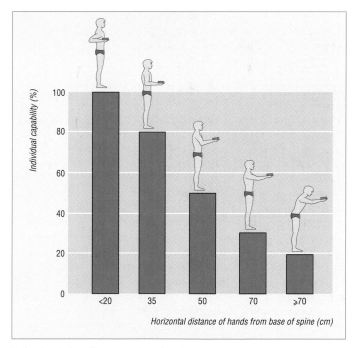

Reduction in handling capacity as hands move away from trunk

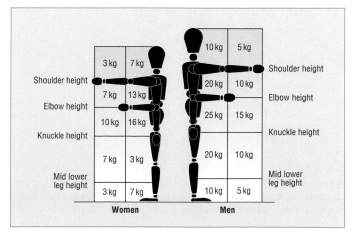

Guide to loads that may be lifted in various positions, assuming that the load is easily grasped with both hands

31

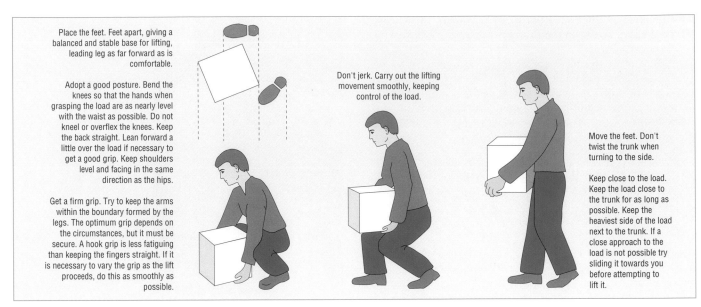

Principles of lifting and carrying a load

progressive motor weakness. However, early referral to a specialist may be required. Patients with possible serious spinal conditions require urgent referral, and emergency referral is needed for those with widespread or progressive neurological changes.

Prognosis

Most patients have simple backache. The exact condition and source of the pain are rarely identifiable, but the principles of management are now well established. Nearly all episodes of acute back pain resolve rapidly. Most patients return to work within a few days, and 90% return within six weeks. Some patients, however, develop chronic back pain, and this small proportion with prolonged disability is responsible for most of the costs associated with back injuries.

With longer time off work, the chances of ever getting back to work decrease rapidly. Only 25% of those off work for a year and 10% of those off work for two years will return to productive employment.

Investigations

Routine radiographs of the lumbar spine should be avoided. Apparent degenerative changes are common and correlate poorly with symptoms: they are better considered as age related changes. Radiographs are necessary when there is the question of possible serious spinal conditions, but a negative result does not exclude infection or tumour.

Imaging with computed tomography or magnetic resonance imaging is of no value for simple backache. These techniques also often display age related changes that correlate poorly with symptoms. The presence of these changes does not influence management.

Management

Simple backache

The early management of acute back pain is important. Much of the traditional management of back pain seems to promote chronicity. In view of the increasing toll of back disability, the Clinical Standards Advisory Group of the UK Departments of Health has published guidelines on managing back problems. These emphasise the importance of maintaining physical activity and minimising the period off work.

Indications for emergency referral

- Difficulty with micturition
- Loss of anal sphincter tone or faecal incontinence
- Saddle anaesthesia about anus, perineum, or genitals
- Widespread (more than one nerve root) or progressive motor weakness in legs or disturbed gait

Characteristics of simple backache

- Onset generally at ages 20-55 years
- Pain in lumbosacral region, buttocks, and thighs
- Pain is mechanical in nature—varies with physical activity and with time
- Patient is well
- Prognosis is good—90% of patients recover from acute attack in six weeks

Characteristics of nerve root pain

- Unilateral leg pain worse than back pain
- Pain generally radiates to foot or toes
- Numbness and paraesthesia in same distribution
- Signs of nerve irritation—reduced straight leg raise which reproduces leg pain
- Motor, sensory, or reflex change—limited to one nerve foot
- Prognosis reasonable—50% of patients recover from acute attack in six weeks

Red flags suggesting possible serious spinal pathology

- Age at onset <20 or >55 years
- Violent trauma—such as fall from height, or road traffic accident
- Constant, progressive, non-mechanical pain
- Thoracic pain
- History of cancer
- Use of systemic corticosteroids
- Misuse of drugs, infection with HIV
- Patient systematically unwell
- Weight loss
- Persisting severe restriction of lumbar flexion
- Widespread neurological signs
- Structural deformity

The natural course of simple backache is spontaneous resolution within a short time. Treatment is directed at relief of symptoms, a minimum period of rest, physical activity, and a rapid return to work.

Pain relief is with simple analgesics such as paracetamol or non-steroidal anti-inflammatory drugs. Narcotics should be avoided if possible, and never used for more than two weeks.

Rest is prescribed only if essential. Bed rest should be limited to three days as longer periods increase the duration of disability.

Early activity is encouraged. Patients should be reassured that exercise promotes recovery. The particular type of exercise is less important. There may be some increase in pain, but the patient should be reassured that hurt does not mean harm, and that those who exercise have fewer recurrences, take less time off work, and require less healthcare in the future.

Physical therapy should be arranged if symptoms last for more than a few days. This may include manipulation, exercises, and encouraging physical activity. Other techniques such as short wave diathermy, infrared treatment, ice packs, ultrasonography, massage, and traction provide only transient symptomatic benefit, but may enable patients to exercise and mobilise more rapidly. Some factories employ therapists so that physical therapy is available early in the work environment. This approach seems promising in promoting quick recovery and reducing risks of chronicity.

Persistent back pain

By six weeks, most patients will have recovered and be back at work. A detailed review is required for those with persistent problems. These patients should undergo a biopsychosocial assessment. There are particular risk factors for chronicity and for back pain and more prolonged disability, and their early identification will help in planning treatment.

Biological assessment includes reviewing the diagnostic triage, seeking evidence of nerve root problems or possible serious spinal conditions with appropriate referral. At this stage, measurement of the erythrocyte sedimentation rate, and radiographs, are indicated.

Psychological assessment should include the patient's attitudes and beliefs about pain. Many patients will not attempt to regain mobility because of unjustified fears about the risks of activity and work. Patients may have psychological distress and depressive symptoms, and develop characteristics of abnormal illness behaviour.

Social assessment includes patients' relationships with their families (who may reinforce the patient's disability), and work problems related to the physical demands of the job, job satisfaction, compensation, and medicolegal issues.

Referral

When a patient with simple backache does not return to work within three months, specialist referral is required to provide a second opinion about the diagnosis, to arrange investigations, and to advise on management, reassurance, multidisciplinary rehabilitation, and pain management. If pain in the back is referred to the buttocks or thighs the appropriate speciality is rheumatology, pain management, or rehabilitation medicine. For nerve root pain, the patient should be referred to orthopaedics or neurosurgery.

Psychological and social factors are increasingly recognised as important, and a multidisciplinary rehabilitation programme is likely to be effective. This may include incremental exercise and physical reconditioning, behavioural medicine, and encouragement to return to work.

Risk factors for back pain becoming chronic

- History of low back pain
- Previous time off work because of back pain
- Radicular pain, possibly with reduced straight leg raise and neurological signs
- Poor physical fitness
- Poor general health
- Smoking
- Psychological distress and depression
- Disproportionate pain behaviour
- Low job satisfaction
- Personal problems—alcohol intake, marital, financial problems
- Medicolegal proceedings

Further reading

- Clinical Standards Advisory Group. *Back pain*. London: HMSO, 1994. *The first UK evidence based review containing broad guidelines for the management of back problems. This publication has led to radical changes in the management of back pain in primary care. Reviewed 1999, see www.rcgp.org.uk*
- Croft PR, Papageorgiou AC, Ferry S, Thomas E, Jayson MIV, Silman A. Psychological distress in low back pain: evidence from a perspective study in general practice. *Spine* 1996;20:2731-7
- Bigos SJ, Battie MC, Spengler D, Fisher LD, Fordyce WE, Hansson TH, et al. A prospective study of work perceptions and psychosocial factors affecting the report of back injury. *Spine* 1991;16:1-6. *These two papers have emphasised the importance of the pre-back pain psychological state in predicting the future development of back problems in both primary care and in industry*
- Heliovaara M, Makela M, Kenkt P, Impivaara O, Aromaa A. Determinants of sciatica and back pain. *Spine* 1991;16:608-14 *Another predictive study highlighting the importance of the back history*
- Health and Safety Executive. *Manual handling. Guidance on regulations*, 2nd ed. London: HSE Books, 1998. *Provides helpful advice on manual handling techniques and provides crude guidelines that are useful in industry*
- Deyo RA, Diehl AJ, Rosenthal M. How many days of bed rest for acute low back pain? *New Engl J Med* 1986;315:1064-70. *The first study indicating that bed rest should be minimised in the management of back pain and that longer periods tend to be harmful*
- Waddell G, Burton AK. *Occupational health guidelines for the management of low back pain at work—evidence review*. London: Faculty of Occupational Medicine, 2000. *The principles underlying the management of back pain in relation to work (whether caused by work or impeding work, or both) have been subject to a number of reviews. This review has been carefully evidence based and is an invaluable source of current knowledge on this subject. Also available at www.facoccmed.ac.uk*

Work modification

Early return to work should be a priority because the physical and psychological consequences of inactivity and unemployment contribute to further dysfunction. Although patients should be encouraged to exercise, some are not capable of undertaking heavy manual work. Careful ergonomic assessment is necessary to avoid excessive stresses on the back. In particular, care should be taken to minimise tasks that require bending, lifting, and twisting. Light work—such as reception or inspection duties that require sitting, standing, and walking but avoid long periods in any one position—may be appropriate. At this point a coordinated approach with an Occupational Health Department is likely to be very helpful.

The figure showing changes in sickness and invalidity benefit for back pain since 1955 is adapted from a report of the Clinical Standards Advisory Group. *Back pain.* London: HMSO, 1994. The figures showing reduction in handling capacity as hands move away from trunk, guide to loads that may be lifted in various positions, and the principles of lifting and carrying a load are all adapted from *Manual handling. Guidance on regulations.* Health and Safety Executive. London: HSE Books, 1998.

7 Upper limb disorders

Mats Hagberg

Improved management of patients with work related neck and arm disorders can reduce the number of working days lost and the incidence of work related illness. A patient's quality of life and potential economic loss is largely dependent on the medical consultation.

The consultation

Every patient who seeks medical attention for neck and arm problems is entitled to a thorough medical examination. It is important for the patient—even when the disorder is non-specific—to get a clear message from the treating physician as to whether progressive disease is present, and for the physician to get the patient to engage with and have control over their rehabilitation and return to work.

The assessment of work related musculoskeletal disorders consists of a clinical examination, an exposure history, a workplace assessment, and suitable further tests.

History

The type, onset, and localisation of symptoms should be explored in detail. The use of a manikin ("bodymapping") to let the patient mark the type and location of pain has good reliability. It is important to distinguish between nociceptive and neurogenic pain. Nociceptive pain usually originates from peripheral pain receptors reacting to mechanical or chemical stimuli. Muscle pain can be regarded as nociceptive. Neurogenic pain is caused by a dysfunction in the nervous system. Accompanying sensory disturbances are common, and they can be caused by entrapment of nerves. Neurogenic pain may follow the sensory distribution of a nerve, whereas nociceptive pain is usually more diffuse and does not correspond to a single nerve distribution. Examples of questions to be asked are: "Does the pain radiate?" "Where to?" Diffuse symptoms may indicate musculoskeletal referred pain, whereas pain radiating towards specific dermatomes suggests a cervical root lesion (radiculopathy). For each single symptom the character, quality, distribution, intensity, frequency, and duration should be described. Information should be elicited about the relation between symptoms and posture, about movements and loading during occupational activity, and the relationship of symptoms to recreational activities and rest.

Special efforts should be made to identify red flags. Examples of red flags are weight loss and severe pain in the mornings. This may indicate a severe systemic disease, endocrine disorder, infection or malignancy. The family and medical history, and questions about morning stiffness and signs of inflammatory activity (joint swellings) may suggest a rheumatoid disorder.

Work and exposure history

A person's job title usually supplies insufficient information to determine whether the disorder is work related and whether the patient can return to their job. The actual work task has to be described in terms of what the patient produces, work posture, repetition, material handling, and work organisation. Any history of sudden events of high energy transfers (formerly termed "accidents") that could have resulted in clinical or subclinical injury should be explored.

Characteristics of non-specific musculoskeletal pain in neck, arm, and hand

History
- Pain and stiffness gradually increase during work and are worst at the end of the working day and week
- Pain localised to cervical spine and the angle between the neck and shoulder or to the upper part of forearm
- Usually no radiation of pain
- Symptoms are improved by heat and worsened by cold draughts

Signs
- Tenderness over neck and shoulder muscles or tenderness over forearm extensor muscles
- Reduced range of active movement of cervical spine (normal passive movement)
- No neurological deficits

Differential diagnosis
- Tendonitis
- Nerve entrapments
- Systemic diseases

Management of work related neck and arm disorders

Clinical management
- Non-steroidal anti-inflammatory drugs can reduce pain and inflammation
- Acupuncture can reduce pain
- Corticosteroids—a single subacromial injection of corticosteroid mixed with local anaesthetic may cure shoulder tendonitis. For tennis elbow and carpal tunnel syndrome, corticosteroids should be used by specialists only
- Heparin (15 000 IU/day in a single intravenous dose) given for 3-4 days is an effective treatment for acute crepitating peritendinitis
- Surgery—surgical division of the carpal ligament is the first choice of treatment for carpal tunnel syndrome. For chronic severe shoulder tendonitis, surgical removal of the lateral part of the acromion may relieve pain at night
- Splints—whether splints should be used to treat early hand and wrist tendonitis and carpal tunnel syndrome is still debated

Modifications to working environment
- Job analysis—to assess work relatedness of a patient's symptoms it is necessary to evaluate working posture, repetition, force and handling of loads, psychological and social factors, and static posture or task invariability
- Job design—job enlargement can reduce the duration and frequency of awkward postures and load handling. Job enrichment reduces poor work content and task invariability. Layout of workplace and technical aids should be improved
- Technique training—ergonomists and supervisors can improve working technique to reduce stressors of postures, motion, and load handling
- Rests and breaks should be organised to allow recovery

For a better assessment of exposure, the patient should be encouraged to bring photographs of their station, products, and tools. Direct observation of the task at the worksite is valuable and can also be used as the basis for suggestions about job redesign and return to work policies during rehabilitation. Direct evaluation can also be enhanced by video recording.

Clinical examination

The physical examination should include the following steps: (1) inspection; (2) testing for range of motion; (3) testing for muscle contraction, pain, and muscle strength; (4) palpation of muscle tendons and insertions; and (5) specific tests. The physician must have a diagnostic strategy to identify and rule out systemic diseases. As a general rule when tests are used for screening or to rule out disease, the test with the highest sensitivity is preferred. When tests are used to confirm or rule in disease, the test with the highest specificity is preferred. Serial (multiple) tests with results that are all normal tend to rule out disease convincingly; serial tests with results that are all abnormal tend to confirm disease convincingly. Several textbooks cover the physical examination of the musculoskeletal system.

Further investigations

Blood tests such as sedimentation rate and rheumatoid factor can be used to rule out general inflammatory disorders. Imaging tests such as radiographs, ultrasound, and magnetic resonance imaging to detect morphological changes should be done if there are red flags present. Radiographic findings such as spinal degeneration, cervical ribs, etc. should be interpreted with caution because they may be normal physiological findings unrelated to back, neck, or arm symptoms. Patients who are told that their radiograph shows that their back or cervical spine is "worn out" may be resistant to rehabilitation. Even advanced magnetic resonance imaging of the spine may show severe degenerative changes that are not related to the patient's symptoms. A patient may deduce from the radiographic findings that they have a progressive disease and thereby become "medicalised." This may, in turn, influence their participation in active rehabilitation and impair the process of returning to work.

Common work related musculoskeletal disorders may constitute a disturbance of sensory neural processing. In the future both neurosensory testing—for example, vibratory perception threshold—and biochemical markers, may become a part of clinical musculoskeletal assessment.

Classification of disease (ICD-10)

The terminology of common musculoskeletal disorders is confusing. The use of terms such as repetitive strain injury (RSI) and cumulative trauma disorder (CTD) should be avoided. The evidence base is often weak or non-existent for these terms. In industrial settings ergonomics may modify the symptoms and signs of disorders and diseases. In a task involving repetitive arm elevation, signs of both tendonitis and non-specific disorders may be present, which are probably related to both concurrent strain on rotator cuff tendons and static strain on neck and shoulder muscles. The occurrence of musculoskeletal symptoms and clinical signs in working and mixed populations has been described. If the different musculoskeletal symptoms and signs do not wholly comply with the criteria for a disease, the recommendation is to choose an ICD label that focuses on the symptoms rather than on the disease. An example of this for non-specific neck and shoulder

Principles of managing hand and arm pain in keyboard operators

- Exclude clear pathological causes such as carpal tunnel syndrome
- Explore psychological profile, including attitudes to work, and support from management and colleagues
- Reassure patient that the condition will improve and is likely to resolve
- Keep the patient physically active and at work. Both aerobic and strength training will reduce pain and increase performance
- If necessary reduce keyboard work
- Liaise with patient's workplace—if possible, with an occupational physician or nurse
- Consider variation of work tasks, reduced work intensity, encouraging short breaks from keyboard work, or job rotation
- Ensure that workstation ergonomics have been evaluated and are satisfactory and that the patient has been taught to use the equipment properly and has the right glasses
- Monitor patient's progress with regular follow up
- When symptoms have subsided advise gradual increase in normal activities
- Exercise may improve blood flow and reduce pain. Strength training may reduce pain and increase performance. Heat application may be worth trying
- Advice from an experienced physiotherapist may assist in rehabilitation
- Those few patients who do not respond to this multidisciplinary management may be at risk of developing chronic symptoms. Revisit the biopsychosocial aspects
- Consider specialist referral (for example, to an occupational physician, rheumatologist, or pain or rehabilitation specialist)
- In extreme cases where long term disablement seems likely, retraining may be necessary. Voice activated software is now widely available

No consensus accepted criteria exist for most ICD-10 (international classification of diseases, 10th revision) musculoskeletal related diagnoses for manual work. When considering the criteria for different musculoskeletal disorders it is reasonable to look first at proposed criteria for surveillance, and epidemiological studies

pain with or without radiation to the forearm would be the label "cervicobrachial syndrome M53.1" (ICD-10, nerve root entrapment is excluded).

Risk factors

Multiple factors
Certain occupations are associated with a high risk for neck and arm pain. Some risk factors can be identified, but the interaction between different risk factors is not understood, and there are not enough data yet to set accurate limits for disease effects. It is important to recognise that personal characteristics and other environmental and sociocultural factors usually play a role in these disorders. A patient with neck pain may be exposed to an awkward posture at work but also to social stress at home: both factors contribute to sustained contraction of the trapezius muscles, inducing pain and stiffness. The cause of a work related disorder can sometimes be attributed to a specific exposure in a job, but there is often simultaneous exposure to several different factors. Individual factors must also be considered when assessing the history of a patient with a work related disorder, and when redesigning a job before such a patient returns to work.

Awkward postures
Working with hands at or above shoulder level counts as an awkward posture and may be one determinant of rotator cuff tendonitis. Awkward postures may cause mechanical trauma or compression, reducing blood flow and tissue nutrition.

The pathogenesis of rotator cuff tendonitis is mainly impingement—compression of the rotator cuff tendons when they are forced under the coracoacromial arch during elevation of the arm. The supraspinatus tendon is forced under the anterior edge of the acromion, causing both a compression that impairs blood circulation through the tendon and mechanical friction to the tendon. Reduced blood flow because of static muscle contraction may contribute to degeneration of the rotator cuff tendons.

Abduction and forward flexion of more than 30° may also constitute a risk factor because the pressure induced within the supraspinatus muscle will exceed 30 mm Hg, impairing blood flow. The vessels to the supraspinatus tendon run through the muscle, and so raised intramuscular pressure can affect the tendon vasculature.

Static postures (task invariability)
It used to be argued that to prevent work related musculoskeletal disorders it was necessary to minimise the load that workers were exposed to. This concept has led to the creation of jobs with low external load, but some of these are still not ideal because poor work content usually leads to a job with invariable tasks, resulting in constrained postures and a low static load for the neck and arms. Ergonomists now try to design jobs that are not only physically variable but also psychologically variable and stimulating.

The health problems caused by task invariability may result from prolonged static contraction of the trapezius muscle during work or daily activity, resulting in an overload of type I muscle fibres, explaining the neck pain. At a low level of muscle contraction, the low threshold motor units (type I fibres) operate. A low static contraction during work may result in a recruitment pattern in which only the type I muscle fibres are used, causing selective fatigue of motor units and damage to the type I fibres. Biopsies of the trapezius muscle from patients with work related trapezius myalgia show enlarged

Risk factors for work related neck and arm disorders
- Working posture
  - Awkward postures or task invariability
  - Static postures
- Repetitive motion
- Force—handling loads or tools
- Psychological and social factors
  - Work organisation
  - Stress
- Working environment

Poultry dressing involves forceful and repetitive manipulation in cold conditions—ergonomic assessment is essential

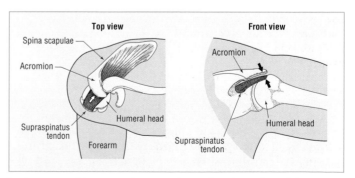

Impingement of the supraspinatus tendon against the surface of the anterior part of the acromion when the arm is raised to shoulder height. Pressure and mechanical friction are centred on the tendon (thick black arrows)

type I fibres and a reduced ratio of type I fibre areas to capillary areas. Strength training improves the performance of the type 2 fibres and there is reduced perceived exertion during work in patients with non-specific neck pain.

Another pain hypothesis is a relative shortage of energy in the muscle cells. When the energy demand in the muscle fibre is excessive, pain can result. The postural pain syndrome associated with sagging shoulders is a type of cervicobrachial pain that may be caused by prolonged stretching of the trapezius muscle or the brachial plexus. In cervical brachial pain syndromes, pain may be triggered by a pain locus in muscles, tendons, joint capsules, ligaments, or vessels. Nociceptors (pain receptors) in these loci may be the origin not only of the neck and shoulder pain but also of the referred pain to the arm and hand. The nociceptive pain may trigger a chronic pain syndrome that can affect the sympathetic nervous system. A possible pathogenic mechanism is that a small injury caused by a strain or a microrupture during some activity (work or leisure time) does not recover properly. Pain receptors induce a pathway of signals to the central nervous system by increasing the susceptibility to stimuli. The neurological response to normal activity is perceived as pain, and a chronic pain syndrome is the result. The predominant clinical symptom is activity related pain. Stiffness and severe pain at extreme postures are also common. The patient affected by chronic pain must be recognised as soon as possible for proper treatment and rehabilitation, preferably in a pain clinic.

Awkward and static postures are common in players of musical instruments. Pain in the neck and arm have been related to gripping an instrument in an awkward posture. Pain in the left shoulder and arm in professional violinists can be the result of static holding of the violin with the left arm.

Neck flexion while working at a visual display terminal may be associated with non-specific shoulder symptoms. A prospective study showed that a non-optimal sight angle with the head overextended was related to neck symptoms, and extreme radial deviation of the hands was related to hand and arm disorders. An exposure-response relation has been found for neck pain and angle of neck flexion in keyboard operators: neck pain was more prevalent among operators who flex their necks more acutely. Incorrect glasses or the need for glasses when working at a visual display terminal may result in neck and shoulder pain, by affecting posture and because of muscle activity in the trapezius muscle caused by a reflex mechanism of oculomotor strain during sustained visual work at short distances.

The development of non-keyboard input devices, such as the computer mouse, has resulted in new postures that may cause a combination of symptoms from the wrist to the shoulder. Work tasks of long duration with a flexed and, to some extent, extended wrist have been reported as risk factors for carpal tunnel syndrome.

Repetition motion

Repetitive motions of the shoulder may constitute a risk for rotator cuff tendonitis. An experimental study showed that women performing repetitive forward flexions of the shoulder developed shoulder tendonitis. Clinical signs of tendonitis were present up to two weeks after the experiments. Repetitive motions by industrial assembly workers (truck making, meat packing, and circuit board assembly) have been associated with the development of shoulder tendonitis, lateral epicondylitis, and tendonitis at the wrist (de Quervain's disease). Excentric exertion with injury of the extensor carpi radialis brevis muscle is one mechanical model for the pathogenesis of lateral epicondylitis.

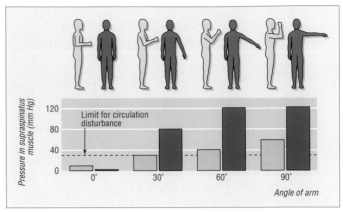

Intramuscular pressure in the supraspinatus muscle at different angles of abduction and forward flexion

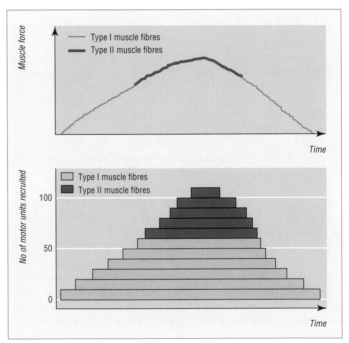

Differential recruitment of muscle fibres with different levels of contraction. At low level static contraction, only type I muscle fibres may be recruited, leading to their selective fatigue and damage

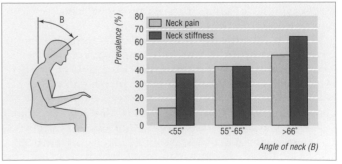

Association between neck flexion and pain and stiffness in the neck

Repetitive motion, being a causal factor for tendonitis, is consistent with the high risk of shoulder tendonitis in competitive swimmers, and epicondylitis in tennis players.

Force—handling load or tools
Only a few studies have investigated the effect of handling loads on neck and arm symptoms. Handling heavy loads seems to be associated with osteoarthrosis and cervical spondylosis. Low frequency vibration exposure of high magnitude is associated with osteoarthrosis of the elbow, wrist, and acromioclavicular joints, and symptoms in the elbow and shoulder. Impacts, jerks, and blows with high energy transfer to the hands at low frequency might have the potential to result in musculoskeletal disorders, considering the general model for injuries. Furthermore, the observed associations with vibration exposure and musculoskeletal disorders might result from the strong dynamic and static joint loading and the repetitive hand and arm motions required in tasks where handheld machines are used.

Psychological and social factors
Psychological and social factors are generally more strongly associated with back pain than with shoulder pain. Furthermore, the association is stronger for non-specific pain than for pain with a specific diagnosis. This means that a diagnosis of general cervicobrachial pain may be more strongly related to psychological and social factors than are carpal tunnel syndrome or shoulder tendonitis. Highly demanding work and poor work content (repetitive tasks with short cycles) have been identified as risk factors for neck and shoulder pain. Psychological factors and personality type may be determinants of muscle tension and the development of myofascial pain.

Piece work is associated with neck and arm disorders when compared with work paid by the hour. This may be because of an increased work pace in addition to high psychological demand and low control in the work situation. Management style, in terms of social support to employees, is claimed to be associated with increased reporting of neck and shoulder symptoms. Social support from management obviously affects turnover of workers, and sick leave.

Psychological stress and burnout are associated with depression. Depressive moods are associated with musculoskeletal pain. It is likely that both psychological stress and chronic musculoskeletal pain can cause depressive moods. When assessing a patient with chronic musculoskeletal pain, a psychological evaluation and identification of possible affective disorders should be done. Treatment of depression can reduce musculoskeletal pain and facilitate return to work.

Individual susceptibility
Individuals may have increased vulnerability to injury because of disease, genetic factors, or lack of fitness. This individual susceptibility may result in a lower threshold for given exposures to cause work related musculoskeletal disorders. Additionally, the exposure may trigger symptoms earlier and at an unusual location because of localised vulnerability in a person who has preclinical systemic disease. As examples, a worker exposed to repetitive flexion in the shoulder developed tendonitis one year before developing rheumatoid arthritis. An electrician exposed to repetitive power grips and vibration developed symptoms and signs of carpal tunnel syndrome: at surgery these were found to be caused by amyloidosis. For work related musculoskeletal disorders individual factors usually have a low magnitude of risk compared with relevant ergonomic factors.

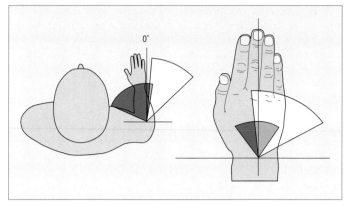

Outward rotation of the shoulder and ulnar deviation of the wrist may be found with use of a computer mouse (yellow) and keyboard (blue)

Work related musculoskeletal disorders found in blue collar and white collar workers

Shoulder pain
Blue collar workers—assembly workers
- Usually shoulder tendonitis due to working with hands above shoulder height
- Repetitive forward flexions

White collar workers—keyboard operators
- Usually non-specific cervicobrachial pain, which may be caused by task invariability leading to static tension of trapezius muscle

Hand and wrist pain
Blue collar workers—assembly workers
- Repetitive power grips may cause repetitive strain of extensor tendons and tendonitis
- Carpal tunnel syndrome may also be related to repetitive power grips

White collar workers—keyboard operators
- Intensive keying may cause repetitive strain of extensor tendons and tendonitis
- Carpal tunnel syndrome may also be related to intensive keying

---

Individual susceptibility to musculoskeletal disorders
Age
- For most musculoskeletal disorders, risk increases with age

Sex
- Among both the general population and industrial workers, women have a higher incidence of carpal tunnel syndrome and muscular pain in the neck and shoulder than men
- Whether this is due to genetic factors or to different exposures at work and at home is not clear

Anatomical differences or malformations
- A rough surface and the sharp edge of the intertubercular sulcus on the humeral head increases wear on the tendon of the long head of biceps muscle, which may make a person more prone to biceps tendonitis
- A cervical rib is a common cause of neurogenic thoracic outlet syndrome: a repetitive task may be the occupational exposure that triggers clinical disease
- Width of the carpal tunnel has been proposed as a risk factor for carpal tunnel syndrome, but there is no consensus

Further reading

- Ohnmeiss DD. Repeatability of pain drawings in a low back pain population. *Spine* 2000;25:980-8
- Lundeberg T. Pain physiology and principles of treatment. *Scand J Rehabil Med Suppl* 1995;32:13-41
- Swenson R. Differential diagnosis: a reasonable clinical approach. *Neurol Clin* 1999;17:43-63
- Black ER, Bordley DR, Tape TG, Panzer RJ, eds. *Diagnostic strategies for common medical problems*, 2nd ed. Philadelphia: American College of Physicians, 1999. *Gives basic information on how to evaluate tests and test performance—for example, predictive values and likelihood ratios*
- Hoppenfeld S. *Physical examination of the spine and extremities.* Connecticut: Appletom Century-Crofts, 1976. *Includes a detailed description of examining different parts of the musculoskeletal system, with extensive illustrations, with emphasis on neurological evaluations*
- McRae R. *Clinical orthopaedic examination.* Edinburgh: Churchill Livingstone, 1983. *Includes brief descriptions of musculoskeletal disorders in addition to extensive illustrations of examination technique*
- Saxton JM. A review of current literature on physiological tests and soft tissue biomarkers applicable to work-related upper limb disorders. *Occup Med (Lond)* 2000;50:121-30. *Concludes by proposing new ways that testing might be implemented during occupational health surveillance to enable early warning of impending problems and to provide more insight into the underlying nature of soft tissue disorders*
- Harrington JM, Carter JT, Birrell L, Gompertz D. Surveillance case definitions for work related upper limb pain syndromes. *Occup Environ Med* 1998;55:264-71. *Describes the consensus case definitions that were agreed for carpal tunnel syndrome, tenosynovitis of the wrist, de Quervain's disease of the wrist, epicondylitis, shoulder capsulitis (frozen shoulder), and shoulder tendonitis. The consensus group also identified a condition defined as "non-specific diffuse forearm pain," although this is essentially a diagnosis made by exclusion. The group did not have enough experience of the thoracic outlet syndrome to make recommendations*
- Hagberg M, Silverstein B, Wells R, Kuroinka I, Smith M, Forcier L, et al. *Work related musculoskeletal disorders (WMSDs): a reference book for prevention.* London: Taylor and Francis Ltd, 1995. *Themes are identification, evaluation, action, and change. The various chapters link work with tendon, nerve, muscle, joint, vascular, and non-specific or multiple tissue disorders; explore individual susceptibility; assess occupational risk factors; describe health and hazard surveillance techniques; discuss the management of change; outline training and education programmes; and give an overview of medical management*
- Health and Safety Executive. *Upper limb disorders in the workplace*, 2nd ed. Sudbury: HSE Books, 2002. *A practical guide on how to assess and minimise workplace risks through positive action*

8 Work related stress

Tom Cox

It is clear from large scale surveys of working people, and of those who have recently worked, that stress is currently one of the two main work related challenges to health. (The other is musculoskeletal disorders.) It is therefore not surprising that a plethora of guidance on work stress is available from government bodies, the social partners, and professional and scientific organisations, and it is unlikely that any individual or organisation could successfully claim ignorance of the topic or a lack of basic knowledge.

What is and what is not stress?

Stress is not an illness; neither is it a meaningful descriptive term to apply to a situation such as a domestic scenario or a workplace, although they might be described as "stressful" or containing "stressors."

Stress is an emotional state that is very real for many people, and poses a major threat to the quality of their lives and to their health. Although that experience is rooted in the way the person sees and thinks about their world, it is essentially *emotional* in nature, normally involving a mixture of negative feelings, such as unpleasant arousal, apprehension, shame, guilt, or anger. It is not necessarily trivial.

Why do people experience stress?

Stress is the emotional state that results from someone's perceptions of an imbalance between the demands (pressures) on them, and their ability to cope with those demands. The control they have over related events and the support that they receive in coping are very important factors in this equation. Demands can be internally (self) generated as well as externally imposed, and a person's needs and expectations can be important in their experience of stress.

Classically, people at risk experience events that place demands on them with which they cannot cope. Their inability to cope may be because of lack of relevant knowledge or skill. They feel out of control and without support. Under these circumstances, they are more likely to experience stress and show the commonly associated patterns of cognitive, behavioural, and physiological change. Interestingly, although some of these changes may represent attempts at coping, others may be detrimental to coping. It is easy to see how a vicious cycle can quickly become established in that the person's ability to cope may be degraded by their experience of stress.

The correlates of stress

The experience of stress alters the way people think, feel, and behave. Many of the changes that occur are modest and potentially reversible, although detrimental to the person's quality of life at the time. Other changes may be more enduring, and have substantial consequences for health.

Behavioural changes may include increases in health risk behaviour, such as smoking and drinking, and decreases in health positive behaviour, such as exercise and relaxation. Many behavioural changes represent attempts to cope with the

---

Myths and facts

"Work related stress is not a serious problem"
Wrong—in the United Kingdom, as many as one in five people report themselves to be suffering from high levels of work related stress. That's around 5 million workers. An estimated half a million individuals report experiencing stress at a level they believe has made them ill. The cost to Britain's economy is estimated at. **6.7 million working days lost per year**. It costs society between about **£3.7 billion and £3.8 billion**

Health and Safety Executive

The Ad hoc Group on Work Stress of the European Commission offered the following definition of work stress

Work stress is the emotional reaction to aversive and noxious aspects of organisations, work, and the work environment. It is a state characterised by extremes of arousal, and by discomfort and distress. It is often characterised by feelings of being out of control and helplessness. Stress can arise as a result of exposure to both physical and psychosocial hazards and may, in turn, affect not only psychological, physical, and social health, but also availability for work and work performance

---

Stress can occur through work. It may be experienced as a result of exposure to a wide range of work related hazards and, in practice, often coexists with adverse influences operating outside the workplace

---

Some factors affecting individual susceptibility to stress

- Individual constitution
- Lifestyle and work style
- Coping mechanisms
- Emotional stability
- Previous experiences
- Expectation
- Self confidence

emotional experience of stress—for example, by drinking more. However, this type of coping can easily become a secondary source of stress and ill health if sustained.

Evidence shows that cognitive stress is associated with poor decision making, impaired concentration, reduced attention span, impaired memory, and confusion. People who report "being stressed" also tend to admit to "not being able to think straight." Social behaviour and interpersonal relations may also be affected, possibly reflecting these and other psychological changes such as exhaustion and increased irritability.

The effects of stress are thought to contribute to a range of disorders as wide as cancer, heart disease, musculoskeletal conditions, skin disease, gastrointestinal disorders, and sexual problems. The evidence is strongest for links between certain types of prolonged stress and ischaemic heart disease, hypertension, and mental illness. Evidence also suggests that stress plays a part in the aetiology, course, and outcome (recovery from disability) of musculoskeletal disorders. Most of the evidence for such links is epidemiological. The pathophysiological mechanisms are not clear—perhaps the effects are direct (chemical mediators, effects on immunity) or indirect (the results of secondary, damaging behaviour).

It is likely that what is bad for the individual employee is also bad for their organisation. Organisational concerns associated with work related stress include high absenteeism, increased staff turnover, low job satisfaction, low morale, poor organisational commitment, poor performance and productivity, possible increased accident and near miss rates, and, in some cases, an increase in employee and client complaints and litigation.

Causes of stress at work

"Psychosocial and organisational" hazards refer to those aspects of the design and management of work and of its social and organisational contexts that are known to contribute to employee stress—so, to a lesser extent, do "physical" hazards such as noise and extremes of temperature. There is a reasonable consensus on the nature of the psychosocial and organisational hazards, and they have been divided into nine broad categories.

Managing stress at work

Work stress can be managed from two different perspectives: the individual and the organisational. The occupational health practitioner has a role to play in each approach.

Education, treatment, and rehabilitation: the individual
Much of little value has been written about individual stress management, and many weird and wonderful treatments are offered commercially. A healthy scepticism is warranted here as few of these treatments are based in scientific knowledge and even fewer have been evaluated.

Three strategies that might help the individual experiencing stress through work are: further education and training in relevant work or life skills, short term treatment for any medical condition, and managed rehabilitation to a normal pattern of working life.

Without doubt, the most effective form of stress management training is through a proper analysis of training needs in relation to the person's job; lifestyle counselling can also be valuable. Fundamental problems in the demands-ability balance may need to be examined. At the same time, reducing health risk behaviour and strengthening health positive

---

Some possible self reported symptoms of work stress
- Anxiety about work, continually agitated
- Continual complaints of unreasonable or unrelenting work demands
- Deep exhaustion
- Disturbed sleep and daytime tiredness
- Expressed dislike of work or work colleagues and low job satisfaction
- Feelings of being out of control or helpless
- Feelings of lack of support and care from others
- Forgetfulness
- Inability to concentrate, continually distracted
- Inability to think straight
- Irritability, being short tempered
- Loss of sexual interest, or impaired sexual performance
- Loss of the "big picture:" unable to get events into perspective
- Repeated absences from work

Psychosocial and organisational hazards: a taxonomy

Content of work
- **Task content:** lack of variety or short work cycles, fragmented or meaningless work, underuse of skills, high uncertainty
- **Workload and workpace:** work overload or underload, lack of control over pacing, time pressure
- **Work schedule:** shift working, inflexible work schedules, unpredictable, long or unsociable hours
- **Control:** low participation in decision making, lack of control over work

Context to work
- **Organisational culture and function:** poor communication, low levels of support for problem solving and personal development, lack of definition of organisational objectives
- **Role in organisation:** role ambiguity and role conflict, responsibility for people
- **Career development:** career stagnation and uncertainty, under or over promotion, poor pay, job insecurity, low social value to work
- **Interpersonal relations at work:** social or physical isolation, poor relations with superiors, interpersonal conflict, and lack of social support
- **Home-work interface:** conflicting demands of work and home, poor support at home, dual career problems

Adapted from Cox (1993)

Work related factors and ill health: the Whitehall II Study

This research concentrated on how the design of work affected people's mental well being and related health outcomes. The key findings were as follows:

- Having little say in how the work is done is associated with poor mental health in men and a higher risk of alcohol dependence in women
- Work requiring a fast pace and the need to resolve conflicting priorities is associated with a higher risk of psychiatric disorder in both sexes, and poor physical fitness or illness in men
- A combination of putting high effort into work and poor recognition of employees' effort by managers is associated with increased risk of alcohol dependence in men, poor mental health in both sexes, and poor physical fitness or illness in women
- A lack of understanding and support from managers and colleagues at work is associated with higher risk of psychiatric disorder. Good social support at work, particularly from managers for their staff, has a protective effect
- Aspects of poor work design is also associated with employees taking more sickness absence

Causes of stress and possible solutions

Poor management culture
Examples of good management are when:
- An organisation is committed to promoting the wellbeing of employees through good management practice
- The people who work in the organisation are valued and respected
- They receive support from the organisation if they wish to raise problems affecting their work

Poor relations
Examples of good relations are when:
- There is good communication between employer and employees, so that the employees understand what is expected, and the employer reacts to any problems experienced by the employees
- Employees are not bullied or harassed, and policies are in place to manage this

Role uncertainty
People understand their role when:
- They know why they are undertaking the work and how this fits in with the organisation's wider aims and objectives
- Jobs are clearly defined to avoid confusion

Too many demands
Demands are at the right level when:
- Staff are able to cope with the volume and complexity of the work
- The work is scheduled sensibly so that there is enough time to do allocated tasks; shift work systems are agreed with employees or their representatives; people are not expected to work long hours over an extended period

Poor management of change
Good change management includes when the organisation:
- Communicates to employees the reason why change is essential
- Has a clear understanding of what it wants change to achieve
- Has a timetable for implementing change, which includes realistic first steps
- Ensures a supportive climate for employees

Lack of control
People feel in control when:
- They are given a say in how they do their work
- The amount of control they have is balanced against the demands placed on them

Lack of training and support, and failure to take account of individual factors
Examples of good practice:
- Employees receive suitable and sufficient training to do their jobs
- Employees receive support from their immediate line management, even when things go wrong
- The organisation encourages people to share their concerns about health and safety and, in particular, work related stress
- The individual is fair to the employer— they discuss their concerns and work towards agreed solutions

---

behaviour such as exercise and relaxation may both improve the person's psychological and physical health, and offer a distraction from their problems.

If the person is affected by anxiety, depression, or some other stress induced illness, then that should be treated in the conventional way, possibly with drugs or psychological treatments, but always appropriately combined with education and rehabilitation. Managed rehabilitation is critical to the success of any treatment for work stress, and necessarily entails a dialogue between the occupational health practitioner and line management.

Prevention and an appropriate response: the organisation

Employers have a duty of care under common law to take reasonable and practicable steps to protect their employees' safety and health at work. This duty clearly extends to psychological as well as physical health, and to psychosocial and organisational as well as physical hazards. It is clear that an employer's failure to consider stress seriously can result in legal challenge. Employers also have duties under statutory health and safety law. Such law has evolved to prevent harm to employees through work, whereas common law allows for financial redress when harm has occurred. These two bodies of law are complementary, as are the duties they impose.

The occupational health practitioner can advise employers on two issues: prevention through risk management, and provision of employee support systems.

According to guidance from the Health and Safety Executive in the United Kingdom and the European Commission, work stress is to be treated as a health and safety issue and dealt with in organisations through the application of a risk management approach (essentially systematic problem solving). Organisations will need to include methods of assessing the risk from exposure to psychosocial and organisational hazards in their routine assessments and develop ways of reducing such risks if necessary. Methods to do this are

---

Expectations of a person experiencing stress through work
- Timely and appropriate support from both management and occupational health
- A professional and sensitive approach
- Help in solving the problem at source: moderating work pressures, providing education and training, increasing control over work events, and improving support
- Advice, if necessary, on lifestyle
- Short term treatment for any associated medical problems
- Active management of rehabilitation to work

available, and occupational health practitioners have a major role to play both as expert advisers and organisational champions.

The successful provision of employee support (to deal with stress) depends on three things: a broad based and competent system, an accessible system, and an integrated system. Most large organisations provide good employee support in theory, but fail themselves and their employees in practice because the overall system is fragmented, often competitive for resources, and territorial, and lacks internal collaboration at the case level. Much can be achieved by bringing existing systems together, by training staff in relation to work stress, and by marketing what is available within the organisation.

The box containing information on psychosocial and organisational hazards is adapted from Cox 1993. The box containing causes of stress and possible solutions is adapted from Health and Safety Executive. *Work related factors and ill health: the Whitehall II study.* Sudbury: HSE Books, 2000 (CRR 266/2000).

Further reading

- Cox T, Griffiths A, Rial-Gonzalez E. *Work-related stress.* Luxembourg: Office for Official Publications of the European Communities, 2000. *A compact overview of the professional and scientific literature on work stress; incorporates a discussion of the risk management approach to dealing with stress problems at work. Can be downloaded free from the website of the European Agency for Safety and Health at Work: http://osha.eu.int*
- Cox T. From environmental exposure to ill health. In: McCaig R, Harrington M, eds. *The changing nature of occupational health.* Sudbury: HSE Books, 1998. *This chapter in an edited volume in memory of Dr Thomas Legge provides a more detailed account of the model of stress referred to here, with more information from the organisational perspective. It also includes further discussion of the individual perspective*
- Griffiths A. The psychosocial work environment. In: McCaig R, Harrington M, eds. *The changing nature of occupational health.* Sudbury: HSE Books, 1998. *This chapter, in what has become known as the Thomas Legge book, focuses on the psychosocial work environment and provides an informed and detailed discussion of the psychosocial and organisational aspects of work, their design, and management. This chapter is usefully read in conjunction with that by the author in the same volume*
- Cox T, Griffiths A, Randall R. A risk management approach to the prevention of work stress. In: Schabracq MA, Winnubst JAM, Cooper C, eds. *Handbook of work and health psychology,* 2nd ed. Chichester: Wiley and Sons, 2002. *A detailed discussion of the risk management approach to work stress; includes a short series of organisational case studies to illustrate that approach in practice. The chapter touches on risk reduction strategies that focus on the individual employee as well as those that operate at the organisational level*
- Griffiths A, Randall R, Santos A, Cox T. Senior nurses: interventions to reduce work stress. In: Dollard M, Winefield A, eds. *Occupational stress in service professionals.* London: Taylor and Francis, 2002. *Provides a relatively detailed case study of an organisational intervention to manage work stress in a group of hospital based senior nurses applying the risk management approach. As with the above chapter, there is some discussion of risk reduction strategies that focus on the individual employee*
- Health and Safety Executive. *The scale of occupational stress: the Bristol stress and health at work study.* Sudbury: HSE Books, 2000 (CRR 265/2000)
- Health and Safety Executive. *Work related factors and ill health: the Whitehall II study—CRR 266/2000,* Sudbury: HSE Books, 2000

9   Mental health at work

Rachel Jenkins

Introduction

Mental illness affects about a tenth of all adults at any one time—about 450 million people worldwide. Lifetime prevalence is much higher. Mental disorders now account for about 12% of the global burden of disease and this is expected to rise to 15% by the year 2020. Neuropsychiatric conditions account for 30% of all years lived with disability.

Mental disorders and substance abuse are important issues in the workplace, partly because they are so common in the general adult population and partly because increasing rates of employment in many countries mean that the less able are entering the workforce. Mental ill health at work seems to be rising and in the United Kingdom at least, it has overtaken musculoskeletal disorders as the main cause of absence from work, long term sickness, and retirement on medical grounds. Whatever the cause of mental disorders, they have consequences for work performance and economic productivity. Appropriately tailored work is generally beneficial for people suffering mental illness, and the workplace can be an important setting for mental health promotion and the prevention of illness.

Positive mental health is not just the absence of mental disorder but has been defined as a positive sense of wellbeing, implying the presence of self esteem; optimism; a sense of mastery and coherence; the ability to initiate, develop, and sustain mutually satisfying personal relationships; and the ability to cope with adversity (resilience). Factors such as these enhance a person's capacity to contribute to family and other social networks, the local community, and society at large. They are also qualities that may be expected to influence work performance.

The spectrum of mental health problems

Mental disorder is common in the adult population of the United Kingdom, as elsewhere in Europe and the rest of the world.

Those who are unemployed have higher rates of mental illness than people in employment, partly because of the socially stressful aspects of unemployment and partly because people with mental illness experience more difficulty in finding and maintaining work.

Rates of mental illness in employed and unemployed, Great Britain 2000

	Working full time	Working part time	Unemployed	Inactive
	Rate per thousand (se)			
Neurosis (per thousand in past week)	136 (7)	161 (11)	196 (30)	270 (12)
Probable psychosis (per thousand in past year)	1 (1)	6 (2)	–	17 (3)
Alcohol dependence (per thousand in past 6 months)	94 (5)	53 (8)	146 (25)	67 (7)
Drug dependence (per thousand in past year)	40 (4)	32 (6)	137 (23)	40 (6)

Source: ONS survey of psychiatric morbidity among adults living in private households, 2000

The spectrum of mental health disorders

Disorder	Rough prevalence
Psychological distress usually connected with various life situations, events, and problems	Most of us from time to time
Common mental disorders (depression, anxiety disorders in adults, and emotional and conduct disorders in children)	10-20% of adults in general population but 40-50% in highly vulnerable populations; 30% of primary care attenders; 10% of children in general population
Severe mental disorders with disturbances in perception, beliefs, and thought processes (psychoses)	0.5% of general population
Substance abuse disorders (excess consumption and dependency on alcohol, drugs, and tobacco)	Highly country specific; 5% and above, increasing
Eating disorders	1-5%; mostly women
Abnormal personality traits that are handicapping to the individual and/or others	Not known; existing studies suggest 5%
Progressive organic diseases of the brain (dementia)	Senile dementia: 5% of over 65s and 20% of over 80s (hence the demographic time bomb)
Tropical organic dementias	Situation specific
AIDS dementia	A growing problem in countries where people with AIDS live long enough to develop it
Toxic organic brain syndromes	Industry specific (mercury, lead, carbon monoxide) or environmental

Prevalence of psychiatric disorders per 1000 population in adults aged 16-64 years in Great Britain 2000

	Women	Men	All adults
	Rate per thousand in past week (se)		
Mixed anxiety and depressive disorders	112 (6)	72 (5)	92 (4)
Generalised anxiety disorder	48 (3)	46 (4)	47 (3)
Depressive episode	30 (3)	26 (3)	28 (2)
Phobias	24 (2)	15 (2)	19 (2)
Obsessive-compulsive disorder	15 (2)	10 (2)	12 (1)
Panic disorder	7 (1)	8 (2)	7 (1)
Any neurotic disorder	202 (8)	144 (7)	173 (6)
	Rate per thousand in past year (se)		
Probable psychosis	5 (1)	6 (1)	6 (1)
Drug dependence	24 (3)	60 (5)	42 (3)
	Rate per thousand in past 6 months (se)		
Alcohol dependence	32 (3)	130 (6)	81 (4)

The prevalence of mental disorders in the workplace

Study	Number studied	Population	Instrument	Male	Female	Total prevalence per 1000
Fraser R, 1947	3000	Light and medium engineering workers	Medical assessment	283	360	300
Heron and Braithwaite, 1953	184	Colliery workers: Sedentary Surface manual Underground workers	Middlesex questionniare	334 452 522		
Jenkins R, et al., 1982	162	Times journalists: 1 month after redundancy notice and 2 months before closure date 3 months after redundancy notice, when redundancy revoked and new owner arrived 12 weeks after threat of redundancy removed	Clinical interview schedule General health questionnaire			378 378 324
MacBride R, et al., 1981	274	Air traffic controllers during an industrial dispute 4 months later 10 months later	General health questionnaire			480 270 310
Jenkins R, 1985	184	Executive officers in civil service	Clinical interview schedule	362	343	
McGrath A, et al., 1989	171	Nurses Teachers Social workers	General health questionnaire			270 310 370
Stansfeld S, et al., 1994	10 314	Whitehall civil servants: Admin grades 1-7 Senior executive officer, Higher executive officer, Clerical	General health questionnaire	248 247 216	353 310 252	

Causes and consequences of mental disorder

Causes

The causation of mental disorder is multifactorial, being half genetic and half environmental for psychoses but largely environmental for the non-psychotic disorders.

Some disorders have a genetic basis, especially the major psychoses. Malnutrition can be a direct cause, whether in childhood or as an adult (for example, pellagra). Rarely, endocrine disorders such as myxodema may be causative. Occupational and environmental causes include infection (for example, encephalitis), the toxic effects of exposures at work (for example, mercury poisoning), and trauma (head injury).

Psychological factors—for example, poor coping skills and persistently low self esteem—also contribute. Such routine adverse life events as bereavement or job loss can lead to at least temporary mental disorder in the vulnerable. Unusually distressing or life threatening events may predispose towards the development of post-traumatic stress disorder. Such mechanisms are exacerbated by inadequate social support networks. Chronic social adversity (unemployment, poverty, illiteracy, child labour, violence, and war) is also often responsible, especially among underprivileged people.

Longitudinal studies have shown that unemployment, redundancy, or even the threat of redundancy cause mental illness, although naturally, employees who are already mentally ill are more likely to lose their jobs—either voluntarily or involuntarily. Given what is known about the mean rates of illness in the population as a whole and a higher rate in the unemployed, one would expect to find comparatively lower rates of illness in people at work. However, those studies that have been done in particular groups of workers have shown quite high rates of mental illness. It has been suggested,

Risk factors associated with common mental disorders: odds ratio (OR) of sociodemographic correlates of revised clinical interview schedule (CIS-R) score of 12 or more; *p < 0.05 **p < 0.01

	Adjusted odds ratio	95% confidence interval
Sex		
Male	1.00	—
Female	1.28**	1.11 to 1.47
Age (years)		
16-24	1.00	—
25-34	1.14	0.89 to 1.45
35-44	1.27	0.99 to 1.64
45-54	1.31*	1.01 to 1.69
55-64	0.71*	0.53 to 0.94
Family unit type		
Couple, no children	1.00	—
Couple with 1 + children	0.89	0.75 to 1.06
Lone parent + child	1.41*	1.08 to 1.83
One person only	1.23*	1.00 to 1.51
Adult with parents	0.44	0.26 to 0.75
Adult with one parent	0.71*	0.53 to 0.95
Employment status		
Working full time	1.00	—
Working part time	1.16	0.96 to 1.39
Unemployed	1.44*	1.02 to 2.01
Economically inactive	2.26**	1.92 to 2.66
Tenure		
Owner-occupier	1.00	—
Renter	1.41**	1.22 to 1.64
Locality		
Semi-rural or rural	1.00	—
Urban	1.16*	1.01 to 1.34

however, that some bias may have occured in studying working populations that were chosen because they are perceived to be particularly stress prone. The table on page 46 shows the strength of some of these risk factors in relation to mental illness in the United Kingdom.

The clinical interview schedule is a semistructured standardised clinical interview for use in epidemiological studies in the community, primary care, and workplace settings. It was originally devised to be used by mental health researchers, but has since been revised for use by lay interviewers with no mental health training.

Consequences

The development of mental illness is often followed by a series of psychosocial problems. Physical illness may occur, partly as a result of self destructive behaviour. Suicide is now the tenth leading cause of death worldwide. A descent in the social order is common, and with this comes poverty and secondary effects on social relationships, especially family ones. These potential developments are paralleled by effects on working life—for example, loss of job status or unemployment. The employer incurs the costs of sickness absence, impaired productivity, and increased devotion of time to human resources issues. The table shows the high level of social disability associated with mental disorder, both psychotic and non-psychotic.

The role of the employer

Whether or not a person's illness is contributed to by work, their workplace bears the consequences of the illness in terms of reduced productivity, sickness absence, labour turnover, accidents, and so on. It should be in the employer's interest to provide a good working environment, supportive if necessary, and to enlist some kind of occupational health service to detect and, sometimes, to help rehabilitate people with mental disorders in collaboration with other health and social agencies. In fact, such is the negative attitude of employers towards potential employees with such an illness that, far from offering support, they usually attempt instead to exclude. Mental disorders that have a substantial impact on everyday life are regarded as disabilities in the United Kingdom, and employers are forbidden to discriminate unreasonably against such people when offering employment. Instead, adjustments to working life must be entertained.

Less serious disorders that have little influence on everyday life, and drug and alcohol dependence, which are not covered by the Disability Discrimination Act, may nevertheless cause immense problems for employers and fellow employees. Mental disorders can be screened for but, rather like back pain, the lifetime prevalence is so high that excluding candidates with a history of mental disorder will simply reduce the potential workforce to unmanageable levels. Certain conditions, if declared, do probably render applicants potentially unfit for certain occupations: psychotic illness, personality disorder, and substance abuse for the caring professions; personality disorder and dependency disorders in safety sensitive jobs.

The role of Government

To support a successful economy and to make an appropriate contribution to the prevention of discrimination against people with mental illness, government agencies and other national bodies may need to take action on environmental conditions at work; access to employment, including sheltered employment for those who need it; opportunities for employment rehabilitation; the promotion of workplace mental health

Difficulties in activities of daily living in household samples

People assessed as having ...	% with any difficulties	N
Suicidal thoughts in the past week	59	45
Probable psychosis in the past year	58	54
Neurosis in the past week	41	1376
None of the above	13	5919

Mental disorder is already prevalent within the workplace. Working conditions are known to have a considerable influence on mental health. Therefore, to minimise the damage from this source to both employees and employers, the most sensible course would seem to be for employers to institute mental health policies as part of their human resources framework

Workplace mental health policy

A workplace mental health policy is agreed between employers, employees, and their representatives—for example, trade unions, and includes:

- A statement that the organisation is committed to a course of action which might include
  - increased understanding of causes of mental health problems in the workforce
  - action to combat workplace stressors and helping staff to manage their stress
  - action to manage mental health problems effectively through early recognition and appropriate management
  - action to manage the return to work of those who have suffered mental health problems to ensure their skills are not lost to the enterprise
- Commitment to a healthy workforce, placing a huge value on both physical and mental health
- Acknowledging that mental health problems may have many causes, including stressors in the workplace and in the outside world
- Listing factors that may lead to increased stress levels in the organisation (customised, based on discussion with staff and needs assessment)
- Recognising that domestic factors (such as housing, family problems, and bereavement) may add to levels of stress experienced by employees

policies; and the provision of occupational health for the workforce. This is especially important now that many governments encourage the return to work of those who have suffered mental health problems, as well as those recovering from physical illness as part of "welfare to work" schemes. In times of full employment this may well increase the proportion of those at work who are psychiatrically vulnerable.

The role of schools in supporting subsequent occupational health initiatives

Besides their primary educational role, schools are important settings for mental health promotion. They can teach children important life skills aimed at reducing acute and chronic social stressors and enhancing social supports, all of which have a direct influence on mental health, and which may be expected to influence subsequent mental health in adult working life. Thus, employers as a body have an interest in encouraging mental health promotion in schools in the same way that they encourage mathematical and literacy skills, as well as physical health. Such mental health promotion should include teaching of coping skills, citizenship skills, exam skills and techniques, stress management, achieving potential in relationships and working situations, recognising and combating bullying, learning to say no to risky behaviours, and education about parenting and child rearing in collaboration with a health education and addiction programme.

The role of health professionals

Health professionals, including occupational health professionals, need to be adept at detecting and assessing mental health problems in the workplace. Managers may suspect mental health problems but they cannot be expected to diagnose or assess them, and they need help from health professionals in understanding and managing them. An occupational physician should be able to take an adequate psychiatric history, identify any possible physical agents responsible or stressors (in or out of work), and then perform a mental state examination to complete a risk assessment.

An occupational health professional's most important and unique contributions to helping manage people at work who have had or are experiencing mental health problems are to try to reduce stigma and discrimination, foster an understanding among managers and work colleagues, and advise on adjustments to the workplace when employees decompensate or when they return after a period off work because of mental illness.

The high rate of suicidal thoughts in people with depression means that teaching good assessment and management techniques to health and social care professionals should be a priority, as should national and local action to minimise environmental risk factors for suicide.

Common mental disorders that may present in the workplace

Mixed anxiety or depression
Mixed anxiety or depression is the commonest disorder seen in occupational settings. People with this disorder may present with one or more physical symptoms—for example, various pains, poor sleep, and fatigue, accompanied by a variety of psychological symptoms. It is a prime cause of absence from

---

> Many schools now teach children "values"—respect for others', feelings, acceptance of differences in race, religion, etc. This can be established equally well in a workplace with a set of "company values" that go beyond the usually facile "mission statement"

Mental state examination
- *Appearance and behaviour*—Grooming, hostility, restlessness, pupils, alcohol smell
- *Communication*—Rapid, sparse, confused
- *Mood*—Low or high, feelings of self worth, hopelessness, concentration, biological aspects (sleep, energy levels, appetite, libido), suicidal ideation
- *Thoughts*—Thought formation, thought content
- *Perceptions*—Hallucinations, etc.
- *Cognitive aspects*—Orientation, short term memory, knowledge of current affairs, neurological deficits
- *Insight*—Individual aware they are ill? Prepared to be treated?

Diagnostic features of mixed anxiety and depression
- Low or sad mood
- Loss of interest or pleasure
- Prominent anxiety or worry
- Multiple associated symptoms
- Disturbed sleep
- Tremor
- Fatigue or loss of energy
- Palpitations
- Poor concentration
- Dizziness
- Disrupted appetite
- Suicidal thoughts and acts
- Dry mouth
- Loss of libido
- Tension and restlessness
- Irritability

work "due to stress." Together with related states, it contributes considerably to the disability accompanying musculoskeletal disorders, especially back pain, and to fatigue states.

Depression

Depression is common, with a lifetime prevalence in the United States of 17% for a major episode. The sufferer may present with physical symptoms, irritability, anxiety or insomnia, worries about social problems such as financial or marital difficulties, increased drug or alcohol use, or (in a new mother) constant worries about her baby or fear of harming the baby. Some groups are at higher risk—for example, those who have recently given birth or had a stroke, and those with physical disorders such as Parkinson's disease or multiple sclerosis.

Differential diagnosis

The differential diagnosis includes acute psychotic disorder if hallucinations or delusions are present; bipolar disorder if there is a history of manic episodes; poisoning or substance misuse if heavy alcohol or drug use has occurred; and chronic mixed anxiety-depression. Some medications may produce symptoms of depression (for example, β blockers, other antihypertensives, H2 blockers, oral contraceptives, corticosteroids). Unexplained somatic symptoms, anxiety, or alcohol or drug disorders may coexist with depression.

Alcohol and drug misuse

Employees (or employers) with alcohol problems may present with depression, nervousness, insomnia, physical conditions such as peptic ulcer, gastritis, liver disease, hypertension, accidents or injuries, poor memory or concentration, and evidence of self neglect (for example, poor hygiene). They may be people in whom treatment for depression has failed. Patients may also have legal and social problems resulting from alcohol—for example, marital problems, domestic violence, child abuse, or missed work. Signs of alcohol withdrawal may be present—for example, sweating, tremors, morning sickness, hallucinations, and seizures. Those with alcohol problems often deny or are unaware of their problems, and it may be others who request professional help.

Management by the occupational health department

Employees may be referred with a suspicion of an alcohol problem or the possibility may be raised at the first interview. Assessment may be aided by simple well validated screening questionnaires such as the CAGE questionnaire and, for less excessive but still harmful drinking, the alcohol use disorders identification test (AUDIT) questionnaire.

The assessment should be conducted in a straightforward non-judgmental way and cover drinking pattern, amount, type, circumstances, and duration, as well as symptoms; convictions for drink driving should be specifically asked about. Laboratory tests may help diagnosis but have a limited use in isolation. They can help in patient education and in monitoring alcohol reduction, as can a drink diary.

Managing alcohol problems at work

This is best done in the context of an alcohol and drugs policy at work, which will always include a ban on the use of illegal drugs at work but which may have a variable attitude to alcohol at work, perhaps allowing alcohol to individuals whose jobs are not safety sensitive, for social occasions, or after the working day is over, etc. Whatever the policy, it needs to be signed up to

---

Diagnostic features of depression

- Low or sad mood
- Loss of interest or pleasure
- At least four of the following:
  - disturbed sleep
  - disturbed appetite
  - guilt or low self worth
  - pessimism or hopelessness about future
  - decreased libido
  - diurnal mood variation
  - poor concentration
  - suicidal thoughts or acts
  - loss of self confidence
  - fatigue or loss of energy
  - agitation or slowing of movement or speech
- Symptoms of anxiety or nervousness are also frequently present

---

Essential information about depression for patient, family, work colleagues, and managers

- Depression is a common illness and effective treatments are available
- Depression is not weakness or laziness
- Depression can affect a person's ability to cope

Information leaflets or audiotapes can be used to reinforce the information

---

Alcohol dependency

The presence of three or more of the following suggests alcohol dependency

- Strong desire or compulsion to use alcohol
- Difficulty controlling alcohol use
- Withdrawal (anxiety, tremors, sweating, hallucinations) when drinking has ceased
- Tolerance—drinking large amounts of alcohol without appearing intoxicated
- Continued alcohol use despite harmful consequences

Presentation of alcohol problems at work

- Poor attendance—frequent sickness absence, certified or uncertified—may be regular—for example, after weekends or breaks
- Lateness for work
- Poor performance—mistakes, slowness, poor judgement, frequent mishaps
- Prolonged lunch hours, afternoon sleepiness
- Poor personal hygiene, scruffiness, smelling of alcohol
- Irrational or noisy behaviour, inappropriate comments, irritability
- Frequent disappearances during the day
- Signs of violence—cuts and bruises
- Dishonesty or deviousness
- Frequent sickness absence because of gastrointestinal upsets

by management and workers' representatives. If there is an Occupational Health Department or some kind of welfare service, then referrals by managers or individuals themselves for alcohol related problems should be possible, and the condition treated initially as a health problem, and only when there is refusal or inability to stop or reduce drinking to reasonable levels are disciplinary procedures invoked. Time off work as sick leave may be required. Referral to a general practitioner or alcohol misuse specialist will be necessary. Compliance with undertakings can be managed by an occupational health department, using random testing if required. The same process can be used for employees who use illegal drugs, although the very illegality of the drugs can lead to disciplinary measures much more quickly.

Both alcohol and drug abuse are chronic conditions, and any employer or Occupational Health Service has to realise the high probability of relapse, although research shows that rehabilitation is more likely to be successful when the problem is dealt with in a work context when the individual is threatened with potential job loss. Early recognition, assessment, and active management of the situation also help.

Alcohol and drug abuse is a serious problem for society and is clearly increasing in incidence; it is also a huge problem for employers. The yearly cost to industry of alcohol misuse has been estimated at about £3 billion in the United Kingdom through accidents, reduced productivity, and absenteeism. Hangovers alone have been estimated to cost industry £50-100 million.

Drugs of abuse other than alcohol can have serious effects on performance, probity, and so on. Testing for drugs at pre-employment or randomly is practised in some safety sensitive industries. The testing has to be done using proper chain of custody techniques and in the context of an agreed drugs policy, which may or may not allow for rehabilitation while still employed. Employers and occupational health professionals who undertake coercive testing for drugs of abuse must ask themselves whether by instituting this programme they are trying to exclude "undesirables" from this workplace or to identify those who, while under the influence of drugs, may present a safety or security risk? This issue raises concerns about human rights.

Women's issues

Women, by virtue of their increased exposure to acute life events, chronic social stresses, lower social status and income, and smaller social networks, are often particularly vulnerable to common mental disorders. This is reflected, hardly surprisingly, in higher rates of sickness absence because of psychological causes. Disorders associated with menstruation, pregnancy, and childbirth are additional disorders specific to women. New mothers often feel pressured to return to work early after childbirth, and one of the most important preventive actions that can be taken in the mental heath arena is to recognise postnatal illness and ensure adequate and prompt treatment.

Eating disorders

An eating disorder may be declared at a pre-employment screening. The two main types, anorexia and bulimia, of which the latter is more common, occur mainly in young women. An individual may present with binge eating and extreme weight control measures such as self induced vomiting, and excessive use of diet pills and laxatives, usually covert. In the case of employees, management may ask occupational health professionals for help because of concerns about an

---

CAGE questionnaire

Four questions:
- Have you ever felt you ought to **Cut** down on your drinking?
- Have people **Annoyed** you by criticising your drinking?
- Have you ever felt bad or **Guilty** about your drinking?
- Have you ever had a drink first thing in the morning to steady your nerves or get rid of a hangover ("**Eye-opener**")?

Over 90% of dependent drinkers answer "yes" to two or more of these questions

---

Alcohol use disorders identification test (AUDIT)

See Saunders JB, Aasland OG, Babor TF, de la Fuente JR, Grant M. Development of the alcohol disorders idenitfication test (AUDIT): WHO collaborative project on early detection of persons with harmful alcohol consumption. *Addiction* 1993;88:791-803

Management of alcohol dependence
Essential information for employees, managers, and families
- Alcohol dependence is an illness with serious consequences
- Ceasing or reducing alcohol use brings mental and physical benefits
- Drinking during pregnancy may harm the baby
- For people with alcohol dependence, physical complications of alcohol abuse or psychiatric disorder, abstinence from alcohol is the preferred goal
- In some cases of harmful alcohol use without dependence, or where the individual is unwilling to quit, controlled or reduced drinking is a reasonable goal
- Relapses are common. Controlling or stopping drinking often requires several attempts. Outcome depends on the motivation and confidence of the patient

Advice and support to patient and family
- Discuss costs and benefits of drinking from individual's perspective
- Give feedback about health risks, including the results of gamma glutaryl transferase and mean corpuscular volume measurements
- Emphasise *personal responsibility* for change and give clear advice
- Consider targeted counselling

For patients willing to stop now
- Set a definite day to quit
- Discuss symptoms and management of alcohol withdrawal (may require time off or even hospitalisation)
- Discuss strategies to avoid or cope with high risk situations (for example, how to face stressful events without alcohol, ways to respond to friends or colleagues who still drink)
- Help identify colleagues, friends, and family who will support ceasing alcohol use
- Discuss support after withdrawal
- Mention self help organisations such as Alcoholics Anonymous, which are often helpful

---

Concern has arisen that a history of such disorders makes candidates unsuitable for caring professions such as nursing or school teaching, but this is not necessarily the case. In this context, attention should be paid to any accompanying behavioural disorders including self harm—for example, and personality disorders, rather than uncomplicated eating disorders

individual's weight loss. Both anorexia and bulimia may present as physical disorders (for example, seizures or cardiac arrhythmias) that may have employment consequences and need treatment. Bulimia is, in general, a much more transitory condition with a better record of successful treatment. Anorexia nervosa is often more chronic and intractable and may involve prolonged sickness absence because of hospitalisation.

Bipolar disorder

Patients may present with a period of depression, mania, or excitement, or referral may be made by others because of the individual's lack of insight.

The diagnostic features of bipolar disorder are given in the box. Periods of either mania or depression may predominate. Episodes may alternate often or may be separated by periods of normal mood. In severe cases, patients may have hallucinations (hearing voices or seeing visions) or delusions (strange or illogical beliefs) during periods of mania or depression. The differential diagnosis includes poisoning or drug or alcohol misuse, which may cause similar symptoms.

Individuals often enter the hypomanic state rapidly, with danger to themselves and to others at work, especially if their job is safety sensitive. Some kind of early warning system should be instituted by the Occupational Health Department with the individual's consent and the cooperation of managers or sympathetic work colleagues.

High risk occupations

Certain occupations are at high risk for work related mental illness (and, incidentally, for fatigue states). These include occupations such as teaching, nursing, and the police force where there is a need for emotional commitment in the personal problems of other people and where there are considerable staff shortages, high demand, and poor locus of control.

Certain occupations are also at high risk for suicide. These include vets, doctors, dentists, pharmacists, and farmers—they have greater access to the means of suicide and better knowledge about effective methods of suicide, as well as being in demanding occupations.

Health professionals lead stressful lives, and epidemiological studies have confirmed the high levels of depression and anxiety in healthcare staff, indicating the need to address the support of this key group.

Employers are becoming increasingly worried—mainly for legal reasons—about the effect of demanding work on the mental health of vulnerable employees. This is a contentious area with little in the way of legal precedent but one where advice is frequently asked of occupational health professionals. Careful psychological assessment, knowledge of the job stressors, and a traditional risk assessment approach offer the best way forward. Attempts have been made, using a partially evidence based approach, to define health standards, including medical criteria, for entry into certain demanding professions—the armed forces, medicine, nursing, teaching, and civil emergency services. This can be helpful.

The potential for violence and bullying at work has also concerned employers, but such behaviour does not in fact usually emanate from those with mental illness but from those with problematic personality types or drug and alcohol problems.

Diagnostic features of bipolar disorder

Periods of mania characterised by
- Increased energy and activity
- Elevated mood or irritability
- Rapid speech
- Loss of inhibitions
- Decreased need for sleep
- Increased importance of self
- Persistent distraction

Periods of depression characterised by
- Low or sad mood
- Loss of interest or pleasure
- Disturbed sleep
- Guilt or low self worth
- Fatigue or loss of energy
- Poor concentration
- Disturbed appetite
- Suicidal thoughts or acts

Further reading

- World Health Organization collaborating centre for research and training for mental Health, eds. *WHO guide to mental health in primary care*. London: Royal Society of Medicine Press, 2000. *This is a pocket guide for the assessment, diagnosis, management, and criteria for referral of common mental disorders at primary care level. It has been specifically tailored for the United Kingdom by the WHO Collaborating Centre at the Institute of Psychiatry and contains the evidence base, resources including voluntary agencies, and a discussion of how to audit training needs*
- Andrews A, Jenkins R. *Management of mental disorders*. Aldershot: Datapress, 2000. *This is a two volume manual for the management of mental disorders, and is suitable for all members of the multidisciplinary team. It contains specific guidance on psychological therapies*
- Jenkins R, Bebbington P, Brugha TS, Farrell M, Lewis G, Meltzer H. British psychiatric morbidity survey. *Br J Psych* 1998;173:4-7. *This paper summarises the key findings from the first national survey of psychiatric morbidity in Britain. It shows the high prevalence of the psychiatric disorder and its association with sociodemographic and social risk factors*
- Jenkins R, Macdonald A, Murray J, Strathdee G. Minor psychiatric morbidity and the threat of redundancy in a professional group. *Psych Med* 1982;12:799-899. *This paper shows the psychiatric impact of the threat of redundancy on* Times *journalists*
- Jenkins R. Minor psychiatric morbidity and labour turnover. *Br J Ind Med* 1985;42:534-9. *The paper shows that the presence of minor psychiatric morbidity (depression and anxiety) is associated with substantially increased labour turnover, with associated costs for employers*
- Jenkins R. Minor psychiatric morbidity in civil servants and its contribution to sickness absence. *Br J Ind Med* 1985;42:147-54. *This paper describes the substantial association between minor psychiatric morbidity and sickness absence both retrospectively (the 12 months before the assessment) and projectively (the 12 months after the assessment), again with associated costs for employers*
- Jenkins R, Warman D, eds. *Developing mental health policies in the workplace*. London: HMSO, 1993
- Jenkins R, Coney N. *Promoting mental health at work*. London: HMSO, 1992. *These two books look at the business case for action to develop mental health policies in the workplace, from the CBI and TUC perspective, and examines a range of good practice examples from different companies*
- Department of Health. ABC of mental health in the workplace. London: HMSO, 1996. *This government publication sets out the key elements of a workplace mental health policy*
- Jenkins R. Public policy and environment. In: Gelder M, ed. *Oxford textbook of psychiatry*. Oxford: Oxford University Press, 2000. *This chapter sets the issue of mental health in the workplace in the context or overall public policy and mental health*
- Miller DM, Lipsedge M, Litchfield P, eds. *Work and Mental Health—an employer's guide*. Gaskell and Faculty of Occupational Medicine, 2002. *Straightforward and comprehensive account of the impact of mental health problems on work and how to deal with them.*

The third area of concern is safety. The potential problems with psychotic or dementing employees and employees who misuse drugs or alcohol will be obvious. The assessment of less serious mental disorders and their relation to safety is a job for the occupational physician using a similar approach to that described for assessing those entering demanding jobs. Psychotropic medication often affects cognition, especially at the beginning of treatment; drowsiness and lack of concentration are common and should be anticipated.

Mental ill health at work is likely to become the dominant occupational health issue of the future. There is enormous scope for research and enormous need for public education and the destigmatisation of mental illness.

The table showing the prevalence of psychiatric disorders and the table showing rates of mental illness employed and unemployed are adapted from ONS survey of psychiatric morbidity among adults living in private households. London: HMSO, 2000. The table showing the prevalence of mental disorders in the workplace is adapted from Jenkins R. Public policy and environment. In: Gelder M, ed. *Oxford textbook of psychiatry*. Oxford: Oxford University Press, 2000. The table showing risk factors associated with common mental disorders and the table showing difficulties in activities of daily living are also adapted from ONS survey of psychiatric morbidity among adults living in private households. London: HMSO, 2000.

10 Human factors

Deborah Lucas

The term "human factors" is often invoked after an accident, whether a minor incident in the workplace or a major disaster entailing significant loss of life. In many respects "human factors" is regarded by the layman as being synonymous with "human failure"—an unavoidable aspect of the human condition. Although there is a long list of major accidents across all hazardous industrial sectors where human failures were causal factors, this is not to imply that human errors are inevitable. Research over the past 20 years has shown much about the origins of different types of error and the best means of reducing their occurrence. However, the loss of life in disasters such as the Clapham Junction rail crash in 1988, the Southall and Ladbroke Grove train crashes in 1997 and 1999, respectively, and the sinking of the Herald of Free Enterprise in 1987 are high in the British public's mind. All of these disasters had human factors as a cause: a maintenance worker not disconnecting a wire, a train driver passing a red danger signal, and a bosun failing to close the bow doors of a ferry. The nuclear industry faced up to the issue of human factors after Three Mile Island in 1979 and the Chernobyl accident in 1986. The oil sector recognised the issue after the Piper Alpha tragedy in 1988. The aviation, rail, and marine transportation sectors are all actively considering the issue of human factors. Proper consideration of human factors is a key ingredient of effective health and safety management in all industrial sectors.

Modern health care is also a complex and, at times, high risk activity where adverse events are inevitable. However, a substantial proportion of adverse events results from preventable human failure by medical staff. Adverse events occur in about 10% of admissions to hospital in the United Kingdom—a rate of 850 000 adverse events a year. In the United Kingdom, 400 people die or are seriously injured every year in adverse events involving medical devices. Hospital acquired infections are estimated to cost the NHS nearly £1 billion every year, but about 15% of such infections may be avoidable. In the United States it is estimated that between 44 000 and 98 000 people die annually because of medical errors. Yet health care is not unique. There are many parallels with other high risk sectors, which have been examining the need to reduce human failures in complex systems for over two decades.

Definition

Human factors are often described as the thread that runs through all the key health and safety management issues, and numerous definitions of human factors and the related term ergonomics exist. The definition given by the UK Health and Safety Executive is "Human factors refer to environmental, organisational and job factors, and human and individual characteristics, which influence behaviour at work in a way that can affect health and safety." Key elements have been identified by psychologists and ergonomists after an incident or accident, and in the military field human factors programmes explicitly consider six aspects or domains during the design or procurement of a system. These domains have been found to be useful in other industrial contexts.

"Human error" is often cited immediately after a disaster

Examples of human failures in medicine

- A patient is inadvertently given a drug that they are known to be allergic to
- A clinician misreads the results of a test
- A child receives an adult dose of a toxic drug
- A patient is given medicine that has a similar sounding name to that prescribed
- A toxic drug is administered by the wrong route—for example, intrathecally
- A heart attack is not diagnosed by emergency room staff in an older patient with ambiguous symptoms

---

Common errors relating to drugs

- Unavailable drug information (for example, lack of up to date warnings)
- Miscommunication of drug orders (for example, through poor handwriting, confusion between drugs with similar names, misuse of zeros and decimal points, confusion between milligrams and micrograms)
- Incomplete patient information (such as not knowing about other medicines they are taking)
- Lack of suitable labelling when a drug is repackaged into smaller units
- Workplace factors that distract medical staff from their immediate tasks (such as poor lighting, heat, noise, and interruptions)

Human factors considered in the development of military systems

Domain	Issue	Issues to consider
Staffing	How many people are needed to operate and maintain the system?	Workload Job descriptions Staffing levels Team organisation
Personnel	What human characteristics, including aptitudes and experience, are needed to operate and maintain the system?	Selection and recruitment Career development Required qualifications, competences, and experience Specific characteristics
Training	What is the best way to develop and maintain the required knowledge, skills, and abilities to operate and maintain the system?	Training needs analysis Documentation Assessment Team training Skill maintenance and update
Human factors engineering	How can human factors be built into the system design to optimise human performance?	Equipment design Workstation design Workplace layout User interface design Maintenance access
Health hazards	What are the short term and long term health hazards from operation of the system?	Minimising exposure to health hazards such as toxic materials, electricity, musculoskeletal injury, noise and vibration, extremes of temperature
System safety	How can safety risks that humans might cause when operating or maintaining the system be avoided?	Sources of human errors Effects of misuse of equipment Abnormal and emergency situations

Human failure

Research across industries has shown much about the types of human failure and the underlying psychological mechanisms. A key distinction can be made between unintended human errors and deliberate rule violations. However, even deliberate violations can result from system pressures such as shortage of time because of a lack of staff, or the correct equipment not being available. In high hazard industries it is no longer acceptable to attribute a safety incident just to a "human error" with the assumption that this was somehow beyond the control of managers and safety management systems. A detailed

Typical causes of human failures in accidents

Job factors
- Illogical design of equipment and instruments
- Constant disturbances and interruptions
- Missing or unclear instructions
- High workload
- Noisy and unpleasant working conditions

Individual attributes
- Low skill and competence levels
- Tired staff
- Bored or disheartened staff
- Individual medical or fitness problems

Organisational aspects
- High work pressure because of poor work planning
- Poor health and safety culture
- One way communications (messages sent but no checks to ensure they are received or are appropriate)
- Lack of safety systems and barriers
- Inadequate responses to previous incidents

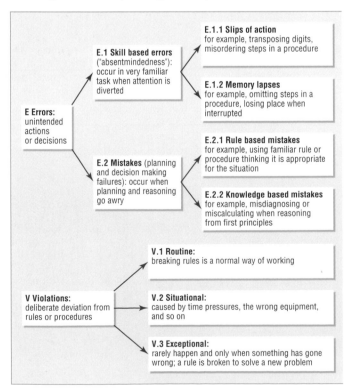

Classification of the types of human failure

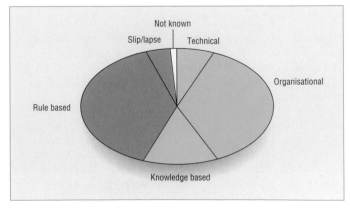

Causes of incidents in a department of surgery

investigation into the causes of incidents involving human failure will show a number of immediate and underlying causes and contributing factors. Many of these will be problems with organisational systems rather than with the individual member of staff.

Control measures

There is no "magic bullet" for the problems of human fallibility. However, thoughtful, multifaceted approaches can reduce the probability of human failures leading to serious consequences. In medicine, knowledge and tools to enhance patient safety are emerging, and much can be learnt from other industries, particularly the high hazard sectors such as the nuclear industry, aviation, and transportation.

Designing for people

Many sources of human error can be removed through effective design of equipment and procedures. Such "error tolerant" designs consider the tasks that the equipment is intended for and the errors the user may make. To give an example, in the early days of automatic teller machines, the user's bank card was returned to them by the machine *after* their cash had been issued. Banks found that many people took their money but forgot to take their card. This error was prevented by returning the card before the cash appeared.

Consideration of human factors is an important aspect of overall design and equipment procurement, and should be considered early in the design process. If left too late, then complicated procedures, added warnings, and requests for the user to "take care" can be the unfortunate result. Compliance with instructions and procedures differs according to the situation, the risks, the element of personal choice, and the probability of being detected. Written warnings are usually noticed, read less often, and complied with infrequently.

Poorly designed equipment can directly influence the chance of human errors occurring. For example, the layout of controls and displays can influence safety if switches are placed so that they can inadvertently be knocked on or off, if controls are poorly identified and can be selected by mistake, or when critical displays are not in the user's normal field of view. The controls of different equipment may not be compatible: for example, a switch in the up position may be "on" in one

Case study: reducing errors in the administration of intravenous heparin

The intravenous administration of heparin (an anticoagulant) is a complex procedure, and this drug has been the subject of serious drug errors. A US hospital wanted to reduce errors in the administration of heparin in cardiac care units. They developed a form that combined the ordering and recording of the use of heparin. In addition, they improved communication with the hospital laboratory, converted all heparin protocols to pharmacy managed protocols, introduced pre-typed heparin orders and the double-checking of pump programming, and encouraged the use of low molecular weight heparin instead of standard heparin. These control measures were claimed to have reduced drug errors by 66%

"Human beings make mistakes because the systems, tasks, and processes they work in are poorly designed"

Dr Lucian Leape, testifying to the US President's Commission on Consumer Protection and Quality in Health Care

---

Examples of ergonomic criteria for procuring equipment
- Does the equipment suit the body size of all users?
- Can users see and hear all they need to easily?
- Is it easy to understand the information displayed?
- Would the equipment cause discomfort if used for any length of time?
- Is it easy to learn how to use the equipment? Are instructions and any warning signs clear? Is the language used appropriate for the users?
- What errors may occur? Can these be detected easily, and corrected?
- Is the equipment compatible with other systems in use?
- Can users reach controls easily?
- Can users move safely between operating positions?
- Is the equipment too noisy, does it vibrate too much, is it paced too fast?

Compliance rates in different situations

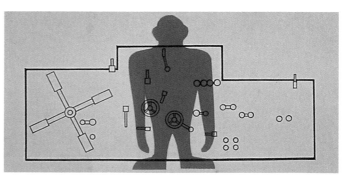

Arrangement of controls on a lathe and the "ideal" operator, who should have the following dimensions—4 feet 6 inches tall, shoulders 2 feet across, and an 8 foot arm span!

case but "off" in another. Alarm systems may be designed so that high priority alarms are not clearly differentiated and are thus easily missed.

Designing tasks, equipment, and workplaces to suit the users can prevent or reduce human errors and thus reduce accidents and ill health. A key message is that effective use of ergonomics will make work safer and more productive.

Sleep and human performance

Although it is often feasible to prevent human failures by the effective design of jobs and equipment, in other situations human performance problems may arise as the result of fatigue, shiftwork, poor communications, lack of experience, or inadequate risk perception. These aspects all need to be managed effectively to reduce the potential risks. One of the most commonly cited problems is lack of sleep for staff carrying out safety critical tasks. The decision to launch the Challenger space shuttle was partly attributed to the effects of fatigue on the decision making team. The rail crash at Selby in the United Kingdom in 2001 occurred because a car driver fell asleep and drove onto a railway line.

A significant proportion of road traffic accidents occur between 2 am and 5 am and are attributed to drivers falling asleep at the wheel. As we are not a nocturnal species, this is the time when our biological clock programmes us to sleep. Such circadian rhythms are hard to adjust to, even when working regular night shifts. Many people work shift systems, do night work, or work very extended hours including significant levels of overtime. Such working patterns can have adverse effects on their health as well as being associated with poorer performance on tasks that need attention or sustained vigilance, decision making, or high levels of skill. Sleep is a powerful biological need, and night work or certain shift systems can disrupt both the quantity and the quality of sleep. Sleeping during the day is never as satisfactory as sleeping at night. Sleep loss of just a few hours over a few days can lead to a build up of a sleep debt and reduced performance, but the person may not be aware of this.

A large body of research on shiftwork exists, but often the findings are not put into practice. Working patterns are usually seen as matters to be negotiated between employees and the employer, and additional overtime can be perceived as a financial advantage, and not as a potential health and safety issue. However, in high hazard industries awareness of the relation between sleepiness and accidents is growing.

Organisational influences

A number of factors within an organisation are associated with good safety performance. These affect not only human factors issues but also the "safety culture" of the organisation. A "culture" means shared attitudes, beliefs, and ways of behaving. An effective culture will be shown through good ways of informing and consulting all staff, recognition that everyone has a role to play in safety, visible commitment by managers to involving all staff, cooperation between members of the workforce, open two way communications, and high quality of training. The organisation that continually improves its own methods, and learns from mistakes (including accidents and "near misses") will tend to have a better safety performance than one that blames individuals for "being careless" when accidents happen.

The relationship between sleepiness and accidents: best practice approaches to managing the problem

- Plan shift rosters to take biological rhythms into account
- Set limits for maximum hours of duty and time needed for recovery afterwards
- Educate shift workers on sleep routines, nutrition, and exercise
- Make environmental changes to the workplace including lighting, temperature, and comfort level, which can all influence alertness
- Plan safety critical tasks to avoid night shifts
- Provide medical advice for shift workers
- Recognise the possibility of true sleep disorders (sleep apnoea, narcolepsy) and referral for investigation and treatment

High hazard industries are becoming increasingly aware of the importance of proper consideration of human factors

The Herald of Free Enterprise sank because no effective system was in place to ensure the bow doors were closed

Key principles

Human factors is a broad concept that can be seen as too complex or difficult to do anything about. However, there are five key principles to be remembered, and these are ones that many regulatory bodies are promoting:

- Recognise that people do not make mistakes because of "carelessness" and accept that even the most experienced members of staff are vulnerable to unintentional errors.
- Learn from adverse events including "near misses." Understand that usually there will be no single cause of an incident but a number of causes and contributing factors.
- Anticipate the influences on human performance. Key themes will include time pressure, experience, staffing levels, fatigue, and risk communications.
- Defend against paths to failure. In particular, appreciate the role of designing equipment and systems that are error tolerant.
- Encourage a "culture of safety."

Further reading

- NHS. *An organisation with a memory*. London: NHS Publications, 2000
- Reason J. *Human Error*. Cambridge: Cambridge University Press, 1990
- van der Schaaf TW, Shea CE. *MECCA: Incident reporting lessons from industry applied to the medical domain*. Conference on examining errors in health care, California: Rancho Mirage, 1996
- Reason J. *Managing the risks of organisational accidents*. Ashgate Publishing, 1997. *Seminal work on the causes of major accidents. A key influence for those looking at medical errors*
- Institute of Medicine. *To err is human: building a safer health system*. Washington DC: IOM, 1999. *Significant US report on medical errors; draws attention to the scale of the problem of potentially avoidable events that result in unintended harm to patients*
- *Building a safer NHS for patients*. London: NHS Publications, 2001. *Describes how promoting patient safety by reducing error is becoming a key priority of health services around the world. Sets out steps to implement a programme to reduce the impact of error within the NHS*
- HSE. *Reducing error and influencing behaviour*. Sudbury: HSE Books, 1999. *Guidance to industry on understanding and control of human factors in health and safety management. Covers understanding human failures, designing for people, and control measures for human errors*
- Noyes J. *Designing for humans*. London: Taylor and Francis. 2001. *Overview of human-machine interaction and the design of environments at work, with focus on health and safety at work*
- Moore-Ede M. *The 24-hour society: the risks, costs and challenges of a world that never stops*. London: Piatkus, 1993. *Introduction to the role of sleep in accidents. Covers biological aspects of sleeping and shiftwork*

11 Physical agents

Ron McCaig

The use of the term "physical agents" is not always clear. Sometimes it is taken to mean dusts and fibres whose effects are determined by their physical properties as well as their chemical composition. However, the term usually refers either to those agents that impart energy to the body by physical means (for example, the effects of radiation, heat, or noise and vibration), or to the effects of environments that differ in their physical characteristics from that existing at ground level on dry land (for example, found in diving and compressed air work, at altitude, and in flight).

The body offers some protection against physical agents experienced in the normal environment, such as heat and radiation—for example, by the physiological changes of heat acclimatisation or, at a cellular level, the operation of DNA repair mechanisms. Such mechanisms are limited in their effectiveness and can be overwhelmed if challenged by an exposure of sufficient magnitude. Even in artificial environments, such as work in compressed air tunnelling or high accelerations in flight, it is possible that a certain amount of physiological adaptation can take place. For example, the incidence of decompression illness often reduces after the first few days of exposure of a work force tunnelling in compressed air—an effect that is thought to be a form of acclimatisation—and some G tolerance can develop with physical fitness training.

Many physical agents have a threshold of exposure below which the body is unlikely to be harmed. Beyond that, it is necessary to restrict exposures, often by administrative controls such as limiting the duration of exposure (as in work rest schedules in the heat), providing shielding or protective clothing and equipment, or limiting the potential for harm by procedures such as staged decompression. Exposures must be carefully managed as some physical agents can kill within quite short periods.

Before exposure to hot, cold, or hyperbaric environments it is important to ensure that individuals have no predisposition to suffer from the effects of the environment. Fitness standards may be available, published by a variety of agencies. For ionising radiation it is important to know that individuals are medically fit for the type of work that they are expected to perform. (They may need to wear protective equipment—for example.)

Heat

Regulation of the central (core) body temperature is an essential physiological function—core temperature must be within the range 36-38°C for the body to perform efficiently. In the face of heat gain from the environment or as a result of exercise, the body defends the core temperature by vasodilatation (increasing skin blood flow) and by sweating.

If heat gain is greater than heat loss by the evaporation of sweat, convective cooling, and thermal radiation, then the body stores heat. As it does so, the temperature of the brain and central organs (such as the liver)—the core temperature—increases and this threatens the survival of the individual. Eventually external cooling must be provided to prevent death. Heat hyperpyrexia (heat stroke) is the most serious effect of exposure to heat. It is generally characterised by a body

> The effects of physical agents have been well studied, and for many of these exposure criteria are now established at an international level. Fatalities are only likely to occur where established safety procedures are broken

Authorities that set exposure standards for physical agents

- International Standards Organisation (ISO)
- American Conference of Governmental Industrial Hygienists (ACGIH)
- International Commission on Radiological Protection (ICRP)
- International Commission on Non-Ionising Radiation Protection (ICNIRP)
- Other national, transnational, and international authorities

The principles of managing work in hot environments

- An assessment of the risk should be undertaken and ways sought to reduce the environmental heat load, paying attention to humidity and radiant heat, as well as air temperature
- Individuals should be screened for medical conditions that may predispose to heat illness, and should be physically fit, well hydrated, and ideally below 40 years of age
- Work-rest regimes should be established from published standards and adhered to, with regular opportunities taken for the worker to cool down
- Workers should be educated about heat illnesses, and first aid facilities should be available
- In planning work, the state of acclimatisation of the workers and the resistance to heat loss provided by their clothing has to be taken into account

> Heat acclimatisation increases the magnitude of these responses. Any factor that impairs either the circulation or the ability to sweat will compromise thermoregulation

temperature of 40-41°C, an altered level of consciousness, and a hot dry skin resulting from failure of the sweating mechanism. These features are not invariable, however, so treatment should not be delayed if heat stroke is suspected.

Heat exhaustion results from a combination of thermal and cardiovascular strain. The individual is tired and may stumble, and has a rapid pulse and respiration rate. The condition may develop into heat stroke if not treated by rest, cooling, and fluids. Other effects are heat syncope (fainting), heat oedema, (often in the unacclimatised), heat cramps, and heat rash (prickly heat). Working in high temperatures can also result in fatigue and an increased risk of accidents.

Workers in fire and rescue services may be exposed to extreme heat in an unpredictable manner. Their safety depends on proper selection, training, and monitoring of the duration of exposure. Personal heat stress monitors are not yet widely available, but their use in these circumstances may confer some benefit.

Cold

In cold conditions the problem is to balance heat produced by physical activity with heat lost to the environment. The rate of heat loss depends on the insulation of the clothing and the external climate, including air temperature and wind velocity. The windchill index (derived in units of kcal/m²/hour) relates to the risk of freezing of superficial tissues, and this, or the related chilling temperature (expressed in °C), is quite widely used as a measure of the discomfort of cold conditions.

The insulation of clothing may be impaired by moisture in the form of condensed sweat or by precipitation. Protection is generally easier in cold dry environments such as mountains or arctic regions than in cold wet conditions. The protection of individuals who are active in cold wet environments, and who need waterproof external garments, is only partly solved by the introduction of "breathable" fabrics. A particular problem occurs in those environments where there is a risk of immersion in cold water, with resulting catastrophic loss of insulation. Where this risk can be anticipated—for example, in helicopter flights over water, protective immersion suits should be used.

Large numbers of workers are employed indoors in conditions of moderate to severe cold, mostly in food preparation and storage. Only a few people are exposed to cold in scientific and testing laboratories. Cold stores can operate at temperatures as low as −30°C. Workers in cold stores must be provided with proper insulated clothing, and they must have regular breaks in warm conditions. A major problem in severe cold, indoors or outside, is to keep the hands and feet warm. The necessary insulation is bulky, which is less of a problem for footwear than for hand wear. Mitts provide better thermal protection than gloves, but limit dexterity.

Indoors, in moderately cold conditions—that is, temperatures below 15°C, it may also be hard to maintain comfort of the extremities, and exposure to draughts can be particularly troublesome. Limited evidence indicates that workers regularly exposed to cold conditions such as these may have worse than average general health.

Serious hypothermia should not occur in occupational settings. If there is a risk, people should not work alone, should have good communications with others, and should be trained in first aid management of the effects of cold. Hypothermia is treated by slow rewarming using the individual's own metabolism, and copious insulation, possibly supplemented by body heat from another person.

Groups of people at risk from heat illness

- Unacclimatised workers in the tropics
- Workers in hot industries who have had a break from exposure
- Workers with an intercurrent illness
- Workers in the emergency services—for example, fire or mines rescue
- People undertaking very heavy physical activity—for example, military recruits
- People working even moderately hard at normal temperatures in all enveloping protective clothing—for example, fire crews dealing with chemical spills
- Older people and the very young when ambient temperatures are raised for prolonged periods

The wet bulb globe temperature

- The wet bulb globe temperature (WBGT) index is an index of heat stress. It is derived from the natural wet bulb temperature (WB), the dry bulb temperature (DB), and the globe temperature (GT) (a measure of radiant heating) in the ratio:

$$WBGT = 0.7\,WB + 0.2\,GT + 0.1\,DB$$

- The WBGT index is measured using a "Christmas tree" array of thermometers, or purpose built electronic sensors and integrating apparatus
- The index was originally derived to protect troops exercising outdoors by relating environmental conditions to the risk of heat illness. It has since been developed and used extensively in industry and is the basis for International Standard 7243 and guidance by the ACGIH. These documents give upper boundaries of WBGT value for continuous and intermittent work of different intensities. Other standards apply in relation to thermal comfort—for example, ISO 7730

Heat stroke

Heat stroke is a medical emergency. The body temperature should be lowered by tepid sponging and fanning with cool air.

Intravenous fluids may be necessary. The following may predispose to heat exhaustion and heat stroke:

- Obesity
- Lack of fitness
- Age 50 years or more
- Drug or alcohol abuse
- History of heat illness
- Drug treatment (for example, antihistamines, tricyclic antidepressants, or antipsychotics)
- Pre-existing disease of cardiovascular system, skin, gastrointestinal tract, or renal system

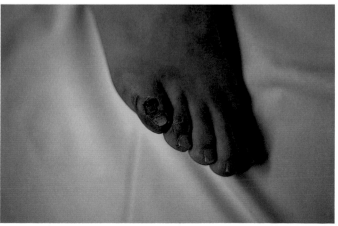

Frostbite in an outdoor worker

The peripheral effects of cold are frost nip, frost bite, and non-freezing cold injury. Frost nip appears as a white area on the skin, and in frost bite the appearance is of marbled white frozen tissue that is anaesthetic to touch. Treatment is by slow rewarming, often using body heat. Non-freezing cold injury often does not manifest until exposure to cold ceases, and it results in warm painful swollen extremities, usually the feet. Chilblains are a minor form of cold injury.

Ionising radiation

Ionising radiation displaces electrons from their normal orbits around the nucleus of the atom. The resulting ionisation alters the nature of biological molecules, especially DNA, resulting in gene mutation or cell death. α Small particles are relatively large and easily stopped. β Small particles are small and can penetrate up to a centimetre in tissue. Neutrons are smaller than α particles but are much more penetrating. γ Small radiation and x rays are packets of energy transmitted as electromagnetic radiation, and are highly penetrating.

External irradiation is that arising from a source—either a radiation generator, such as an x ray machine, or a radioactive substance—that is separate from the body. The irradiation ceases when the generator is switched off or the source is moved away or shielded. The body can be *contaminated* by particles of radioactive material that lie on the skin externally or are incorporated into the tissues, resulting in *internal* irradiation. The latter will persist as long as the radioactive material is in the body. Alpha emitters such as plutonium are particularly harmful sources of internal irradiation.

Large doses of ionising radiation cause death by damage to the brain, gut, and haemopoietic system. Such exposures only occur in the event of accidents or deliberate release in nuclear warfare. Lower doses can damage the skin or the lens of the eye. This may occur if sources are mishandled or exposures are prolonged—for example, in industrial radiography or interventional radiography. The *direct* effects of radiation are considered to have a dose threshold for their occurrence, and the severity of the effect is related to the dose received.

The *stochastic* effects of radiation (including the induction of cancer and hereditary effects) do not have a threshold, and the likelihood of the effect is related to the dose. Risk estimates for the stochastic effects of radiation have been derived from epidemiological studies (cancer) and animal studies (hereditary effects). The most important epidemiological data are from the Life Span Study of survivors of the atom bombs used in 1945. The risk estimates are published by a number of bodies of which the ICRP is the most influential. The ICRP also publishes dose limits derived from the risk estimates, and these are the basis of the statutory dose limits applied in many countries. Risk estimates and dose limits are regularly updated as the underlying science develops.

Workers who are substantially exposed to ionising radiation are subject to regular medical surveillance. This is to ensure that they are fit for their proposed work with radiation—for example, the need to work with unsealed sources or to use respiratory protective equipment. They are also subject to dose monitoring. Exposure to ionising radiation should be as low as reasonably practicable (ALARP) by the provision of appropriate controls, including shielding and reduction of exposure time. As legislative controls have been tightened, so the typical exposure to ionising radiation of workers has fallen. In the United Kingdom, average annual occupational doses are 1-2 millisieverts per year (about the same as background radiation).

Conditions that preclude work in moderate to severe cold
- History of ischaemic heart disease
- Peripheral vascular disease
- Hypertension or Raynaud's phenomenon
- Asthma
- Metabolic disorders
- Sickle cell disease
- Arthritis

Doses and units of radiation
- Absorbed dose—the energy of ionising radiation a body absorbs, measured in gray
- Dose equivalent—an adjustment of the absorbed dose, using a quality factor for the type of radiation involved, to take account of the effectiveness of the different types of radiations in harming biological systems; measured in sieverts
- Effective dose—an integrated index of the risk of harm, derived by multiplying the dose equivalent for each of the major tissues by a weighting factor based on the tissue's sensitivity to harm by radiation. The weighted values are summed. The unit is the sievert

The probabilities of harm from exposure to ionising radiation derived by the ICRP

Values are expressed as percentage risk per sievert dose received (the values in the table are multiplied by $10^{-2} Sv^{-1}$ to give the actual risk)

	Whole population	Working population
Fatal cancers	5	4
Hereditary disorders	1	0.6
Total risk	6	4.6

The ICRP recommends an effective dose limit of 20 mSv (averaged over a defined five year period) for workers, and 1 mSv per year for the public. Limits are also set for exposure of the eye lens, the skin, and the hands and feet. The dose limit for the fetus is the same as the public dose limit of 1 mSv a year

Studies of large cohorts of workers occupationally exposed to radiation consistently show a healthy worker effect. Nevertheless, cases of cancer of types known to be produced by ionising radiation do occur in these populations, sometimes with a slight excess. Individuals may be compensated for such disease on the basis of presumption of origin or probability of causation.

Electromagnetic fields

Electromagnetic fields with wavelengths shorter than 0.1 mm—that is, ultraviolet and below, contain insufficient energy to break molecular bonds and so do not result in ionisation. This "non-ionising radiation" does, however, have other frequency dependent effects on biological tissues. Broad divisions of this radiation include microwave and radio frequency radiation, as well as extremely low frequency, which includes the frequencies of power distribution.

At high frequencies—for example, microwaves used in communication systems—the main effect is tissue heating, a phenomenon made use of in the microwave oven. This effect is quantified by the specific absorption rate of energy into the body, and in most situations there are unlikely to be ill effects. This might not be the case where the individual is also working hard, or is exposed to a hot environment. At lower frequencies the effects of electric and magnetic fields are considered separately. Exposure to magnetic fields can set up circulating currents within the body, which have the potential to interfere with physiological processes if sufficiently great. For example, muscle activation could potentially occur during magnetic resonance imaging. Low frequency electric fields do not penetrate the body, but can generate charges on the body surface.

Other recognised but rarer effects include the phenomenon of microwave hearing. Some people hear repeated clicks when exposed to pulsed sources of electromagnetic fields, usually radars. A visual illusion of flickering lights (magnetophosphenes) can be produced when the retina is exposed to intense magnetic fields. Exposure standards, which reflect the frequency dependence of effects, have been derived to protect against the established effects of electromagnetic fields.

Since the late 1970s there has been increasing public concern about exposure to electromagnetic fields. This was prompted by epidemiological studies of the association between childhood cancer and residential exposure to magnetic fields. In 2001 the International Agency for Research on Cancer concluded that there was limited evidence that residential magnetic fields increase the risk of childhood leukaemia, resulting in a classification of "2B" "possibly carcinogenic" for extremely low frequency magnetic fields. It is thought that any risk relates to those exposed to fields at or above 0.4 microtesla, which are relatively large. The UK Childhood Cancer Study (UKCCS), the world's largest case control study on the causes of childhood cancer, found no evidence to support the association between residential magnetic field exposure and childhood leukaemia or other cancers. Any real effects must be very small in magnitude.

Public concern also extends to the possible effects of exposure to electromagnetic fields from mobile phone hand sets and base stations. In the United Kingdom an independent expert group was commissioned to study the evidence in relation to mobile phone technology. This group concluded that exposure to radio frequency radiation below the ICNIRP guidelines did not adversely affect population health, but in

---

Typical magnetic and electrical fields

Typical magnetic fields
- Natural fields—70 microtesla (static)
- Mains power—200 nanotesla (if not close to power lines), 20 microtesla (beneath power lines)
- Electric trains—50 microtesla
- Cathode ray tubes—700 nanotesla (alternating)

Typical electric fields
- Natural fields—200 V/m (static)
- Mains power—100 V/m (in homes), 10 kV/m (under large power lines)
- Electric trains—300 V/m
- Cathode ray tubes—10 V/m (alternating), 15 kV/m (static)

ICNIRP 1998 Exposure guidelines to time varying electric and magnetic fields

- These specify basic restrictions in terms of current density for the head and trunk, whole body and localised specific absorption rates, and power density
- Reference levels below which the basic restrictions are unlikely to be exceeded are specified in terms of electric field strength (E), magnetic field strength (H), magnetic flux density (B), and power density (S). These are given separately for occupational exposure and for the general public, with lower values for the latter. Reference levels are also given for contact currents from conductive objects and for induced current in any limb

---

Exposure from mobile phones and base stations

- Public exposures from base stations are low; typical power densities have been measured as 1 mW/m² , with maximum power densities of 10 mW/m²
- For comparison, the ICNIRP public exposure guidelines are a power density of 4.5 W/m² at 900 MHz and 9 W/m² at 1.8 GHz
- Power densities can exceed guidelines very close to the antenna, and for this reason public access to these antennae has to be controlled
- Hand sets can generate power densities of up to 200 W/m² , but the resulting fields inside the body are appreciably less then those measured externally

---

Units for electromagnetic fields

- Electric field strength (E)—volts per metre
- Magnetic field strength (H)—amps per metre
- Power density (S) (vector product of E and H)—watts per square metre
- Magnetic flux density (B)—Tesla (1 Tesla is about equal to 10 000 Gauss)

view of other biological evidence it concluded that it was not possible to say that exposures below current guidelines were totally without potential adverse health effects. The group therefore advocated a precautionary approach in the use of this technology—for example,, suggesting that the use of mobile phones by children for non-essential calls should be discouraged.

There is no evidence that exposure to electromagnetic fields from the use of display screen equipment has any harmful effects.

Optical radiations

Optical radiation comprises ultraviolet, visible, and infrared radiation, which have wavelengths between 100 nm and 1 mm. Their harmful effects are largely restricted to the skin and the eye. Ultraviolet radiation is implicated in non-melanoma and melanoma cancers. Outdoor workers—for example, farmers and the deck crews of ships—have an increased risk of non-melanoma cancer. Fortunately this is usually curable. As a sensible precaution, all those who work outdoors should avoid overexposure of the bare skin to sunlight and sunburn in order to reduce their risk of melanoma cancer. Some evidence suggests that exposure to ultraviolet radiation can impair the function of the immune system.

Ultraviolet radiation is responsible for the painful symptoms of arc eye (photokeratoconjunctivitis), which occurs some hours after exposure to a bright source of ultraviolet radiation such as a welding arc. Often, bystanders who are adventitiously exposed get this condition.

Infrared radiation can cause thermal damage to the skin and eyes, both of which are easily protected, the latter with appropriate goggles. In developed countries occupational cataract from exposure to infrared radiation is largely of historical interest, given proper protection. In developing countries, however, cataracts may occur as a result of overexposure to infrared radiation, possibly exacerbated by episodes of dehydration.

Sources of optical radiation where the light waves are in phase (for example, from lasers) can cause serious thermal damage to the retina, and skin burns. Engineering and administrative controls and personal protection are needed to prevent damage where high powered lasers are in use. Routine eye examination is not appropriate for laser workers, although a baseline assessment of visual acuity is useful to identify the functionally monocular individual, for whom a greater duty of care exists.

If unusual skin symptoms are reported in workers exposed to optical radiation the possibility of photosensitisation should be considered, as can occur with exposure to plant products—for example, psoralens released in parsley cutting. Photosensitisation can also occur from certain drugs. If workers complain of "sunburn" from working in the vicinity of ultraviolet sources such as insect killing lamps, it is important to check that the bulbs have the correct frequency spectrum.

Altered ambient pressure

Compressed air is used in civil engineering to stabilise the ground and to remove water from workings. Alternative methods of doing so are available, and should always be considered before opting to use compressed air. The effects of hyperbaric exposure in diving and compressed air work are different. Surface diving usually entails short exposures to high pressures, whereas compressed air work generally entails

---

Possible effects of optical radiation on the eye

- Ultraviolet C/B—arc eye
- Ultraviolet B—pigmentation of lens
- Ultraviolet A—retinal damage in aphakia
- Visible—accelerated ageing (high power sources), burns of retina (lasers)
- Infrared—corneal burns, usually prevented by blink reflex, cataract, retinal burns, from infrared A sources including lasers

---

Wavelengths of optical radiation

- Ultraviolet C (UVC)—100-280 nm
- Ultraviolet B (UVB)—280-315 nm
- Ultraviolet A (UVA)—315-400 nm
- Visible—400-760 nm
- Infrared—760 nm − 1 mm

The most potent sources of optical radiation are those in which the light waves are coherent or in phase, typically coming from laser sources

---

Working at pressure

- Atmospheric pressure is 14.7 psi
- 1 atmosphere, 1 bar, 10 m (or 33 feet) of sea water, are broadly equivalent pressures
- Absolute pressure is that of the working environment added to atmospheric pressure
- Decompression illness is very rare at pressures below 1.7 bar absolute. There is no risk from slight elevations of pressure such as in clean rooms
- Typical pressures experienced in civil engineering works are in the range 2-3.5 bar absolute
- Saturation diving techniques become necessary at depths below 50 m, 6 bar absolute

prolonged exposures at relatively low pressures. In diving, the physical effort required for the task may be limited, often using only the arms, whereas heavy manual work may be undertaken in compressed air work.

One effect that differs little in either situation is barotrauma—damage to an air containing organ by pressure exerted across a structure, typically in the ear or respiratory tract. Individuals exposed to raised pressures must be able to equalise such pressures—for example, by steady exhalation, during ascent from diving. The risk of barotrauma is minimised by excluding individuals with upper respiratory tract infections and by careful control of the rate of change of pressure during compression and decompression.

Decompression illness and osteonecrosis

More serious health effects are decompression illness and osteonecrosis. Under pressure, inert gas (principally nitrogen) dissolves in the tissues. When the pressure is reduced, this gas will come out of solution and form bubbles, in much the same way that bubbles form when pressure on carbonated drinks is released. These bubbles in turn cause effects which, if they are in the circulation or central nervous system, can be life threatening.

Decompression illness occurs in two types: pain only (previously type 1), in which symptoms occur in the skin (niggles) or around joints (bends), and serious (previously type 2), in which symptoms can occur in the circulation or nervous system. Symptoms can arise from gas bubbles in the pulmonary or coronary circulations (for example, the chokes), or from damage to the brain or spinal cord (for example, the staggers). Serious decompression illness can be life threatening.

To reduce the potential for bubble formation during decompression, pressure is reduced in a controlled, staged manner, the details of which depend on the duration and pressure of the preceding hyperbaric exposure. At its simplest this can be achieved by a series of timed stops at specified depths during ascent to the surface.

Decompression regimens inevitably entail a compromise between the long times needed for nitrogen to evolve from the tissues and the practical constraints arising from keeping a group of workers (in the case of civil engineering work) in the decompression chamber for long periods. The decompression chamber is an airlock between the working chamber and the external environment. Workers remain seated, resting, while the ambient pressure is reduced in a controlled fashion over one or more hours. Breathing oxygen during decompression helps to remove nitrogen from the body and shortens decompression times. As exposures increase in terms of both depth and time, longer decompression periods are required. At some of the higher pressures encountered in diving, the only practical approach is to adopt saturation methods, where individuals live and work under pressure for long periods, avoiding the need to decompress between working exposures.

With careful control of decompression and oxygen breathing, the incidence of decompression illness in offshore diving work has been kept very low. Further advances are needed in civil engineering work, where oxygen decompression is not yet always routine.

When decompression illness occurs it should always be treated by therapeutic recompression, as such events increase the risk of osteonecrosis. This serious complication of hyperbaric work results from compromise of the blood flow within bone structures. A section of normal bone dies and is replaced by softer material. If this occurs below the surface of a joint, such as the hip joint, there is a real risk of the joint surface collapsing, resulting in permanent disability.

Deep sea diver

Decompression chamber

Guidance on exposures, and international standards

- ICNIRP. Guidelines for limiting exposure to time-varying electric, magnetic, and electromagnetic fields (up to 300 GHz). *Health Phys* 1998;74:494-522
- ICRP. 1990 *Recommendations of the international commission on radiological protection*. Annals of the ICRP 21,1-3. Oxford: Pergamon Press, 1991
- International Standards Organisation. *Hot environments— estimation of the heat stress on working man, based on the WBGT index (wet bulb globe temperature)*. Geneva: ISO, 1989 (ISO 7243)
- International Standards Organisation. *Moderate thermal environments—determination of the PMV and PPD indices and specification of the conditions for thermal comfort*. Geneva: ISO, 1993 (ISO 7730)
- International Standards Organisation. *Ergonomics of the thermal environment—Medical supervision of individuals exposed to extreme hot or cold thermal environments*. Geneva: ISO, 2001 (ISO 12894)

Risk factors for osteonecrosis are not clearly established. It can occur after one "bad" decompression but is normally seen only after higher pressure exposures. Risk factors in compressed air work include the number of hyperbaric exposures and the number of episodes of decompression illness.

Barotrauma and decompression illness may occur in aviation environments. They are most likely to occur if an aircraft pressurisation system fails at an altitude above 20 000 feet, after a high altitude ejection, or after flight at altitude in an unpressurised aircraft. The risks can be minimised by breathing 100% oxygen (denitrogenation) before flights or training exposures in an altitude chamber carrying a risk of decompression illness. Osteonecrosis after decompression in aviation is exceedingly rare.

Living and working at altitude

Living and working at altitude carries different risks—namely, acute mountain sickness, high altitude pulmonary oedema (HAPE), and high altitude cerebral oedema (HACE). Symptoms of acute mountain sickness can occur at altitudes of 2500 m, with the prevalence reaching 40% at altitudes over 4000 m. The symptoms include headache, nausea and vomiting, sleep disturbance, and muscle weakness, and are thought to arise from a mild oedema of the lungs, the splanchnic circulation, and the brain. The condition is treated by descent to a lower altitude. Breathing oxygen, and taking acetazolamide and dexamethasone can also help. The main preventive measure is to limit the rate of ascent to altitude. Unlike acute mountain sickness, both high altitude pulmonary oedema and high altitude cerebral oedema are life threatening. The former is treated by descent and the use of oxygen.

People who live at high altitude show physiological adaptations to their environment, although even these may fail with time. Chronic mountain sickness (Monge's disease) is a loss of tolerance to hypoxia, which occurs particularly in middle aged men. It results in an erythropoiesis, with the haematocrit rising as high as 80%. Clinical effects include cyanosis, dyspnoea, cough, palpitations, and headache. The condition can only be alleviated by moving to a lower altitude.

Acceleration

Exposure to sustained acceleration is experienced on fairground rides (2-3 G) or in flight, and then only significantly in aerobatic or military flying. Radial acceleration occurs during banked turns. When the head is to the inside of the turn the acceleration is positive in the "z" axis. With the head on the outside of the turn the acceleration is negative in the same axis. Positive G increases the hydrostatic weight of the column of blood above the heart, reducing arterial pressure and perfusion of the retina and the brain. Negative G has the opposite effect, increasing arterial pressure and resulting in engorgement of the head and neck

Protection from positive G is provided by posture, keeping the body nearer the horizontal plane than the vertical, by lifting the legs up and lowering the backrest. Valsalva type manoeuvres are used slightly in anticipation of acceleration to increase the pressure in the arterial system, and protective anti-G suits are routinely worn by military pilots. These prevent pooling of blood in the peripheries and limit the descent of the heart and diaphragm under acceleration

Further reading

- Ashcroft F. *Life at the extremes*. London: Flamingo, 2001. *A journalistic account by a professor of physiology of the science of survival, including chapters on altitude, diving, heat, and cold*
- Case RM, Waterhouse JM. *Human physiology: age, stress and the environment*. Oxford: Oxford University Press, 1994. *An undergraduate textbook with a series of short chapters on topics including the thermal environment, altitude, diving, and acceleration. Useful academic introduction to the areas covered*
- Edholm OG, Weiner JS. *The principles and practice of human physiology*. London: Academic Press, 1981. *A bit dated, but still a valuable reference on the physiology of diving, altitude, the thermal environment, and other topics. Covers the basics in much more detail than Case and Waterhouse*
- Bennett PB, Elliott DH. *The physiology and medicine of diving*, 4th ed. London: WB Saunders, 1993. *A comprehensive textbook, which includes a chapter on compressed air work. A standard reference covering all aspects of hyperbaric exposures including clinical hyperbaric oxygen therapy*
- Cummin AR, Nicholson AN. *Aviation medicine and the airline passenger*. London: Arnold, 2002. *A multiauthored text considering the aeromedical implications of a range of common medical conditions*
- Ernsting J, Nicholson AN, Rainford DJ. *Aviation medicine*, 3rd ed. London: Butterworths, 2000. *A comprehensive text covering all aspects of aviation physiology, psychology, and clinical aviation medicine; suitable for students of specialised aviation medicine diplomas*
- Harding RM, Mills FJ. *Aviation medicine*, 3rd ed. London: BMJ Publishing Group, 1993. *An introductory text for the general reader which gives a good overview of the main topics relevant to clinical practice*
- Mettler FA, Upton AC. *Medical effects of ionising radiation*, 2nd ed. Philadelphia: WB Saunders, 1995. *A comprehensive and well referenced review of the science underlying the medical effects of ionising radiation. Covers direct effects and carcinogenesis at length*
- National Radiation Protection Board. *Living with radiation*. London: NRPB and HMSO, 1998. *A book written for the lay reader which sets out a good introduction to the science and social context of exposures to both ionising and non-ionising radiations*
- Parsons K. *Human thermal environments*, 2nd ed. London: Taylor and Francis, 2002. *A standard text on responses to hot, moderate, and cold thermal environments, presented as an integrated approach incorporating physiology, psychology, and environmental physics*
- Report of the Advisory Group on Non-ionising Radiation. *ELF Electromagnetic fields and the risk of cancer*. London: NRPB 2001;Doc12:3-179. *Scientific report covering exposures to electromagnetic fields, studies on cancer induction, epidemiological studies, and occupational exposures. Includes recommendations for further research*
- Stewart W. *Mobile phones and health*. Chilton Independent Expert Group on Mobile Phones, 2000. *Report of a Government appointed review group with good coverage of mobile phone technology and the scientific evidence for health effects. Makes numerous recommendations for action*
- Ward MP, Milledge JS, West JB. *High altitude medicine and physiology*, 3rd ed. London: Arnold, 2000. *A comprehensive review covering history, physiology, biochemistry, and the clinical effects of altitude and cold*
- Barry PW, Pollard AJ. Altitude illness. *BMJ* 2003;326:915–9. *A well-referenced up-to-date clinical review*

Effects of positive headwards acceleration

- 3-4 G—darkening of visual fields
- 3.5-4.5 G—loss of peripheral vision
- 5-6 G—loss of consciousness

If the rate of onset of acceleration is high, loss of consciousness will be the first symptom

12 Noise and vibration

Paul Litchfield

Sound is generated when a vibrating source transmits energy to the surrounding air, creating small changes in pressure. If the frequency of the sound produced lies between about 20 and 16 000 Hz it may be perceived by the hearing mechanism and is classed as being "audible." Sound levels are measured in decibels (dB), a logarithmic unit in which the faintest sound detectable by the human ear is set at 0 and the level doubles for every 3 dB. In assessing audible sound it is conventional to use a weighted scale that filters the actual pressure level in specified octave bands by an agreed amount to resemble the response of the ear over those frequencies. The most commonly used weighting is the "A" network, and resultant units are expressed as dB(A). Noise is simply unwanted sound.

The body is also susceptible to non-acoustic vibration transmitted by direct contact with oscillating surfaces. As with sound, frequency is important: vibration below 2 Hz and above 1500 Hz is not thought to be harmful; motion between 5 Hz and 20 Hz is considered potentially most damaging. Vibration can be measured in various ways, but is normally expressed as acceleration in metres per second squared (m/s^2) averaged over the three axes. As vibration at frequencies below 2 Hz and above 1500 Hz is not thought to cause damage, weighting is applied to measurements of vibration magnitude to allow for this frequency dependence of the risk of harm.

Health effects of noise

The principal hazard from noise is impairment of hearing. This may be confined to a reversible alteration in hearing levels, known as temporary threshold shift, which resolves spontaneously in the quiet. It may last from a few minutes to months depending on the noise level encountered. If exposure to high noise levels is sustained for a prolonged period a permanent shift can occur, termed noise induced hearing loss. Short bursts of very high intensity sound (such as an explosion or gunfire), known as impulse noise, can also cause additional harm to the ear by rupturing the tympanic membrane or even disrupting the ossicles.

There has been considerable interest in recent years in the non-auditory effects of noise. Comprehensive literature reviews

---

Non-auditory health and physiological effects of noise

- *Cardiovascular effects*: in laboratory studies, noise has been shown to produce increases in diastolic blood pressure. However, there is no clear evidence that long term exposure to noise is a risk factor for hypertension
- Some studies suggested an association between noise exposure or noise annoyance and the frequency of *psychiatric symptoms* but these findings have been questioned in later studies. There is some evidence that noise sensitivity is an indicator of vulnerability to minor psychiatric disorder, and that annoyance responses are stronger among individuals with psychiatric disorders
- The effect of noise on *performance* is complex. Some research found no clear evidence of effects at noise levels below 95 dB, whereas other research suggests that performance may be affected at much lower levels
- *Fatigue, headaches, and irritability* have been found to be over-represented in groups exposed to noise, but methodological flaws in study design have made valid conclusions difficult

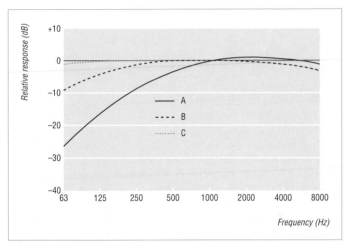

The human ear is more sensitive to certain frequencies, and in order to approximate the response of the ear it is possible to suppress certain frequencies and boost others in the electronic circuitry of sound level meters. This technique is known as "weighting," and the most commonly quoted weighting network is the A weighting

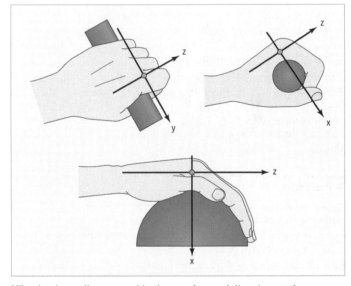

Vibration is usually measured in three orthogonal directions at the interfaces between the body and the vibrating surface

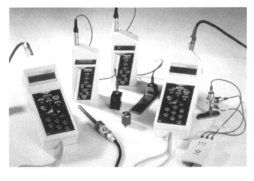

Range of instruments for measuring noise and vibration levels

have been published, but much of the evidence remains weak or equivocal.

Noise induced hearing loss

Noise induced hearing loss is caused by damage to the cilia on the basilar membrane in the organ of Corti in the inner ear. This damage is progressive and irreversible and results in loss of both absolute sensitivity of the ear and in frequency selectivity. Characteristically, loss is initially predominant in the higher frequencies (3-6 kHz) and classically, a depression at 4 kHz may be seen on audiometry. With continuing exposure hearing loss extends to both higher and lower frequencies and is frequently superimposed on the effects of age related hearing loss, also known as presbyacusis.

The development of noise induced hearing loss is insidious, and deafness may be considerable by the time an individual seeks assistance. Initially those affected describe difficulty in hearing conversations against a noisy background. Because consonants have a higher frequency than vowels, they are more difficult for a person with noise deafness to recognise, with resultant degradation of discrimination of speech. Hearing loss is frequently associated with tinnitus, which may be more disabling than deafness. On examination, the tympanic membranes usually seem normal, but testing with a tuning fork shows a sensorineural deafness. Industrial noise usually gives rise to bilateral hearing loss but specific activities, such as use of firearms, may produce unilateral deafness depending on the location of the noise source in relation to the ears. Audiometry shows a hearing loss that is predominantly high frequency, although in severe cases lower frequencies are affected. This latter case produces far greater disability because of the impact on the speech range (0.5-2.0 kHz).

Noise induced hearing loss is common. Data from the UK National Household Survey indicate that in excess of 130 000 people have hearing problems arising from noise at work, and the Occupational Safety and Health Administration estimates that there are 10 million people with similar hearing problems in the United States. Manufacturing industry has been the source of most cases in the past, but noise levels can be high for those working in many other sectors including construction, transport, and the armed forces. More recently, concern has been raised in relation to call centre operatives, but any potential problems seem to relate to extraneous noises received through headsets (acoustic shock) rather than to ambient noise levels.

Risk management

Noise induced hearing loss is a preventable condition and, as with any hazard, the first step is to assess the risk. As a general guide, noise levels are likely to be hazardous if communication without shouting is difficult at a distance of two metres. If there is reason to believe that there may be a problem then noise levels should be measured by a competent person. The risk of developing noise induced hearing loss is a function of both the level of noise exposure and its duration. Noise levels are therefore often expressed as daily personal noise exposure (L EP,d), which averages the dose over an eight hour working day. L EP,d action levels of 85 dB(A) and 90 dB(A) have been set in both the United States and European Union, above which certain control measures are mandatory. However, at the time of writing, negotiations are far advanced in Europe for a new Noise Directive, which will replace the existing directive (86/188/EC, implemented in the United Kingdom by the Noise at Work Regulations 1989) with tougher legislation that will reduce the action levels to 80 dB(A) and 85 dB(A), and introduce a limit value on exposure of 87 dB(A).

The best means of hazard control is elimination, and machinery noise can often be reduced substantially by better

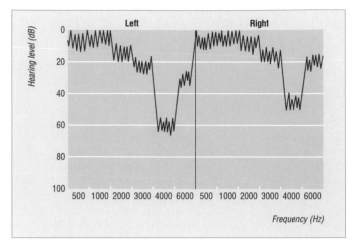

Audiogram showing noise induced hearing loss with classical depression at 4 kHz

Noise induced hearing loss in the United Kingdom (adapted from Health and Safety Executive statistics 2000-1)

- UK Health and Safety Executive statistics are obtained from a variety of sources, including the occupational physicians reporting activities (OPRA), occupational surveillance scheme for audiologists (OSSA), and industrial injuries scheme (prescribed diseases)
- The industry groups with the highest annual average incidence rates of new cases qualifying for benefit were extraction, energy, and water supply (7.9 cases per 100 000 employees), manufacturing (3.9), and construction (2.3) (based on 1999 and 2000 data). Of cases qualifying for benefit, 11% were in shipbuilding, repair, or breaking, and 9% were in the coal mining industry. Of new cases qualifying for benefit in 2000, 52% were in the occupational group of metal machinery and related trades workers
- Noise induced hearing loss is not reportable under the Reporting of Injuries, Diseases and Dangerous Occurrence Regulations 1995 (RIDDOR)

	Number of cases (OSSA/OPRA, estimated for 2000)
Sensorineural hearing loss	627
Tinnitus	161
Balance problems	5
Tympanic disorder	3
Other problems	1
Total	797 (648 individuals)
Prescribed diseases*	226

*To qualify for benefit, there must be at least 50 dB of hearing loss. The degree of disability is calculated from the hearing loss in such a way that 50 dB in both ears equates to 20% disability. Under current guidelines, a worker must have been employed for at least 10 years in specified noisy occupations. Of the almost 2000 disallowed claims in 1998, 800 claimants had 35-49 dB hearing loss

Differential diagnosis of noise induced hearing loss

- Conductive—Wax, acute otitis media, chronic otitis media, otosclerosis, tympanic membrane injury, barotrauma, ossicular dislocation

- Sensorineural—Presbyacusis, congenital (maternal rubella, hereditary, perinatal anoxia), infective (measles, mumps, meningitis), vascular (haemorrhage, spasm or thrombosis of cochlear vessels), traumatic (head injury), toxic (streptomycin, neomycin, carbon monoxide, carbon disulphide), Meniere's disease, late otosclerosis, acoustic nerve tumours (usually unilateral)

Main requirements of the UK Noise at Work Regulations 1989

Action required where L EP,d* is likely to be:	<85 dB(A)	85 dB(A) First action level	90 dB(A) Second action level†
Empolyers' duties			
General duty to reduce risk			
Risk of hearing damage to be reduced to the lowest level reasonably practicable*	√	√	√
Assessment of noise exposure			
• Noise assessments to be made by a competent person		√	√
• Record of assessments to be kept until a new one is made		√	√
Noise reduction			
Reduce exposure to noise as far as is reasonably practicable by means other than ear protectors			√
Provision of information to workers			
• Provide adequate information, instruction, and training about risks to hearing, what employees should do to minimise risk, how they can obtain ear protectors (if they are exposed to an L EP,d between 85 and 90 dB(A)), and their obligations under the Regulations		√	√
• Mark ear protection zones with safety signs, so far as reasonably practicable			√
Ear protectors			
Ensure so far as is practicable that protectors are:			
• Provided to employees exposed to an L EP,d of 85 dB(A) or above and less than 90 dB(A), who ask for them		√	
• Provided to all exposed above the second action level			√
• Maintained and repaired		√	√
• Properly used by all exposed			√
Ensure so far as is reasonably practicable that all who go into a marked ear protection zone use ear protectors			√‡
Maintenance and use of noise control equipment			
Ensure so far as is practicable that:			
• All equipment provided under the Regulations is used, except for the ear protectors provided between first action level and second action level	√	√	√
Ensure all equipment is maintained	√	√	√
Employees' duties			
Use of equipment; so far as is practicable:			
• Use ear protectors			√
• Use any other protective equipment	√	√	√
• Report any defects discovered to employer	√	√	√
Machine makers' and suppliers' duties			
Provision of information			
Provide information on the noise likely to be generated	In theory if equipment provided to comply with*	√	√

*The dB(A) action levels are values of daily personal noise exposure L EP,d.

†All the actions indicated at 90 dB(A) are also required where the peak sound pressure is at or above 200 pascals.

‡This requirement applies to all who enter the zones, even if they do not stay long enough to receive an exposure of 90 dB(A) L EP,d.

design and maintenance. Damping and enclosure of vibrating machinery can greatly reduce exposure, or people can be provided with well insulated noise refuges in otherwise noisy environments. As a last resort, people can be issued with hearing protection: ear muffs (which completely cover the ear), ear plugs (which are inserted into the auditory canal), or semi-inserts (which cover the entrance to the ear canal).

It is important to ensure not only that any ear protection offered provides adequate noise attenuation but also that it does not interfere with any other protective equipment required, and that those using it understand that even short periods of non-use will greatly reduce the protective value.

Health surveillance

Health surveillance (including audiometry), although not a legal requirement, can provide a useful adjunct to risk management and is considered good practice where the second action level (see table) is exceeded. Hearing conservation

Noise hazard sign to indicate that use of hearing protection is mandatory and standard design of ear muffs

programmes will normally include a structured interview to gather relevant health data. This should cover relevant medical history based on the differential diagnosis for noise induced hearing loss, and a history of previous noise exposure such as previous employment in noisy industries, service in the armed forces, and leisure pursuits such as shooting or regular clubbing. The ear canal and tympanic membrane should be examined. Personal protective equipment should be inspected, and workers reminded of its correct use. Audiometric testing should be undertaken in a soundproof booth, and the screening results should be fully discussed, with onward referral if required.

Such programmes aim to identify at an early stage individuals particularly susceptible to noise damage, and to reinforce hazard information together with the use of control measures. The UK Health and Safety Executive has produced comprehensive guidelines on the conduct of audiometric testing programmes, including a helpful categorisation scheme that provides a template for the management of individuals according to the degree of hearing loss identified. The five categories within the scheme and the suggested action for each, and a chart of age related hearing loss at low and high frequencies are given in the two tables.

Classification of audiograms into warning and referral levels

| Age in years | Sum of hearing levels | | | |
| | 0.5, 1, 2 kHz | | 3, 4, 6 kHz | |
	Warning level	Referral level	Warning level	Referral level
20-24	45	60	45	75
25-29	45	66	45	87
30-34	45	72	45	99
35-39	48	78	54	111
40-44	51	84	60	123
45-49	54	90	66	135
50-54	57	90	75	144
55-59	60	90	87	144
60-64	65	90	100	144
65	70	90	115	144

The Health and Safety Executive categorisation scheme

Category	Symptom	Suggested action
1	Rapid change in hearing threshold has occurred (that is, a change in the sum of the hearing levels for either the low or high frequencies of 30 dB, compared with the previous audiogram, or 45 dB if the period between the tests is more than three years). This change may be due to noise exposure or disease	Referral
2	This is usually related to medical factors. Unilateral hearing loss is not normally noise induced and may indicate auditory nerve disease. Unilateral hearing loss is considered to exist if the difference in the sums of the hearing levels between the two ears exceeds 45 dB for the low frequencies, or 60 dB for the high frequencies	Referral
3	Results show a pattern that could suggest significant noise inducing hearing loss (that is, where the sum of either the low or high frequencies, or both, in either ear, exceeds the value given for the appropriate age band)	Referral
4	Hearing has deteriorated beyond the level that might be accounted for by age alone, but not to the extent that medical referral is required	Warning. Formally notify the employee of the presence of hearing damage. Employee to understand that they have suffered some hearing loss; it is essential that they comply with the employer's hearing conservation measures. Assess rate of progression of hearing loss
5	Within normal limits	None, but assess rate of progression of hearing loss

Health effects of vibration

Vibration and noise often emanate from the same source. Vibration may reach the body through a number of pathways, but consideration of adverse health effects centres on whole body vibration and hand arm vibration. As with noise, the risk of harm is a function of both the magnitude of exposure and of its duration: "doses" are therefore adjusted to a standard reference period of eight hours to allow comparison, and this figure is termed A(8). Measuring vibration is complex and should only be undertaken by those with specialist training.

Whole body vibration
Interest in the effects of whole body vibration stems from the middle of the 20th century when mechanisation, particularly of transport, became more prevalent. Vibration is transmitted either from a machine platform through the feet, or from a

Use of a vibrating tool for road breaking

seat through the buttocks. Exposure is most likely to occur with vehicle use and this includes road, off road, rail, air, and maritime use: it is estimated that as many as 9 million people in the United Kingdom are regularly exposed to whole body vibration. The disorders reported in groups exposed in this way include gastric problems, vestibular dysfunction, circulatory changes, menstrual disturbance, and psychological effects. However, the main problem associated with whole body vibration is back pain, and the UK Health and Safety Executive estimates that up to 21 000 cases may be caused by exposure, with a further 13 500-31 500 cases of exacerbation of a pre-existing condition. The evidence base for a causal link between whole body vibration and back pain nevertheless remains weak, and has recently been comprehensively reviewed.

Hand arm vibration

Vibration may be transmitted to the hands and arms by the use of hand held power tools, hand guided machinery, or by holding materials being processed by machines. Exposure is particularly common in agriculture, construction (particularly scabbling), mining, engineering, forestry, public utilities, and shipbuilding. It is estimated that about 1 million people in the United Kingdom are exposed to potentially harmful levels of hand arm vibration in their work, and as many as 300 000 may have developed adverse health effects as a result.

The health effects of exposure to hand arm vibration have been recognised for many years and have been ascribed a variety of labels. There is now general consensus on the use of the term "hand arm vibration syndrome" to describe the vascular (sometimes also known as vibration white finger), neurological, and musculoskeletal symptoms that can result. Acute vibration exposure causes vasoconstriction of the blood vessels supplying the fingers and, if prolonged, it may damage the endothelium and stimulate smooth muscle proliferation so that the lumen of the vessels gradually narrows. Damage also occurs to the peripheral nerves, with acute oedema and chronic demyelination. Muscular weakness in the hand is common, carpal tunnel syndrome is recognised in some cases, and there is evidence to indicate that premature osteoarthrosis of the wrist and elbow may occur. The precise relation between these elements of the syndrome remains a matter for debate, but there is no doubt that the vascular and neurological components can occur separately.

In the early stages of vibration injury the only symptom may be a tingling in the fingers, most noticeable at the end of the working day. This may be associated with a loss of sensation and periodic blanching of the tips of the fingers when exposed to cold. As the condition progresses the blanching extends to the root of the fingers, although the thumbs are rarely affected. In more severe cases there is considerable pain, with a loss of grip strength and dexterity, and attacks may occur even in warm surroundings. Rarely the condition can progress to the extent that circulation is permanently impaired and the fingers become cyanosed—exceptionally, cases of vibration induced gangrene have been reported.

Risk management

Assessment of risk is based on the type of vibrating equipment employed and its pattern of use. In the United Kingdom the action level for introducing preventative measures is if exposure regularly exceeds an A(8) of 2.8 m/s^2 (dominant axis). It is important to recognise that this is not a "safe" level: some individuals are likely to develop hand arm vibrations with prolonged use even if this threshold is not exceeded. A new European Vibration Directive has recently been adapted (to be transferred into UK law in 2005), which sets a limit value

Vibration induced disorders in the United Kingdom

- A UK survey on behalf of the Health and Safety Executive gave an estimate for the national prevalence estimate of vibration white finger (VWF) of 288 000
- The industry with the highest annual average rate of new assessments of disability at 1% in 1999-2000 was extraction, energy, and water supply, because of the relatively high number of claims made by current or former coal miners. Of the new assessments made in other industries, 3% were in shipbuilding, repair, or breaking; 5% were in other manufacturing industry; and 4% in construction
- In 1999-2000, coal mining accounted for 46% of cases for carpal tunnel syndrome, construction for 12%, and shipbuilding, repair, or breaking for 4%

	No of cases*
Raynaud's phenomenon or hand arm vibration or vibration white finger	935
RIDDOR† (2000-1 provisional)	
Carpal tunnel syndrome	119
Hand arm vibration	905
Prescribed diseases (1999-2000)	
Vibration white finger	3212
Carpal tunnel syndrome	475

*Musculoskeletal occupational surveillance scheme (MOSS), reporting by rheumatologists or occupational physicians reporting activities (OPRA), estimated for 2000.
†RIDDOR, Reporting of Injuries, Diseases and Dangerous Occurrence Regulations 1995 (adapted from Health and Safety Executive statistics 2000-1).

Differential diagnosis

Vascular conditions

- Connective tissue disease—scleroderma, mixed connective tissue disease, systemic lupus erythematosus, rheumatoid arthritis, dermatomyositis, polyarteritis nodosa, Sjogren's disease
- Traumatic—after injury or surgery, hand transmitted vibration, frostbite, thoracic outlet syndrome
- Arterial disease—thromboangitis obliterans, thromboembolism, arteriosclerosis
- Toxins and drugs—vinyl chloride, ergot, β blockers, clonidine
- Dysglobulinaemia—cryoglobulinaemia
- Neurogenic—poliomyelitis, syringomyelia, hemiplegia

Neurological conditions

- Peripheral nerve entrapment—carpal tunnel syndrome, ulnar nerve entrapment at elbow or wrist, thoracic outlet syndrome
- Central nervous system disorders—compression myelopathy (spondylosis or spinal cord tumor), subacute combined degeneration of the cord, multiple sclerosis
- Peripheral neuropathy—diabetic, alcoholic, toxic (for example, organophosphates, thallium, acrylamide, carbon disulphide, n-hexane, methyl butyl ketone, diethyl thiocarbamate, lead)
- Drug induced (for example, chloramphenicol, isoniazid, streptomycin, polymyxin, ethambutol, nitrofurantoin, metronidazole, gold, indomethacin, vincristine, perhexiline, phenytoin)

on exposure of $5\,\mathrm{m/s^2}$ (sum of three axes) and an action value of $2.5\,\mathrm{m/s^2}$ (sum of three axes).

Manufacturers of vibrating tools may be able to provide useful data on levels under standard conditions, but care must be taken because actual levels in field use can differ substantially from those generated in a controlled environment. Similarly, field measurements can vary widely depending on mode of use and the materials being worked. In practice it is therefore usual to institute a preventive programme wherever there is prolonged use of tools likely to be hazardous.

Prevention programmes aim to eliminate or substitute the hazardous process where possible. Where this is not possible, the procurement of low vibration machinery, fitting of vibration reducing adaptations (such as vibration reducing handles), regular maintenance and re-engineering of processes to avoid the need for prolonged tight gripping of high vibration parts will reduce exposure. Keeping the hands and body warm helps to maintain a good blood supply to the fingers and thereby reduces the risk of injury. Vibration reducing gloves are available but their efficacy is limited. A key element in a preventive programme is the provision of training and information about the hazard and the means of reducing risk.

Health surveillance

Health surveillance aims to identify those who develop early symptoms so that progression can be avoided and it is appropriate if exposure levels are likely to trigger a prevention programme. Pre-employment screening is helpful in identifying individuals with conditions such as Raynaud's disease that are a contraindication to work with vibrating tools, in establishing baseline measurements, and in educating workers about measures to minimise risk—not least the avoidance of smoking. It is good practice to repeat the assessment for newly exposed workers to identify those who may be particularly susceptible. Thereafter, annual review is recommended, with any symptoms being reported to a designated person as soon as they occur.

Assessment should comprise a structured history and relevant clinical examination that will identify early hand arm vibration syndrome and assist with differential diagnosis, as a number of constitutional conditions give rise to similar symptoms. Guidelines from the UK Health and Safety Executive (see Further reading) give a sample questionnaire and guidance on tests that may be helpful for examination. Various methods of grading signs and symptoms have been devised and those of Taylor and Pelmear, and Griffin have been widely used. However, the most commonly used system of classification for hand arm vibration syndrome is currently the Stockholm Workshop scale, which grades the vascular and sensorineural components by severity. This scale, and the speed of progression along it, can helpfully be used to guide the management of affected workers. No effective treatment is available for this condition: management relies on adjustments to work, and limitation of vibration exposure. Cessation of vibration exposure may well compromise an individual's continuing employment, and great care is therefore required before making any such recommendation. A number of additional test measurements (detailed Lindsell CJ and Griffin MJ, 1988) can be carried out by specialist centres to help confirm the degree of incapacity, and referral should be considered in such circumstances.

The photographs showing the range of instruments for measuring noise and vibration and showing a vibrating tool for road breaking are courtesy of Castle Instruments. The figure showing how vibration is measured is adapted from HS(G)88.

Vibration induced gangrene

Stockholm workshop classification

Vascular component		
Stage	**Grade**	**Description**
0		No attacks
1V	Mild	Occasional attacks affecting only the tips of one or more fingers
2V	Moderate	Occasional attacks affecting distal and middle (rarely also proximal) phalanges of one or more fingers
3V	Severe	Frequent attacks affecting all phalanges of most fingers
4V	Very severe	As in stage 3 with trophic changes in the fingertips

Sensorineural component	
Stage	**Description**
0SN	Vibration-exposed but no symptoms
1SN	Intermittent numbness with or without tingling
2SN	Intermittent or persistent numbness, reduced sensory perception
3SN	Intermittent or persistent numbness, reduced tactile discrimination or manipulative dexterity or both

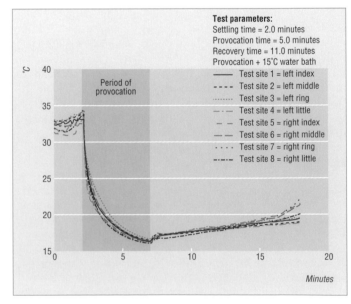

Results of cold provocation showing an abnormal response as found in vascular damage from hand arm vibration syndrome

Further reading

- Butler MP, Graveling RA, Pilkington A, Boyle AL. *Non-auditory effects of noise at work: A critical review of the literature post 1988. HSE Contract Research Report 241/1999.* Sudbury: HSE Books, 1999. *A review of the literature relating to the non-auditory effects of noise since 1988, updating earlier work by Smith and Broadbent, considering behavioural and psychological elements as well as physiology and health*

- Health and Safety Executive. *A guide to audiometric testing programmes. Guidance Note MS 26.* Sudbury: HSE Books, 1995. *Practical guidance on the conduct of occupational audiometry*

- Stayner RM. *Whole body vibration and shock: A literature review.* Sudbury: HSE Books, 2001. (HSE Contract Research Report 333/2001) *Review of the effects of whole body vibration, comparing the state of knowledge with noise induced hearing loss and hand transmitted vibration; concentrates on the relationship with low back pain*

- Health and Safety Executive. *Hand-arm vibration. HS(G)88.* Sudbury: HSE Books, 1994. *Practical guidance on the hazards, assessment methods and controls for hand transmitted vibration*

- Lindsell CJ, Griffin MJ. *Standardised diagnostic methods for assessing components of the hand-arm vibration syndrome.* Sudbury: HSE Books, 1988 (HSE Contract Research Report 197/1988) *Lindsell and Griffin define a standardised battery of tests for detecting the various components of hand arm vibration syndrome*

- Faculty of Occupational Medicine of the Royal College of Physicians of London. *Hand-transmitted vibration: clinical effects and pathophysiology.* London: Faculty of Occupational Medicine of the Royal College of Physicians of London, 1993. *Part one summarises the evidence relating to hand arm vibration syndrome and recommends assessment methodologies; part two outlines in some detail the evidence base for the report. Currently being revised; publication is planned for 2004*

- OHSA. *Noise and Hearing Conservation.* Occupational Safety and Health Administration. US Department of Labor. Revised 15 February 2002. http://www.osha-slc.gov/SLTC/noisehearingconservation/. *The OSHA site provides links to a wide range of US Government documents relating to noise and hearing conservation*

- Palmer KT, Coggon D, Griffith MJ, Haward BM. *Hand-transmitted vibration: occupational exposure and their health effects in Great Britain.* Sudbury: HSE Books, 1999 (HSE Contract Research Report 232/1999)

13   Respiratory diseases

Ira Madan

The pattern of occupational lung disease is changing in industrialised countries. A reduction in manufacturing industries and stricter health and safety legislation during the past 50 years have resulted in a sharp decline in the incidence of silicosis, asbestosis, and other pneumoconioses. Asthma is now the most common occupational respiratory disorder in these countries. By contrast, the traditional occupational lung diseases are commonly seen in developing countries, and occupational asthma is reported less often. However, the true prevalence of asthma attributable to occupation in these countries remains unknown.

Since 1989, the understanding of the epidemiology of occupational lung disease in the United Kingdom has been greatly enhanced by the Surveillance of Work related and Occupational Respiratory Disease (SWORD) and Occupational Physicians Reporting Activity (OPRA) projects. Occupational and respiratory physicians systematically report new cases of occupational lung diseases, together with the suspected agent, industry, and occupation. The projects have provided an estimate of the incidence and pattern of occupational lung disease in the United Kingdom.

Occupational asthma

Occupational asthma is a disease characterised by variable airflow limitation and airway hyper-responsiveness caused by specific agents inhaled in the workplace. It does not include activation of pre-existing asthma or airway hyper-responsiveness induced by non-toxic irritants or physical stimuli such as cold air.

Two types of occupational asthma are recognised: immunological asthma appears after a latent period of occupational exposure; non-immunological occupational asthma develops without a period of latency and is associated with exposure to high concentrations of irritants. This latter type is referred to as reactive airways disease and is discussed separately. To date, more than 250 agents capable of causing immunological occupational asthma have been reported. In some jobs, such as hairdressing and farming, workers are exposed to many potential sensitisers and sensitisation may occur through interaction of several agents.

Substances that induce occupational asthma are classified as either high (>5 kDa) or low molecular weight allergens. High molecular weight substances are usually protein derived allergens such as natural rubber latex and flour. It is thought that some low molecular weight chemicals, such as diisocyanates, act as haptens and combine with a body protein to form a complete antigen.

Atopic individuals seem to be at increased risk of developing occupational asthma from some agents that induce specific immunoglobulin E (IgE)—for example, rat urinary proteins, and protease enzymes derived from *Bacillus subtilis* (detergent workers). However, atopic workers who are exposed to other agents—for example, isocyanates and plicatic acid (Western red cedar) seem to be at no more risk than non-atopic workers. Tobacco smokers are at greater risk of developing asthma after occupational exposure to several agents such as platinum salts, acid anhydride, and green coffee bean; the mechanism of this modifying effect is unknown.

Estimated number of cases of work related and occupational respiratory disease reported to SWORD/OPRA by diagnostic category, 1998-2000

Diagnostic category	1998	1999	2000
Benign pleural disease	625	1243	1080
Asthma	807	1129	797
Malignant mesothelioma	701	1018	964
Pneumoconiosis	225	320	292
Other diagnosis	187	239	218
Inhalation accidents	178	154	119
Bronchitis/emphysema	58	29	144
Lung cancer	112	81	126
Infectious disease	87	63	77
Allergic alveolitis	29	42	37
Total number of diagnoses	3009	4418	3854
Total number of individuals*	2934	4298	3787

*Individuals may have more than one diagnosis.

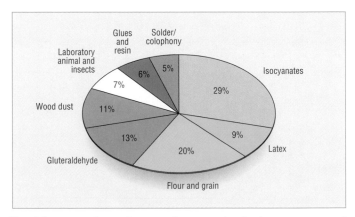

Top eight suspected causative agents for occupational asthma cases reported to SWORD/OPRA 1998-2000

Farmers are at particular risk of developing occupational asthma because they are often exposed simultaneously to an array of potential sensitisers, such as animal derived allergens, arthropods, moulds, plants, and fungicides

Tobacco smoking and atopy are common among the working population. If these risk factors are found at pre-employment assessment the individual should not automatically be excluded from working with a respiratory sensitiser

Diagnosis

Between 5% and 10% of adult asthma is attributable to occupational factors. A detailed history of past and present occupational exposures is therefore essential in the assessment of a patient with adult onset asthma. Coughing at work or at the end of a shift is often the first symptom and precedes wheezing. Concurrent nasal congestion, lacrimation, and conjunctivitis may be associated with exposure to high molecular weight substances. The symptoms generally improve at weekends and holidays, but at advanced stages the respiratory symptoms may persist. Where possible, advice should be sought from the patient's employer's occupational health service, as they will have information on the substances that the employee is exposed to and will know if other workers have developed similar respiratory symptoms.

Investigations

Patients should record the best of three measurements of peak expiratory flow made every two hours from waking to sleeping over a period of one month (charts are available from Clement Clarke International Limited). Ideally, this period should include one or two weeks away from work. A drop in peak expiratory flow or substantial diurnal variability on working days but not on days away from work supports a diagnosis of occupational asthma. If there is any doubt, the patient should be referred to a specialist centre for further investigation.

A bronchial provocation test (inhalation test) with the suspected agent may be required to give the patient advice about future employment. The test may precipitate severe bronchospasm, so the procedure must be undertaken in a specialist hospital unit with inpatient facilities. The individual is exposed to the suspected sensitiser in circumstances that most closely resemble their exposure at work. Forced expiratory volume in one second (FEV1), forced vital capacity, and responsiveness to histamine or methacholine are measured serially and then compared with serial measurements taken during a control challenge test performed on a separate day. An increase in airway hyper-responsiveness, particularly a late response, caused by the putative agent in concentrations that occur at work is taken as evidence of an allergic response. Although bronchial provocation testing is considered the gold standard test for the diagnosis of occupational asthma, false negatives can arise if the testing is conducted with the wrong material or if the concentration of the suspected agent is too low.

Management

Treatment of acute occupational asthma is the same as for asthma generally, but it is important to remove the sensitised individual from exposure to the substance causing their asthma, as subsequent exposure to even minimal quantities of the sensitising agent may precipitate severe bronchospasm. If their job entails working with the causative agent, relocation to another area will need to be considered. The employer's occupational physician will be able to advise on suitable areas for redeployment and will be in a position to liaise with the employee's manager. The employer should review their statutory risk assessments and control measures in the area

Examples of high and low molecular weight substances that may cause occupational asthma

Chemicals (low molecular weight)	Occupational group at risk/industrial use
Toluene di-isocyanate	Car or coach paint spray
Colophony (pine resin)	Electronics industry
Complex platinum salts	Platinum refinery workers
Proteins (high molecular weight)	
Flour or grain	Bakers
Rodent urinary proteins	Laboratory workers
Salmon proteins	Fish processing plant workers
Natural rubber latex	Healthcare professionals

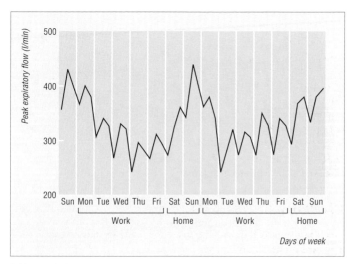

Self recorded peak expiratory flow measurements showing a classic pattern of occupational asthma

Specialist investigation of occupational asthma

(a) Identification of atopy: skin prick tests with common allergens—for example, grass pollen, *Dermatophagoides pteronyssinus*, and cat fur
(b) Skin prick tests with specific extracts of putative sensitising agent
(c) Serology: radioallergosorbent tests (RAST) to identify specific IgE antibody
(d) Bronchial provocation test with the suspected causative agent

A worker who develops occupational asthma should avoid further exposure to the causative agent. As this often means relocation or loss of current employment, it is essential that the specific cause is identified accurately where the affected employee was working to prevent other workers being similarly affected.

Reactive airways disease

Exposure to gases

Although fatalities from exposure to gases in the workplace are now rare in industrialised countries, inhalation accidents still occur relatively often. Accidental inhalation of gas (most commonly chlorine), fume, or vapour with irritant properties can lead to reactive airways disease. Frequently, individuals complain of a burning sensation in their nose and throat within minutes of exposure. The symptoms of asthma develop within 24 hours. The airway irritability usually resolves spontaneously but can persist indefinitely, and it may be provoked by a range of irritants or other provoking factors—for example, cold. The key to preventing the syndrome is good health and safety management.

On a wider scale, industrial accidents involving the release of a toxic irritant gas may cause pulmonary injury or even death in the surrounding population. The release of methylisocyanate from the Union Carbide pesticide plant in Bhopal, India, in 1984 resulted in many deaths from acute pulmonary oedema. Survivors still have chronic respiratory ill health.

Byssinosis

The symptoms of byssinosis occur as a result of hypersensitive airways and an acute reduction in FEV1 in susceptible individuals when they are exposed to dusts of cotton, sisal, hemp, or flax. It occurs most commonly in cotton mill workers and is probably a response to inhaled organic contaminants of the cotton boll, such as cotton bract (leaves at the base of the cotton flower that become hard and brittle during harvesting and comprise a major constituent of cotton dust in the mill). Smokers are at increased risk of developing the disease, but the pathogenic mechanisms underlying the disease remain obscure.

Characteristically, individuals experience acute dyspnoea with cough and chest tightness on the first day of the working week, three to four hours after the start of a work shift. The symptoms improve on subsequent working days, despite continued exposure to the sensitising agent. As the disease progresses the symptoms recur on subsequent days of the week, and eventually even occur at weekends and during holidays. Exposure of textile workers to cotton and flax dust per se does not seem to cause a significant loss of lung function. However, if the subset of workers who develop byssinosis are not removed from further exposure, they go on to develop long term respiratory impairment and subsequently have an excess risk of mortality from respiratory disease.

Pneumoconiosis

Pneumoconiosis is the generic term for the inhalation of mineral dust and the resultant diffuse, usually fibrotic, reaction in the acinar part of the lung. The term excludes asthma, neoplasia, and emphysema.

Silicosis is the commonest type of pneumoconiosis worldwide. It is caused by inhalation of crystalline silicon dioxide, and may affect people working in quarrying, mining, stone cutting and polishing, sandblasting, and fettling. Silicosis

---

Diagnostic criteria for reactive airways disease syndrome
- History of inhalation of gas, fume, or vapour with irritant properties
- Rapid onset of asthma like symptoms after exposure
- Bronchial hyper-responsiveness on methcholine challenge test
- Individual previously free from respiratory symptoms

The Bhopal disaster in India highlighted the need for rapid access to expert advice in the event of a chemical disaster

Harvested cotton consists of leaves, bracts, stems, bacteria, fungi, and other contaminants. Steaming or washing it before processing can reduce the biological activity of cotton

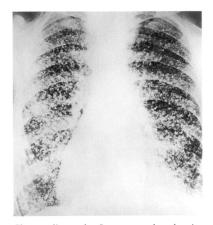

Chest radiograph of quarry worker showing extensive simple silicosis

occurs in several different forms depending on the level and duration of exposure.

Simple nodular silicosis is the most common form, and is similar clinically and radiographically to coal worker's pneumoconiosis. Chronic silicosis presents with increasing dyspnoea over several years and chest radiography shows upper lobe fibrosis or calcified nodules. Acute silicosis results from a brief but heavy exposure: patients become intensely breathless and may die within months. Chest radiographs show an appearance resembling pulmonary oedema. Accelerated silicosis occurs as the result of less heavy exposure and presents as slowly progressive dyspnoea caused by upper lobe fibrosis.

Coal worker's pneumoconiosis is caused by inhalation of coal dust, which is a complex mixture of coal, kaolin, mica, silica, and other minerals. Simple coal worker's pneumoconiosis usually produces no symptoms or physical signs apart from exertional dyspnoea. The diagnosis is made by a history of exposure and the presence of characteristic opacities on chest radiographs. A small proportion of individuals with simple coal worker's pneumoconiosis go on to develop progressive massive fibrosis which, when sufficiently advanced, causes dyspnoea, cor pulmonale, and ultimately death. Coal worker's pneumoconiosis is disappearing in developed countries as mines close and working conditions improve; however, it remains widespread in China and India.

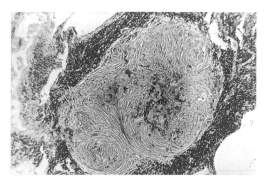
Silicotic nodule

Classification of radiographs for pneumoconiosis is based on the 1980 International Labour Office (ILO) system. This is a method of describing the pattern and severity of the change in groups of workers. The classification has been used worldwide for epidemiological research, surveillance, and medical checks of dust exposed workers

Chronic obstructive pulmonary disease and mining

The relationship between occupational exposure to coal dust and loss of ventilatory function is well established. However, after accounting for the effects of smoking and dust exposure, some miners still develop a severe decline in FEV1; the reasons for this are not fully understood. In the United Kingdom, chronic obstructive pulmonary disease due to coal dust is a prescribed industrial disease in those who have worked underground for at least 20 years and whose FEV1 is at least 1 litre below the predicted value.

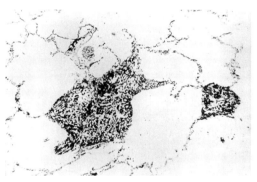
Coal miners' pneumoconiosis

Asbestos related diseases

Exposure to asbestos causes several separate pleuropulmonary disorders, including pleural plaques, diffuse thickening of the pleura, benign pleural effusions, asbestosis, bronchial cancer, and malignant mesothelioma. Bronchial cancer and malignant mesothelioma are discussed in chapter 15.

Asbestosis is a diffuse interstitial pulmonary fibrosis caused by exposure to fibres of asbestos, and its diagnosis is aided by obtaining a history of regular exposure to any form of airborne asbestos. The presence of calcified pleural plaques on a chest radiograph indicates exposure to asbestos and helps to distinguish the condition from other causes of pulmonary fibrosis. Once the diagnosis is made, workers should be removed from further exposure. As there may be a synergistic effect between smoking and asbestosis in the development of lung cancer, workers should be encouraged to stop smoking.

Occupational groups at greatest risk of developing asbestos related diseases

- Carpenters and electricians
- Builders
- Gas fitters
- Roofers
- Demolition workers
- Shipyard and rail workers
- Insulation workers
- Asbestos factory workers

Extrinsic allergic alveolitis

Extrinsic allergic alveolitis is a granulomatous inflammatory reaction caused by an immunological response to certain inhaled organic dusts and some low molecular weight chemicals. Farmer's lung and bird fancier's lung remain the most prevalent forms of the disease.

Blue asbestos fibres (left); white asbestos fibres (right)

Acute extrinsic allergic alveolitis usually occurs after exposure to a high concentration of the causative agent. After a sensitising period, which may vary from weeks to years, the individual develops flu-like symptoms after exposure to the sensitising antigen. Prolonged illness may be associated with considerable weight loss, but symptoms usually improve within 48 hours of removal from the causative agent.

Chronic extrinsic allergic alveolitis is caused either by chronic exposure to low doses of the causative antigen, or as a consequence of repeated attacks of acute alveolitis over many years. It results in irreversible pulmonary fibrosis, and the dominant symptom is exertional dyspnoea. Weight loss may be considerable but other systemic symptoms are usually absent.

Diagnosis principally depends on a history of relevant exposure and on identification of a potential sensitising agent at home or at work. Inspiratory crackles may be heard on examination of the chest, and chest radiography in acute extrinsic allergic alveolitis may show a ground glass pattern or micronodular shadows. In chronic extrinsic allergic alveolitis lung shrinkage in the upper lobes is usually apparent. The diagnosis is confirmed by detailed pulmonary investigations and the demonstration of precipitating antibodies (precipitins) to the causal antigen in the serum.

Some causes of extrinsic allergic alveolitis

Disease	Source of antigen	Antigen
Farmer's lung	Mouldy hay and straw	*Micropolyspora faeni* *Thermoactinomyces vulgaris*
Bird fancier's lung	Bird excreta and bloom	Bird serum proteins
Bagassosis	Mouldy sugar cane	*Thermoactinomyces sacchari*
Ventilation pneumonitis	Contaminated air conditioning systems	*Thermophilic actinomycetes*
Malt worker's lung	Mouldy barley	*Aspergillus clavatus*
Mushroom worker's lung	Spores released during spawning	*Thermophilic actinomycetes*
Cheese washers' lung	Mould dust	*Penicillium casei*
Animal handler's lung	Dander, dried rodent urine	Serum and urine proteins
Chemical extrinsic allergic alveolitis	Polyurethane foam manufacture and spray painting	Toluene (TDI) and diphenylmethane di-isocyanate (MDI)

Farmers and pigeon fanciers often deny a relation between causative exposure and symptoms for fear of compromising their livelihood or hobby

Characteristic abnormalities of lung function in extrinsic allergic alveolitis

- Total lung capacity—reduced
- Residual volume—reduced
- Vital capacity—reduced
- Forced expiratory volume in one second (FEV1)—reduced
- FEV1/forced vital capacity—normal or increased
- Transfer factor for carbon monoxide—reduced*
- Gas transfer coefficient—reduced

*Sensitive indicator of the disease

Further reading

- Meyer JD, Holt DL, Chen Y, Cherry NM, McDonald JC. SWORD 1999. Surveillance of work-related and occupational respiratory disease in the UK. *Occ Med* 2001;51:204-8. *This paper reports on the 1999 SWORD results and findings*
- Mapp CE. Agents, old and new, causing occupational asthma. *Occup Environ Med* 2001;58:354-9. *An up to date review of the causative agents of occupational asthma, including detailed discussion on isocyanates, latex, flour, enzymes, glutaradehyde, and acrylates. The paper concludes with an extensive reference list for further reading*
- Kogevinas M, Anto JM, Sunyer J, Tobias A, Kromhard H, Burney P. Occupational asthma in Europe and other industrialised areas: a population based study. *Lancet* 1999;353:1750-4. *The results of a study of 15 637 young adults in Western European and other industrialised countries. The aim was to verify which occupations carry a high risk of asthma, and to estimate the proportion of asthma cases in the general population attributable to occupational exposures*
- Health and Safety Executive. Proposals for reducing the incidence of occupational asthma, including an Approved Code of Practice: Control of substances that cause occupational asthma. Sudbury: HSE Books, 2002. *This publication details the Health and Safety Executive's current strategy for reducing the incidence of occupational asthma in the United Kingdom*
- Baxter PJ, Adams PH, Aw TC, Cockcroft A, Harrington JM. *Hunter's diseases of occupations.* London: Edward Arnold, 2000. *A multiauthor textbook that contains several chapters on occupational lung disease written by leading experts in the field*

The picture of victims of the Bhopal disaster is reproduced with permission of Rex Features. The table showing the estimated number of cases of work related and occupational respiratory disease is adapted from Health and Safety Executive Statistics 2000-1

The photograph of a harvester is reproduced with permission from Jeremy Walker/Science Photo Library. The photograph of cotton is with permission from Bill Barksdale/Agstrct/Science Photo Library. The photograph of the Bhopal disaster is reproduced with permission from Rex Features Ltd.

14 Occupational infections

Dipti Patel

The pattern of infectious hazards at work changes constantly. Occupational infections, although not common, can be serious and easy to miss unless there is a high index of suspicion combined with an understanding of infectious disease. Furthermore, infections that are predominantly of historic interest in the developed world continue to pose a considerable problem in the developing world, and the changing pattern of travel means that those who visit or work overseas remain exposed. Drug resistance, the resurgence of certain diseases, and the emergence of new or previously unrecognised organisms further complicate matters, as does an increasing number of immunocompromised individuals. A detailed occupational history is therefore essential, as this will often point to the diagnosis of unusual illnesses caused by infectious hazards.

Occupational infections may be work specific or may be common in the general population, but they occur more often in those with occupational exposure. Like all occupational diseases, they are mostly preventable.

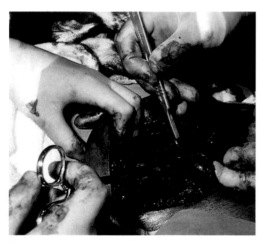

Healthcare workers are at risk acquiring infections from human sources such as bloodborne viruses

The traditional model of infectious disease causation

The epidemiological triangle
- An external agent—the organism that produces the infection
- A susceptible host—attributes that influence an individual's susceptibility or response to the agent—for example, age, sex, lifestyle
- Environmental factors that bring the host and agent together—factors that affect the agent and opportunity for exposure—for example, climate, physical surrounding, occupation, crowding

Basic concepts in infectious disease
- The *infectivity* of an agent is the proportion of exposed people who become infected (attack rate)
- The *pathogenicity* is the proportion of people exposed who develop clinical disease
- The *virulence* is the proportion of people with clinical disease who become severely ill or die
- The *infectious dose* is the number of organisms that are necessary to produce infection in the host, and this will vary according to the route of transmission and susceptibility of the host

Occurrence
- An infectious disease is *endemic* if there is a persistent low to moderate level of occurrence
- It is *sporadic* if the pattern of occurrence is irregular with occasional cases
- When the level of disease rises above the expected level for a period of time, it is referred to as an *epidemic*
- An *outbreak* is two or more cases of illness that are considered to be linked in time and place

Reservoir
This is any person, animal, arthropod, soil, etc. in which the infectious agent normally resides

Mode of transmission
This is the mechanism by which an infectious agent is spread from source or reservoir to a susceptible person—that is, direct (touching, biting, eating, droplet spread during sneezing, etc.), indirect (inanimate objects, fomites, vector borne) transmission, or airborne spread (dissemination of microbial aerosol to a suitable port of entry, usually the respiratory tract)

Main occupational groups at risk of infection

The three main categories of occupational infections are zoonoses, infections from human sources, and infections from environmental sources

Zoonotic infections
About 300 000 workers are at risk in the United Kingdom. Zoonotic infections include anthrax, leptospirosis, Q fever, Lyme disease, orf, and psittacosis. Workers at risk:

- Farmers and other agricultural workers
- Veterinary surgeons
- Poultry workers
- Butchers and fishmongers
- Abattoir workers and slaughtermen
- Forestry workers
- Researchers and laboratory workers—that is, animal handlers
- Sewage workers
- Tanners
- Military staff
- Overseas workers

Infections from human sources
About 2 million people are employed in the health service sector in the United Kingdom. Infections in this category include tuberculosis, erythema infectosum, scabies, bloodborne viruses, and rubella. Workers at risk:

- Healthcare workers
- Social care workers
- Sewage workers
- Laboratory workers
- Overseas workers
- Archaeologists (during exhumations)

Infections from environmental sources
Examples include legionellosis and tetanus. Workers at risk:

- Construction workers
- Archaeologists
- Engineering workers
- Military staff
- Overseas workers

The European Union has introduced the Biological Agents Directive (ongoing with updates since 1993), which is designed to ensure that the risk to workers from biological agents in the workplace is prevented or adequately controlled. In the United Kingdom this directive has been implemented via the Control of Substances Hazardous to Health (COSHH) Regulations 2002

Assessment of health risks of an infectious hazard, and its prevention or control should include:

- Details of the hazard group the agent belongs to
- The diseases it may cause
- How the agent is transmitted
- The likelihood of exposure and consequent disease (including the identification of those who may be particularly susceptible—for example, asplenic individuals, those with generalised immune deficiency, pregnant staff), taking into account the epidemiology of the infection within the workplace
- Whether exposure to the hazard can be prevented
- Control measures that may be necessary
- Monitoring procedures
- Need for health surveillance, which may include assessment of worker's immunity before and after immunisation

Hazard classification
In the United Kingdom biological agents are classified into four hazard groups according to their ability to cause infection

- *Group 1*—unlikely to cause human disease—for example, *Bacillus subtilis*
- *Group 2*—can cause human disease and may be a hazard to employees; it is unlikely to spread to the community, and there is usually effective prophylaxis or treatment available—for example, *Borrelia burgdorferi*
- *Group 3*—can cause severe human disease and may be a serious hazard to employees; it may spread to the community, but there is usually effective prophylaxis or treatment available—for example, *Bacillus anthracis*
- *Group 4*—causes severe human disease and is a serious hazard to employees; it is likely to spread to the community and there is usually no effective prophylaxis or treatment available—for example, *Ebola* virus

When a biological agent does not have an approved classification, the COSHH Regulations 2002 contain guidance on how biological agents should be classified. If in doubt, a higher classification should be assigned

Epidemiology

As with all occupational ill health statistics, no single source of information provides comprehensive data on occupationally acquired infections. In the United Kingdom, the principal data sources, although useful, underestimate the true incidence of occupational infections.

Data from UK reporting schemes. The industry with the highest estimated rates of infection per 100 000 workers per year for 1998-2000 was health and social care, followed by fishing, and agriculture and forestry. Diarrhoeal illnesses were the most frequently reported conditions

Disease	No of cases of infectious disease SIDAW 2000 (estimated)
Diarrhoeal illness	367
Hepatitis	–
Legionellosis	4
Leptospirosis	7
Ornithosis	4
Pulmonary tuberculosis	4
Q fever	–
Other (for example, scabies)	175
SIDAW total	**561**
SWORD/OPRA 2000	**77**
EPIDERM/OPRA 2000	**88**
RIDDOR (2000-1 provisional)	**93** Anthrax (1), chlamydiosis (2), hepatitis (4), legionellosis (14), leptospirosis (12), Lyme disease (3), Q fever (1), tuberculosis (15), others (41)
Prescribed diseases (1999-2000)	**7** Leptospirosis (1), tuberculosis (4), viral hepatitis (2)

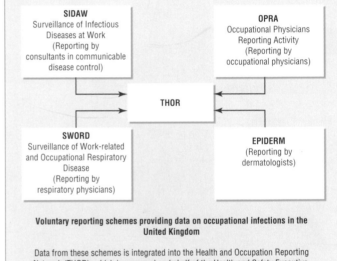

Voluntary reporting schemes providing data on occupational infections in the United Kingdom

Data from these schemes is integrated into the Health and Occupation Reporting Network (THOR), which is managed on behalf of the Health and Safety Executive. With the exception of SIDAW, reporting is based on a sampling process whereby participating doctors are asked to report incident cases for one month per year.

Statutory reporting schemes

- Reporting of Injuries Diseases and Dangerous Occurrences Regulations (RIDDOR) 1995.
- Social Security (industrial injury) (prescribed disease) Regulations 1985. (See chapter 1)
- Public Health (control of diseases) Act 1984.

Main information sources for occupational infections in the United Kingdom

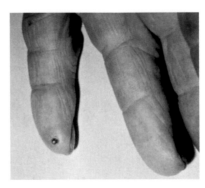

Typical painless blister of Orff

Zoonoses

These are infections that are naturally transmissible from vertebrate animals to man. The World Health Organization estimates that there are over 200 zoonoses worldwide, and around 40 occur in the United Kingdom.

Protection of workers exposed to zoonotic infections relies on a number of control measures

Control of the disease in the animal reservoir
- Stock certification and vaccination (for example, anthrax or brucellosis)
- Quarantine measures (for example, for psittacine birds)
- Infection free feeds (for example, *Salmonella* free feed for poultry)
- Avoidance of contamination of animal drinking water
- Test and slaughter policies (for example, for bovine tuberculosis)
- Good standards of hygiene in stock housing
- Regular stock health checks by vets
- Meat inspection

Safe work practices
- Safe handling of animals or animal products (for all zoonotic infections)
- Safe disposal of carcasses and animal waste (for example, hydatid disease)
- Avoidance of equipment likely to cause cuts, abrasions, and grazes

Strict personal hygiene
- Covering existing wounds with waterproof dressings before work
- Prompt cleaning of any cuts or grazes that occur while handling animals
- Regular and correct hand washing, and avoidance of contact between unwashed hands and the mouth, eyes, or face

Personal protective equipment
- Waterproof aprons or parturition gowns
- Obstetric gauntlets for lambing or calving
- Face protection if there is a risk of splashing from urine or placental fluids
- Plastic or synthetic rubber gloves for oral or rectal examinations
- Gloves, overalls, and face protection for slaughtering animals or dressing carcasses
- Chainmail gloves for butchers

Other measures
- Immunisation of at risk worker (anthrax, Q fever)
- Provision of health warning cards (leptospirosis)

NB

For protection of laboratory workers advice on control measures has been provided by the Advisory Group on Dangerous Pathogens

(Adapted from Health and Safety information sheet "Common zoonoses in agriculture")

Anthrax

Also known as malignant pustule, Woolsorter's disease, and Ragpicker's disease, anthrax is a notifiable disease, a prescribed disease, and RIDDOR 1995 reportable. It is an acute infection caused by *Bacillus anthracis* (a spore forming Gram positive bacterium), and the normal animal reservoirs are grazing mammals such as sheep, cattle, and goats. Human anthrax is primarily an occupational hazard for workers who process hides, hair, wool, bone, and bone products, but it also occurs in vets and agricultural workers who handle infected animals. It is rare in the United Kingdom (only three cases of anthrax were reported in England and Wales between 1998 and 2001), occurring in those who work directly or indirectly with infected animal products from epizootic areas. Most cases of anthrax occur in Africa, the Middle East, and the former Soviet Union.

Cutaneous anthrax accounts for 95-8% of cases, and occurs when the organism enters a cut or an abrasion. After an incubation period of one to seven days, a small papule develops at this site. Over 24-48 hours, it enlarges, eventually forming a characteristic black ulcer (eschar). If not treated, cutaneous anthrax may progress to bacteraemia, meningitis, and death.

Pulmonary and gastrointestinal anthrax occur infrequently, and are the result of inhalation and ingestion of anthrax spores, respectively. In pulmonary anthrax (Woolsorter's disease) non-specific upper respiratory tract symptoms follow an incubation period of one to six days. Rapid deterioration in respiratory function and death generally follow unless treatment is started promptly. Gastrointestinal anthrax is characterised by severe abdominal pain, watery or bloody diarrhoea, and vomiting. Progression to bacteraemia is usually two to three days. Case fatality in both these forms of anthrax is high.

Most naturally occurring strains of anthrax are susceptible to penicillin, although doxycycline and ciprofloxacin have been used recently. Immunisation is also available for at risk workers, and oral antibiotics (ciprofloxacin and doxycycline) have been used as prophylaxis for individuals exposed to anthrax spores.

Leptospirosis

Leptospirosis is also known as Weil's disease, canicola fever, haemorrhagic jaundice, mud fever and swineherd disease. It is a notifiable disease, prescribed disease, and RIDDOR 1995 reportable. Leptospirosis is a rare cause of septicaemia caused by pathogenic leptospires belonging to the genus

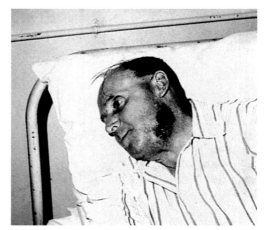

Patient with cutaneous anthrax

Anthrax has recently received attention because of its potential for use in bioterrorism. Other potential bioterrorism organisms include:

Organism (disease)	Potential source	Ability to cause disease
Brucella (Brucellosis)	Aerosol or food	High
Clostridium botulinum toxin (Botulism)	Food, water, or aerosol	High
Coxiella burnetii (Q fever)	Aerosol or food supply	High
Variola virus (Smallpox)	Aerosol	High
Vibrio cholerae (Cholera)	Food, water, or aerosol	Low

Leptospira interrogans (*Li*). The genus has over 200 serovars; of most importance in humans are *Li hardjo* (cattle associated leptospirosis), *Li icterohaemorrhagiae* (Weil's disease), and *Li canicola*. The principal animal reservoirs are cattle, rats, and dogs, respectively.

The distribution of human disease depends on the local prevalence of animal infection and local environmental conditions. At risk occupational groups include agricultural workers, farmers, vets, miners, abattoir workers, and sewer and canal workers. In 2001 there were 25 notified cases of leptospirosis in England and Wales (predominantly caused by *Li hardjo*).

Leptospirosis is usually acquired by direct contact with infected animals or their urine, contaminated soil, food, or water (a hazard for those indulging in watersports). The incubation period is usually five to 14 days, and symptoms, which are not serotype specific, typically consist of fever, flu-like symptoms, headache, myalgia, photophobia, and conjunctival injection. In severe cases (often associated with *Li icterohaemorrhagiae*) haemorrhage into skin and mucous membranes, vomiting, jaundice, and hepatorenal failure may occur.

Mild infection is often self limiting, but penicillin, erythromycin, and doxycycline are all effective treatments. For more severe disease, intensive and specialised therapy is necessary.

Immunisation of animals is possible for certain serovars, and in some countries (Japan, Italy, Spain) immunisation of at risk workers against certain serovars is available. In the United Kingdom, workers who may be exposed to leptospires usually carry an alert card provided by their employer to warn their doctors should they develop such symptoms.

Transmissible spongiform encephalopathies (TSEs)
Prion disease

These are a group of progressive and fatal neurological disorders occurring in humans and certain animal species. TSEs are thought to be caused by infectious proteins (prions) that are unusually resistant to conventional chemical and physical decontamination. They do not seem to be highly infectious and, with the exception of scrapie, do not seem to spread through casual contact.

Bovine spongiform encephalopathy (BSE) was first recognised in British cattle in 1986. Its origin is still uncertain, but it probably originated in the early 1970s, developing into an epidemic because of changing practices in rendering cattle offal to produce animal protein in the form of meat and bonemeal, which was included in compound cattle feed. This resulted in the recycling and wide distribution of BSE. In 1996, a previously unrecognised form of Creutzfeldt-Jakob disease (CJD) occurring in younger patients (range 14-53 years, mean 28 years), with a different symptom profile and different postmortem changes in the brain tissue, was identified in the United Kingdom.

The Government's Spongiform Encephalopathy Advisory Committee concluded that the most likely explanation for the emergence of this variant CJD (vCJD) was that it had been transmitted to humans through exposure to BSE as a result of consumption of contaminated bovine food products.

A major concern now is the risk of transmission in a healthcare setting. Although there have been no reported cases of nosocomial transmission of vCJD, an expert group has been established by the UK government to advise on prevention and management of possible exposures.

Farm workers are at increased risk of catching animal borne diseases

---

Transmissible spongiform encephalopathies (TSEs)

Human TSEs
- Creutzfeldt-Jakob disease (CJD)
- Variant CJD (vCJD)
- Gerstmann Sträussler Scheinker syndrome
- Kuru
- Fatal familial insomnia

Animal TSEs
- Scrapie (sheep and goats)
- Bovine spongiform encephalopathy (BSE) (cattle)
- Transmissible mink encephalopathy (farmed mink)
- Chronic wasting disease (deer)
- Feline spongiform encephalopathy (domestic cats and captive exotic felines)
- Spongiform encephalopathy (captive exotic ungulates)

A number of measures have been taken to minimise disease transmission among animals and humans, and although there is no clear evidence of occupational risk, advice on safe working practices has been provided by the Advisory Committee on Dangerous Pathogens. Those potentially at risk include workers in abattoirs, slaughterhouses and rendering plants; farmers; neurosurgeons; pathologists; and mortuary technicians

The incubation period of vCJD is unknown, but is likely to be several years. The infectious dose is also unknown, and is likely to be dependent on the route of exposure. However, by February 2002, a total of 114 individuals throughout the United Kingdom (106 dead and 8 alive) were considered to have had definite or probable vCJD. There is currently no evidence to link any cases of vCJD with surgical procedures or with transmission by blood, but the possibility cannot be ruled out.

It is already current practice to dispose of instruments used on anyone showing symptoms of vCJD. A problem, however, occurs in those who have presymptomatic disease; precautions to avoid this theoretical risk of transmission are therefore essential. Any assessment of risk of transmission from instruments must consider a wide range of scenarios, and precautionary measures should be taken against risks that might occur, even if the level of risk is not known. The key message in reducing any risk of vCJD transmission is the rigorous implementation of washing, decontamination, and general hygiene procedures.

In January 2001, a recommendation that single use instruments were used for tonsillectomy and adenoidectomy surgery was made. This recommendation was withdrawn in December 2001 because adverse incidents (mainly haemorrhage, but also one death) were reported after the introduction of single use instruments. It was felt that on balance, the single use instruments represented an actual risk to patients, whereas the concerns regarding vCJD transmission were only theoretical. Further information is available at http://www.open.gov.uk/doh/coinh.htm.

Infections from human sources

These infections are of most relevance to healthcare workers. They are important because healthcare workers are at high risk of acquiring infections occupationally and they are also a potential source of infection to their patients, particularly those who are immunologically impaired.

Bloodborne viruses
Occupational exposure to blood or body fluids poses a small risk of transmission of bloodborne pathogens. Those presenting the greatest crossinfection hazard are HIV, and hepatitis B and hepatitis C viruses. Although healthcare staff are at greatest risk, other occupational groups (for example, police officers) may also be exposed.

The risk of infection depends on the type and severity of the exposure, the infectivity of the source patient, the immune status of the exposed healthcare worker, and the availability of treatment after exposure.

Prevention entails minimising exposure to blood or body fluids, and consists of strict infection control, adherence to universal precautions, immunisation against hepatitis B, and prompt management of any occupational exposure.

Healthcare workers infected with bloodborne viruses can potentially transmit infection to their patients, and although the risk is small, guidelines exist in many countries to reduce this risk further. In the United Kingdom, all healthcare workers who perform exposure prone procedures are required to provide evidence that they are immune to hepatitis B as a result of immunisation, or that they are not HBe antigen (HBeAg) positive. Because of transmissions of HBV associated with codon 28 precore mutations, those who are HB surface antigen positive, but HBeAg negative, must now be tested for hepatitis B virus DNA; they may perform exposure prone work provided that their HB viral load is below 10^3 genome equivalents per millilitre, and this is subject to annual testing.

> Although it is likely that most of the UK population has been exposed to BSE, the true number of individuals who have been infected is not known

---

Reasons that vCJD might be spread from person to person in healthcare settings

- Classical CJD has been transmitted from person to person by a range of medical procedures including surgery, grafts or transplants, and treatment with pituitary extracts, and about 1% of classical CJD cases in the past are considered to have been iatrogenic
- Abnormal prion protein has been shown in the lymphoreticular tissue (tonsils, spleen, and lymph nodes) of patients with established vCJD
- Abnormal prion protein has been shown in the appendix of a patient who subsequently developed vCJD
- Although, to date, the transmissible agent has not been shown in blood, it is possible that abnormal prion protein, at concentrations not detectable with current techniques, may be associated with circulating B lymphocytes and with other cells of the immune and circulatory systems
- Abnormal prion protein has been shown to be highly tenacious and may not be inactivated by conventional sterilisation and decontamination procedures

---

> Exposure prone procedures are invasive procedures where there is risk that injury to the worker may result in the exposure of a patient's open tissues to the blood of the worker. These incude procedures where a healthcare worker's gloved hand may be in contact with sharp instruments or tissues inside a patient's open body cavity, wound, or confined anatomical space where the hands may not be completely visible at all times

Risk of transmission of bloodborne viruses

High risk body fluids
- Cerebrospinal fluid
- Peritoneal, pleural, pericardial fluid
- Synovial fluid
- Amniotic fluid
- Breast milk
- Vaginal secretions
- Semen
- Saliva associated with dentistry
- All visibly blood stained fluid
- Unfixed organs or tissues

Estimated risk of seroconversion after percutaneous exposure
HIV: 0.32% (based on data of 6202 healthcare workers). Risk of mucous membrane exposure is 0.09%, and there have been no transmissions associated with exposure of intact skin. In the United Kingdom there have to date (March 2002) been five definite occupationally acquired transmissions of HIV. Worldwide by 1999, 102 definite and 217 possible cases of occupationally acquired HIV had been reported

The risk of percutaneous exposure is increased if the injury is deep, the device is visibly blood stained, the injury is from a needle placed in artery or vein, or the source patient has terminal HIV infection

Post-exposure prophylaxis (PEP)
HIV
Most countries now recommend a four week course of zidovudine with lamivudine, and many recommend the addition of a protease inhibitor. The choice of drugs, doses, route of administration, and the length of PEP are somewhat empirical. However, because most studies indicate a time limited response to PEP, the need for timely and early therapy is vital. In the United Kingdom, HIV PEP generally consists of zidovudine and lamivudine (Combivir) with nelfinavir, indinavir, or soft gel saquinavir (March 2002)

Hepatitis B virus
Hepatitis B virus immunoglobulin (HBIG) is available for passive protection and is normally used in combination with hepatitis B vaccine to confer passive-active immunity to susceptible individuals after exposure. The post-exposure efficacy of combination HBIG and hepatitis B vaccine has not been evaluated in the occupational setting, but increased efficacy (85-95%) has been observed perinatally. Although HBIG may not completely inhibit virus multiplication, it may prevent severe illness and the development of a chronic carrier state

Low risk body fluids (unless visibly bloodstained)
- Urine
- Faeces
- Vomit

Significant exposures
- Percutaneous injury
- Exposure of broken skin
- Exposure of mucous membrane

Hepatitis C virus: 1.8%
Hepatitis B virus: 37-66% from HBeAg positive source; 23-37% from HBsAg positive source
Effective immunisation is available for hepatitis B virus and 80-90% of individuals mount an adequate response

Hepatitis C virus
No effective PEP exists. Recommendations for post-exposure management are therefore intended to achieve early identification of infection, with appropriate specialist referral. Although consistent data are lacking, one uncontrolled trial has shown a substantially better response rate of early treatment using interferon compared with treatment of patients with chronic disease

Individuals who, as a result of testing, are found to be hepatitis C RNA positive should not perform exposure prone procedures. However, hepatitis C infected workers who have been successfully treated with antiviral therapy and remain hepatitis C virus RNA negative six months after finishing treatment should be able to resume exposure prone procedures or start professional training for a career that relies on the performance of exposure prone procedures.

HIV testing is not compulsory for healthcare workers in the United Kingdom and many other countries. In the United Kingdom, professional regulatory bodies state that workers who may have been exposed to HIV have an ethical responsibility to be tested. If found to be HIV infected, exposure prone work is prohibited. The UK Department of Health is currently reviewing their policy.

Tuberculosis
Tuberculosis is a notifiable disease, a prescribed disease, and RIDDOR 1995 reportable.

Mycobacterium tuberculosis continues to be the leading cause of adult death from any single infectious agent worldwide.

Recent UK guidance for hepatitis C
- Healthcare workers who carry out exposure prone procedures and already know themselves to be infected with hepatitis C should be tested for hepatitis C virus RNA (if not already done)
- All healthcare professionals intending to undertake professional training for a career that relies on the performance of exposure prone procedures should be tested for hepatitis C infection
- Those who perform exposure prone procedures and believe that they may have been exposed to hepatitis C should seek and follow confidential and professional advice on whether they should be tested for hepatitis C

Bloodborne viruses and risk to patients

HIV

- In the United Kingdom, the Expert Advisory Group on AIDS (EAGA) provides guidance on look-back procedures for HIV. As UK studies of over 30 000 patients after look-back exercises have shown no evidence of transmission of HIV to patients, it is likely that look-back procedures for HIV in the United Kingdom will stop
- Two incidents of transmission from a healthcare worker to a patient have been reported: a Florida dentist who infected six patients, and a French orthopaedic surgeon who infected one patient
- Dr Patrick Ngosa, an HIV positive obstetrician, was removed from the UK General Medical Council's Register in 1997 when it was discovered that he had refused to have an HIV test and continued to perform exposure prone procedures after learning that a former sexual partner was HIV positive. A total of 1750 women on whom he had operated were sent letters informing them that there was a possibility that they had been exposed to HIV

Hepatitis B virus

- A number of look-back studies involving surgical staff from 1975 to 1990 have identified transmission risks of 0.9-20%
- The most recent look-back exercise for hepatitis B virus in the United Kingdom was in 2001. About 350 patients were contacted in Fife, when infection in two patients was traced back to one healthcare worker
- A surgeon infected with hepatitis B (Dr Gaud) who lied about his infectivity was convicted and jailed for the common law charge of "public nuisance" after knowingly operating on patients and putting them at risk of infection

Hepatitis C virus

- In the United Kingdom there have been five patient notification exercises after investigations of hospital acquired hepatitis C infection. Since 1994 there have been 15 documented transmissions of hepatitis C virus to patients from infected healthcare workers during exposure prone procedures

---

The emergence of multidrug resistant tuberculosis (MDRTB), with its high case fatality, its prolonged sputum positivity (and consequently, high transmission risk), and its complex treatment has re-emphasised the importance of tuberculosis control.

Tuberculosis remains a hazard in the healthcare setting, and incidence in healthcare workers parallels (but is higher than) that in the community; a study in the mid-1990s found about a twofold increased risk of tuberculosis among healthcare workers in England and Wales. Healthcare workers should therefore be protected against infection, and measures should be taken to detect tuberculosis in new or existing staff in order to protect their patients and colleagues. Protection begins at pre-employment, and continues with strict infection control measures for nursing infected patients.

In the United Kingdom, protection of healthcare workers should follow the guidelines produced by the Joint Tuberculosis Committee of the British Thoracic Society.

Adults with non-pulmonary tuberculosis can usually be nursed on general wards, but those with pulmonary tuberculosis should initially be admitted to a single room vented to the open air until their sputum status is known. Those with smear positive sputum should be managed as infectious. In the case of known or suspected MDRTB, particular care must be taken, and patients should be admitted to a negative pressure single isolation room until MDRTB is excluded or until sputum smears have been negative on three consecutive occasions over 14 days.

Outbreaks of MDRTB in the United States and Europe have emphasised the importance of control. These outbreaks have occurred predominantly in institutional settings (prisons, residential homes, and hospitals) and have mainly been in HIV infected patients. Contributory factors in these outbreaks included lapses in respiratory isolation, inadequate ventilation in isolation rooms, and "immunocompromised convergence" (the assembling of immunocompromised HIV infected patients in institutions).

Multidrug resistant tuberculosis (MDRTB)

MDRTB is tuberculosis resistant to at least isoniazid and rifampicin

Effective control of MDRTB requires a multidisciplinary approach involving the hospital infection control team, microbiologist, tuberculosis physician, consultant in communicable disease control, engineers, and occupational health

- Visitors to patients with known or suspected MDRTB should be kept to a minimum
- The number of healthcare workers exposed to MDRTB patients should be kept as low as possible
- All who enter the rooms of MDRTB patients should wear suitable particulate masks that filter down to particles of 1 micron in diameter
- Staff should wear masks during aerosol generating procedures, such as sputum induction, bronchoscopy, and pentamidine therapy. These procedures should only be performed in suitably ventilated facilities
- Individuals who have not been checked for immunity to tuberculosis, or those with a negative skin test who have not received BCG vaccination should avoid contact with MDRTB patients, as should those who are immunocompromised

The decision to discontinue strict isolation and infection control procedures should only be made after discussion between the clinician with responsibility for the patient, the hospital infection control team, occupational health, and a consultant in communicable diseases

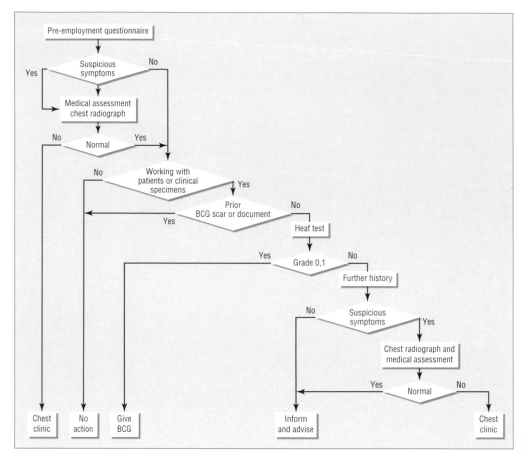

Protection of healthcare workers with tuberculosis

When a patient or member of staff is found to have tuberculosis, infection control and occupational health staff have to assess the need for contact tracing. In the United Kingdom, most staff are not considered to be at special risk and should be reassured and advised to report any suspicious symptoms. Those who are immunocompromised, have undertaken mouth to mouth resuscitation, prolonged high dependency care, or repeated chest physiotherapy without appropriate protection should be regarded as close contacts and followed up according to national guidelines. Similar precautions should be taken if the index case is highly infectious.

Chickenpox

Chickenpox is a systemic viral infection resulting from primary infection with varicella zoster virus. It is highly infectious and transmitted directly by personal contact or droplet spread, and indirectly through fomites. Shingles (herpes zoster) is a reactivation of dormant virus in the posterior root ganglion and can be a source of infection generally by contact with the skin lesions, but occasionally by the respiratory route in immunocompromised individuals.

Primary infection in adults can be severe, resulting in a higher frequency of complications such as pneumonia, encephalitis, and hepatitis, but its main importance is the risk to non-immune pregnant women and the immunosuppressed.

Although the prevalence of seropositivity for varicella zoster virus in healthcare workers in temperate climates is high (90-98%), nosocomial exposure to the virus is a major occupational health problem requiring non-immune healthcare workers to be excluded from patient contact from day 8 to 21 after a substantial exposure. A live attenuated vaccine is now available in many parts of the world.

Complications of varicella zoster virus

- Severe disease due to fulminating varicella pneumonia is more likely in adults, especially pregnant women, and smokers
- Pregnant women are at greatest risk late in second or early third trimester
- In the immunocompromised and neonates, disseminated or haemorrhagic varicella is more likely
- The risk to fetus and neonate from maternal infection relates to gestation at time of infection
  - *First 20 weeks*—congenital varicella syndrome (limb hypoplasia, microcephaly, hydrocephalus, cataracts, growth retardation, and skin scarring)
  - *Second and third trimester*—herpes zoster in otherwise healthy infant
  - *A week before to a week after delivery*—severe and even fatal disease in the neonate (particularly premature babies)
- Human varicella zoster immunoglobulin (VZIG) is available and can be given for post-exposure prophylaxis in individuals who fulfill the following conditions:
  - a clinical condition that increases risk of varicella infection
  - no antibodies to varicella zoster virus
  - substantial exposure to chickenpox or herpes zoster
- A substantial exposure to varicella zoster virus depends on:
  - the type of infection in the index case—for example, the risk of acquiring infection from an immunocompetent individual with non-exposed shingles is remote
  - the timing of the exposure in relation to onset of rash in the index case—the critical time for chickenpox or disseminated zoster is 48 hours before the onset of rash until crusting of lesions for varicella zoster virus, and day of onset of rash until crusting in localised zoster
  - closeness and duration of contact—contact in same room >15 minutes, or face to face contact
- The recommendation that VZIG is used for exposed non-immune pregnant women during the first 20 weeks of pregnancy is based on biological plausibility. No evidence exists showing that the risk of congenital varicella syndrome is reduced
- VZIG is not recommended for healthy healthcare workers, but in the United States, varicella vaccine is recommended for use in susceptible individuals after exposure; data from hospital and community settings suggest that it is effective in preventing illness or modifying severity if used within three days of exposure

Other infections

Other infections worth mentioning include skin infection in engineers associated with the re-use of cutting oils (which can lead to oil mists being contaminated with bacteria and fungi), pseudomonal otitis externa in deep sea divers who use saturation techniques, and legionellosis (which can occasionally be occupationally acquired). Finally, travel associated infections are becoming an important cause of occupationally acquired disease with the increase in international business travel and overseas workers (see *ABC of Healthy Travel*).

Legionellosis (Legionnaire's disease, Pontiac fever)

This infection is RIDDOR 1995 reportable. It is an acute bacterial infection caused by a Gram negative bacillus belonging to the genus *Legionella*. Two clinical presentations are recognised: Legionnaire's disease and Pontiac fever, and the majority of infections are due to *L. pneumophila*. The bacillus is an ubiquitous aquatic organism that thrives in warm environments (25-45°C, but preferably at 30-40°C), and is often isolated from natural habitats (rivers, creeks, hot springs) and from artificial equipment where the temperature is maintained at levels favouring bacterial proliferation.

Transmission of infection is from inhalation of contaminated aerosols, and both Legionnaire's disease and Pontiac fever present initially with non-specific flu-like symptoms. Pontiac fever occurs after an incubation period of 4 to 66 hours, and is a self limiting non-pneumonic form of the infection. By contrast, the incubation period for Legionnaire's disease is two to ten days. Initial symptoms of fever, malaise, anorexia, and myalgia are followed by progression to pneumonia and associated multisystem involvement, with diarrhoea, vomiting, confusion, and renal failure. Case fatality can range from 5% to 15%, but may be higher in outbreaks.

Treatment generally consists of erythromycin (although rifampicin may be used as an adjunct). If infection is confirmed, local public health authorities need to be notified as contacts may need to be identified, and the source of infection needs to be established and appropriately controlled.

Conclusion

The extent of occupationally acquired infections is unknown, but it is likely that they are extremely common, particularly mild infections in agricultural and healthcare workers. Preventing infection is an important aspect of occupational health practice as it will impact favourably on communicable disease in the general population. Similarly, the control of communicable disease in both the general (and animal) population will decrease the risk to certain occupational groups.

The table showing Data from UK reporting schemes depicting the industries with the highest estimated rates of infection is adapted from Health and Safety Executive Statistics 2000-1. The figures showing the protection of workers with tuberculosis are adapted from the guidelines of the Joint Tuberculosis Committee of the British Thoracic Society. Control and prevention of tuberculosis in the United Kingdom: code of practice 2000. Http://www.brit-thoracic.org.uk

---

Legionnaire's disease

- Travel abroad is a major risk factor for Legionnaire's disease in the United Kingdom, with nearly 50% of cases being contracted abroad
- About 15% of UK cases are linked to local outbreaks (caused by wet cooling systems or hot water systems), and roughly 2% are hospital acquired. Many cases are sporadic, or from an unidentified source
- Hospital outbreaks in particular have high case fatalities
- The highest risk of infection occurs with water systems leading to the aerosolisation of water that is stored at temperatures of 25-45°C. This includes:
  – wet cooling systems (for example, cooling towers and evaporative condensers)
  – hot water systems (especially showers)
  – whirlpool spas
  – indoor and outdoor fountain and sprinkler systems
  – humidifiers
  – respiratory therapy systems
  – industrial grinders
- Prevention of infection relies on ensuring that equipment and systems are kept as clean as possible, and disinfected regularly. Where possible, water temperatures should be kept above 50°C or below 20°C. Use of biocides may also need to be considered. In the United Kingdom, the Health and Safety Executive provides guidance on the prevention and control of legionellosis

---

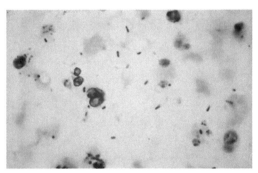

Legionella bacteria

Further reading

- Heponstall J, Cockcroft A, Smith R. Occupation and infectious diseases. In: Baxter P, Adams PH, Cockcroft A, Harrington JM, eds. *Hunter's diseases of occupations*. London: Edward Arnold, 2000:489-517. *This chapter provides comprehensive information on occupational infections*
- Hawker J, Begg N, Blair I, Reintjes R, Weinberg J. *Communicable disease control handbook*, 1st ed. Oxford: Blackwell Science Ltd, 2001
- Chin J. *Control of communicable diseases manual*, 17th ed. Washington: American Public Health Association, 2000. *Both these references, although aimed at public health practitioners, provide extensive detail on communicable diseases, their epidemiology, clinical features, prevention, and control*
- http://www.who.int
- http://www.cdc.gov
- http://www.phls.co.uk
  These websites are excellent resources for information on infectious diseases (both occupational and non-occupational)
- http://www.open.gov.uk/doh/dhhome.htm *The UK department of health website is particularly useful for information on bloodborne viruses and BSE*
- http://www.hse.gov.uk *This site provides practical and clear information on prevention and control of a variety of infectious hazards in the workplace, and is also a source of occupational ill-health statistics*

15　Occupational cancers

John Hobson

The first report of cancer caused by occupational exposure was in 1775 by Percival Pott, a British surgeon who described scrotal cancer in boy chimney sweeps. A century later, in 1895, Rehn, a German surgeon working in Frankfurt, treated a cluster of three cases of bladder cancer in workers at a local factory producing aniline dyestuffs from coal tar.

Occupational cancer is any malignancy wholly or partly caused by exposures at the workplace or in occupation. Such exposure may be because of a particular chemical (such as β-naphthylamine), a physical agent (such as ionising radiation), a fibre like asbestos, a biological agent (such as hepatitis B virus), or an industrial process in which the specific carcinogen may elude precise definition (such as coke production).

Overall it is estimated that 4% of all cancers are caused by occupation (range 2-8%), but for bladder cancer this may be as high as 20%. In the working population as many as one in five cancers may be attributable to exposure in the workplace. In England and Wales at least 3000 men die each year from potentially preventable malignancies.

The International Agency for Research on Cancer (IARC) was set up to identify carcinogenic hazards to humans. To date, 874 chemicals, groups of chemicals, complex mixtures, occupational exposures, cultural habits, and biological and physical agents have been evaluated. The findings have been published in 79 monographs and eight supplements.

Mechanisms of cancer

Cancer is a genetic disorder of somatic cells and can be triggered by the genotoxic action of carcinogens. There are five or six independent stages of carcinogenesis, each of which is rate limiting. The best available model is colorectal cancer, which requires seven independent genetic events. The three key stages are initiation (by a mutagen), promotion (where development of tumours is enhanced by other stimuli to cell proliferation such as lung fibrosis), and progression (development of malignant tumours from benign neoplasms).

Mutations in tumour suppressor genes (for example, *p53*) are particularly important, and half of all cancers contain *p53* mutations, of which there are 6000 possible point mutations. Several environmental and occupational carcinogens are linked to *p53* mutations—for example, ultraviolet light and skin cancer, and tobacco and oral cancer. Other factors linked with *p53* include alcohol, vinyl chloride, and asbestos.

Most carcinogens are genotoxic (DNA reactive) and cause mutation. There is no threshold below which they are not carcinogenic and therefore exposure levels are set at acceptable levels. Tests for genotoxicity such as Ames and fluorescent in situ hybridization (FISH) are now well established. The Ames test is the most widely used procedure for assessing the mutagenicity of chemicals. The relative mutagenic potency of an agent is indicated by the number of bacterial colonies growing on a plate containing the toxic agent relative to those growing on a plate containing normal medium. FISH is used to assess chromosomal abnormalities.

Epigenetic carcinogens (also known as non-genotoxic or cocarcinogens) act more directly on the cell itself, through

Foundry workers may be exposed to a complex mixture of carcinogenic agents in fumes

Of all the occupationally related diseases, cancer evokes particular concern and strong emotions, because of the opportunity afforded for attribution, blame, and compensation. However, occupational cancers also have unique potential for prevention

International Agency for Research on Cancer (IARC) classifications to date

Group		Number
1	Carcinogenic	87
2A	Probably carcinogenic	63
2B	Possibly carcinogenic	233
3	Unclassifiable as to carcinogenicity in humans	490
4	Probably not carcinogenic to humans	1 (caprolactam)

hormonal imbalances, immunological effects, or promoter activity, to cause abnormal cell proliferation and chromosomal aberrations that affect gene expression. These carcinogens have a threshold dose for carcinogenicity and it is possible to set exposure levels. There is probably a minimal threshold dose as well as a clear dose-response relation influencing the occurrence of cancers. For example, all workers involved in distilling β-naphthylamine eventually developed tumours of the urothelial tract, whereas only 4% of rubber mill workers who were exposed to β-naphthylamine (a contaminating antioxidant (at 0.25%) used in making tyres and inner tubes) developed bladder cancer over a 30 year follow up.

Polymorphisms are different responses to the same factor such as a drug. Slow acetylators who are heavy smokers are 1.5 times more likely to get bladder cancer if exposed to carcinogens. Certain polymorphisms increase the risk of mesothelioma 7.8 times. It will be possible in the future to rapidly and cheaply test individuals for polymorphisms and genotypes.

Thick walled mesothelioma of pleura with haemorrhagic cavitation in a former insulation worker

Sites of cancers

Carcinogens are organotropic. In the United Kingdom the most commonly affected sites are the lung (mesothelium) (75%), bladder (10%), and skin (1%). Other sites affected are the haemopoietic system, nasal cavities, larynx, and liver.

Natural course of cancers

Occupationally related cancers are characterised by a long latent period (that is, the time between first exposure to the causative agent and presentation of the tumour). This latency is not usually less than 10 to 15 years and can be much longer (40-50 years in the case of some asbestos related mesotheliomas): presentation can therefore be in retirement rather than while still at work. However, susceptibility to occupational carcinogens is greater when the exposure occurs at younger ages. An occupationally related tumour does not differ substantially, either pathologically or clinically, from its "naturally occurring" counterpart.

Diagnosis of work related cancer
- Detailed lifelong occupational history
- Comparison with a checklist of recognised causal associations
- Confirmation of requisite exposure
- Search for additional clues: shift to a younger age, presence of signal tumours, other cases and "clusters," long latency, absence of anticipated aetiologies, unusual histology or site

Recognition and diagnosis

For a group of workers, occupational cancer is evidenced by a clear excess of cancers over what would normally be expected. Some common malignancies that can be work related also have a well recognised and predominant aetiology related to other agents, diet, or lifestyle (for example, lung cancer from smoking). There are, however, some features that may help to distinguish occupational cancers from those not related to work.

History taking
Taking a patient's occupational history is paramount. It should be defined in detail and sequentially. For example, a holiday job in a factory that lasted only a few months could easily be overlooked, but it may have included delagging a boiler or handling sacks of asbestos waste.

Signal tumours
Several uncommon cancers are associated with particular occupations. Thus, an angiosarcoma of the liver may indicate past exposure to vinyl chloride monomer in the production of polyvinyl chloride, although there have been no cases in workers exposed since 1969. A worldwide registry of all exposed workers exists.

Rubber workers in mill room

Age

A younger age at presentation with cancer may suggest an occupational influence. For example, a tumour of the urothelial tract presenting in anyone under the age of 50 years should always arouse suspicion.

Patients' information

Patients may speak of a "cluster" of cancer cases at work, or they may have worked in an industry or job for which a warning leaflet has been issued.

Prevention

Primary prevention seeks to prevent the onset of a disease. Secondary prevention aims to halt the progression of a disease once it is established. Tertiary prevention is concerned with the rehabilitation of people with an established disease to minimise residual disabilities and complications or improve the quality of life if the disease itself cannot be cured.

Cystoscopic view of papillary carcinoma of the bladder in a 47 year old rubber worker

Levels of prevention

| | Stages | | | Outcomes | | |
	Health	**Asymptomatic**	**Symptomatic**	**Disability**	**Recovery**	**Death**
Intervention strategies	Health education, immunisation, environmental measures and social policy	Presymptomatic screening	Early diagnosis and prompt effective treatment	Rehabilitation		
Level of prevention	Primary	Secondary		Tertiary		

Adapted from Donaldson and Donaldson, 1999.

Primary prevention of occupationally related cancers depends essentially on educating employers and employees; firstly about recognising that there is a risk, and then about the practical steps that can be taken to eliminate or reduce exposure and to protect workers. Modern risk based legislation now directs these educational and practical measures.

Secondary prevention

Screening procedures may enable earlier diagnosis, but there is little evidence to suggest that most screening makes a difference to outcome. Screening is of proven benefit in cutaneous cancers of occupational origin, mainly because of the excellent prognosis afforded by treatment. Routine skin inspections should be initiated where there is exposure to known skin carcinogens. Routine urine cytology has been carried out in many industries where there has been previous exposure to known carcinogens. It is possibly of benefit but this has not been proven. β-Naphthylamine was withdrawn from use by 1950, but many former workers continue to participate in urine cytology screening programmes. Once commenced, surveillance should be lifelong. In the United Kingdom it is recommended workers exposed to 4,4-methylene-bis-(2-chloroaniline) (MbOCA) should have their urinary levels of MbOCA and its N-acetyl metabolites checked, but periodic urine cytology for those exposed remains controversial. Screening for lung and liver cancer is not of benefit.

Action for primary prevention of occupational cancers

- Recognition of presence of hazards and risks
- Education of management and workforce
- Elimination of exposure by substitution and automation
- Reduction of exposure by engineering controls (such as local exhaust ventilation and enclosure, changes in handling, and altering physical form in processing)
- Monitoring of exposure and maintaining plant
- Protection of workers with personal protective equipment
- Limiting access
- Provision of adequate facilities for showering, washing, and changing
- Legislative provisions

Criteria for screening

- Is the condition an important health problem?
- Is there a recognisable early stage?
- Is treatment more beneficial at an early stage than at a later stage?
- Is there a suitable test?
- Is the test acceptable to the population?
- Are there adequate facilities for diagnosis and treatment?
- What are the costs and benefits?
- Which subgroups should be screened?
- How often should screening take place?

Legislation and statutory compensation

Essential legislative provisions in the United Kingdom and the European Union are comprehensive. Ten types of cancer are prescribed diseases and are eligible for industrial injuries benefit. Some cancers are reportable under the Reporting of Injuries, Diseases, and Dangerous Occurrence Regulations 1995 (RIDDOR), although many occur in those who have retired. Most occupational cancers recorded or eligible for benefit are mesotheliomas. In 2000, 652 people received benefits in the United Kingdom for mesothelioma, which is less than half the number of deaths recorded as caused by this disease (1595 deaths in 1999). About 80 people with other occupational cancers receive benefits each year, these being split between bladder cancer and asbestos related lung cancer. Bladder cancers have slowly increased over the past decade, whereas lung cancers have decreased. The figure for asbestos related lung cancers substantially under-represents the true number.

Specific carcinogens

Metals and metalliferous compounds
Arsenic, beryllium, cadmium, chromium(VI), nickel, and iron are considered to be proven human carcinogens, either as the metal itself or as a derivative. The risk from iron is related only to mining the base ore and is caused by coincidental exposure to radon gas. In foundries, where there is concomitant exposure to several agents in a complex mix of emanating fume, the responsible agents are not clearly defined.

With all the metallic carcinogens, the lung is the main target organ, but other potential sites are shown in the table. The main occupational exposures occur in the mining, smelting, founding, and refining of these metals, and less commonly in secondary industrial use.

Aromatic amines
Aromatic amines are among the best known and most studied of chemical carcinogens. The bladder is the main target organ, but any site on the urothelial tract composed of transitional cell epithelium can be affected—that is, from the renal pelvis to the prostatic urethra. Tumours of the upper urothelial tract (renal pelvis or ureter) are very rare, and a cluster of these signal tumours usually heralds an underlying risk of occupational cancer. The carcinogenic potential of aromatic amines lies not in the parent compound but in a metabolite formed in the liver and excreted through the urinary system.

The occupations classically associated with risk from these chemicals were in the industries' manufacturing chemicals and dyestuffs. In the early 1950s an investigation of bladder cancers in workers in British chemical industries showed that individuals exposed to benzidine and 2-napthylamine had a 30 times greater risk of developing bladder cancer than the general population. Occupational bladder cancer became a prescribed disease in 1953.

Antioxidants contaminated with β-Naphthylamine were used in the rubber and cable making industries until the end of 1949 (when they were universally withdrawn), and they caused an excess of bladder cancer. The level of contamination was only about 0.25%, yet it almost doubled the risk for the workforce so exposed. People who started work in the rubber industry after 1951 seem to have no excess risk.

There is now increasing evidence that some polycyclic aromatic hydrocarbons can act as urinary tract carcinogens.

Benefits and disadvantages of screening
Benefits
- Improved prognosis for some cases detected by screening
- Less radical treatment for some early cases
- Reassurance for those with negative test results

Disadvantages
- Longer morbidity for cases whose prognosis is unaltered
- Over treatment of questionable abnormalities
- False reassurance for those with false negative results
- Anxiety and sometimes morbidity for those with false positive results
- Unnecessary medical intervention for those with false positive results
- Hazard of screening test
- Resource costs: diversion of scarce resources to screening programme

---

Main legislative provisions in the United Kingdom
- Control of Substances Hazardous to Health (COSHH) Regulations 2002 and associated approved code of practice on the Control of Carcinogens
- European Commission Carcinogens Directive (90/934/EEC)
- Chemical Agents Directive (98/24/EC)
- Chemicals (Hazard Information and Packaging) Regulations 1999 (CHIP)
- Ionising Radiations Regulations (1999)
- Control of Asbestos at Work Regulations (1998)
- Reporting of Injuries, Diseases, and Dangerous Occurrences Regulations (RIDDOR) 1995

Metalliferous carcinogens

Agent	Target organ
Arsenic	Lung and skin
Beryllium	Lung
Cadmium	Lung, prostate gland
Chromium (hexavalent)	Lung
Nickel	Lung, nasal sinuses
Iron in:	
Haematite mining (radon)	Lung
Iron and steel founding	Lung, digestive tract

Aromatic amine carcinogens
Proved
- 4-Aminobiphenyl (xenylamine) and its nitro derivatives
- β-Naphthylamine
- Benzidine
- Auramine and magenta

Probable
- Polycyclic aromatic hydrocarbons

Possible
- The hardener MbOCA (4,4-methylene-bis-(2-chloroaniline))

This is reflected in excesses seen in aluminium refiners and in painters exposed to solvents.

Asbestos

Few natural materials used in industry have been the subject of more epidemiological and pathological research than the fibrous mineral, asbestos. Lung cancer because of asbestos was first reported in the 1930s and its association was confirmed in the 1950s. In 1960, Wagner and colleagues reported 33 cases of the "rare" tumour mesothelioma in workers exposed to asbestos in South Africa.

In asbestos workers who have developed asbestosis the risk of lung cancer is increased at least five times. For chrysotile there is a linear relationship between exposure and risk of lung cancer. Each additional fibre exposure (every ml a year) is equivalent to a 1% increase in the standardised mortality ratio.

Between 0.6% and 40% of lung cancers have been attributed to occupation, depending on place and time. Chlormethylesters, used in ion exchange resins, increase the risk of lung cancer 20 times and have a short latent period of 10-15 years. The type of cancer is small cell, also caused by uranium and beryllium (which also causes adenocarcinoma). Painters have a 30-100% increase in lung cancer. This may be caused by heavy metal salts or chromates, organic solvents, or exposure to silica and asbestos.

Over 40% of people with asbestosis die of lung cancer, and 10% die of mesothelioma. Mesotheliomas, which are predominantly of the pleura (ratio of 8:1 with peritoneum), have usually been growing for 10 to 12 years before becoming clinically evident. This latency can be very long—often 30 years and sometimes up to 50 years. However, median survival from the time of initial diagnosis is usually short—three to 12 months.

The amphibole fibres in crocidolite (blue asbestos) and amosite (brown asbestos) carry the greatest risk of causing mesothelioma, but the serpentine fibres in chrysotile (white asbestos) can also do so, especially if they contain tremolite. In about 90% of patients with mesothelioma, close questioning will usually show some earlier exposure to asbestos. The possible risk to neighbourhoods outside asbestos factories from discharged asbestos dust or contaminated clothing brought home should not be forgotten.

The annual number of deaths from mesothelioma has increased rapidly from 153 in 1968 to 1595 in 1999. The latest projections suggest that male deaths from mesothelioma may peak in about 2011, at about 1700 deaths every year. Occupations with the highest risk of mesothelioma for men include metal plate workers (including shipyard workers), vehicle body builders (including rail vehicles), plumbers and gas fitters, carpenters, and electricians.

Occupations causally associated with urothelial tract cancers

- Dyestuffs and pigment manufacture
- Rubber workers (in tyre, tube, and cable making before 1950)
- Textile dyeing and printing
- Manufacture of some chemicals (such as 4,4-methylene-bis-(2-chloroaniline) (MbOCA))
- Gas workers (in old vertical retort houses)
- Laboratory and testing work (using chromogens)
- Rodent controllers (formally using (alpha)-naphthylthiourea)
- Painters
- Leather workers
- Manufacture of patent fuel (such as coke) and firelighters
- Tar and pitch workers (roofing and road maintenance)
- Aluminium refining

Asbestos related cancers

- Lung
- Malignant mesothelioma—most commonly of pleura, occasionally peritoneal, and rarely of pericardium
- Larynx
- Possibly gastrointestinal tract

Smoking and asbestos

Asbestos	Tobacco	Lung cancer rate per 100 000
−	−	11
+	−	58
−	+	123
+	+	590

Smoking with concomitant exposure to asbestos greatly increases the risk of developing lung cancer: compared with non-smokers not exposed to asbestos, a smoker exposed to asbestos has a 75-100 times greater risk if exposure was sufficient to cause asbestosis, otherwise the risk is about 30-50 times higher. This multiplicative theory on effects of asbestos exposure and smoking, however, has recently been disputed

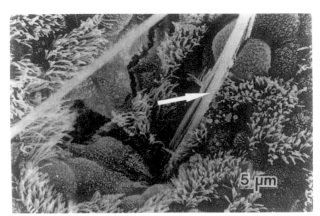

Blue asbestos

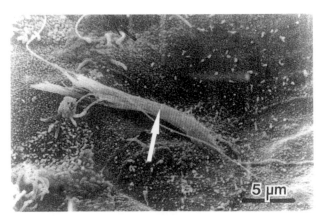

White asbestos

Asbestos legislation

Asbestos is controlled in the United Kingdom by three complementary sets of regulations:

- **The Asbestos (Licensing) Regulations** (amended 1998) require work with the most dangerous types of asbestos (coating, lagging, and asbestos insulating board) to be carried out only by contractors who have a licence issued by the Health and Safety Executive
- **The Control of Asbestos at Work Regulations** (amended 1998) lay down the practices that must be followed for all work with asbestos, including that which requires a licence. Employers must prevent the exposure of employees to asbestos or, where this is not reasonably practicable, reduce exposure to a level that is as low as possible
- **The Asbestos (Prohibitions) Regulations** (amended 1999) prohibit the importation into the United Kingdom, and the supply and use within Great Britain, of amphibole asbestos—crocidolite (blue) asbestos and amosite (brown) asbestos—and, since 1999, of chrysotile (white) asbestos

The supply and fitting of vehicle brake linings containing asbestos is prohibited in **The Road Vehicles (Brake Linings Safety) Regulations 1999**, and the European Union has amended the **Marketing and Use Directive (76/769/EEC)**, which prohibits the marketing and use of chrysotile asbestos throughout the EU after 1 January 2005, with one derogation for diaphragms for the chlor-alkali process

Forthcoming legislation will require employers to manage the risk from asbestos in non-domestic premises

The latest amendments to the Control of Asbestos at Work Regulations 1987 (which came into force in 1999) target workers who come across asbestos accidentally, such as electricians, plumbers, other maintenance workers, and demolition workers. The Amendment Regulations also tighten the law on control of exposure to asbestos by lowering the action level and the control limit for chrysotile

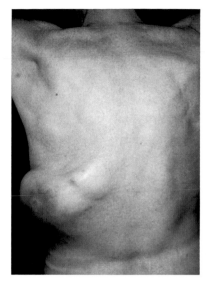

Mesothelioma extending through needle biopsy tract

Occupations involving exposure to asbestos

- Manufacture of asbestos products
- Thermal and fire insulation (lagging, delagging)
- Construction and demolition work
- Shipbuilding and repair (welders, metal plate workers)
- Building maintenance and repair
- Manufacture of gas masks (in second world war)
- Plumbers and gasfitters
- Vehicle body builders
- Electricians, carpenters, and upholsterers
- Armed forces (historical)

Tyndall beam photography showing asbestos fibres released by handling of asbestos boards (left), emphasising the need for proper protection when dealing with asbestos (right)

Ultraviolet radiation

Ultraviolet radiation from exposure to sunlight causes both melanotic and non-melanotic skin cancers (basal cell and squamous cell carcinomas), but an excess of skin cancers in outdoor workers is seen only in those with fair skin. Initial presentation may be that of solar keratoses or a premalignant state. Immunosuppression can increase the risk; other possible additive factors are trauma, heat, and chronic irritation or infection.

Premalignant melanosis (lentigo maligna) in a man who retired after a lifetime of working outdoors

Mineral oils

The classic epithelioma of the scrotum or groin caused by contact with mineral oil is rarely seen today, but these tumours can appear at other sites (such as arms and hands) if contamination with oil persists.

Other occupational carcinogens

Ionising radiation is a carcinogen at low doses (0.2 gray or a dose rate of 0.05 mSv per min). Cancer or hereditary defects are known as stochastic effects and can only be minimised. Cataract, sterility, and skin disorders are deterministic effects and can be prevented by keeping exposure below threshold. The recommended dose limit is 20 mSv a year averaged over five years for occupational exposures and 1 mSv for the public.

Epithelioma of groin caused by past exposure to mineral oil

Proven human carcinogens

Miscellaneous proved human carcinogens	Site of cancer
Aluminium production	Lung, bladder, skin
Benzene in petroleum associated industries	Haemopoietic
Bis-(chloromethyl)-ether in production of ion exchange resin	Lung
Benzene and leather dust in boot and shoe making and repair	Haemopoietic, nasal
Polycyclic aromatic hydrocarbons and aromatic amines in coal gasification and coke production	Lung, bladder, skin
Coal tars and pitch in roofing and road maintenance	Lung, bladder, skin
Ethylene oxide as medical steriliser and chemical intermediary	Lung, bladder, skin
Formaldehyde and hardwood dust in furniture and cabinet making	Nasal, paranasal
Isopropyl alcohol manufacture	Nasal, paranasal
Mineral and shale oils in engineering and metal machining, past exposure to mule spinning in cotton industry and jute processing	Skin, scrotum
Solvents and pigments in painting and decorating	Lung, bladder, stomach, oesophagus
Mists of strong inorganic acid (sulphuric acid) in acid pickling and soap making	Nasal, larynx
Radon in underground mines	Lung
Soots from chimney sweeping and flue maintenance	Lung, skin
Antineoplastic agents	Bladder, haemopoietic

Frieben documented the first case of skin cancer on the hand of an *x* ray tube factory worker in 1902. Cancer risk estimates on nuclear workers are still not conclusive, and the Gardener hypothesis that the children of radiation workers have an increased risk of leukaemia has not been supported. However, incidence may be increased in emergency workers. The epidemiological evidence from studies concerning airline crew who may receive the equivalent of 100 mSv over a 20 year period from cosmic radiation are inconclusive. No excess cancer has been reported among therapeutic or diagnostic radiologists.

All studies on electromagnetic radiation show inconsistencies and seldom indicate dose-response trends. This may mean that there is no association between electromagnetic fields and cancer, or that there is a risk but studies have not been able to show it. Particular aspects studied so far have been leukaemia, brain cancer, male breast cancer, electrical workers, and welders, but a broader research hypothesis is needed.

Studies of manmade mineral fibres have looked only at small exposures in terms of fibres and years of exposure. An increased risk of lung cancer was found in rock wool workers but it was not possible to conclude that it was caused by manmade mineral fibres. No risk was found in glass wool or glass filament workers. Five deaths from mesothelioma have

Further reading

- McDonald C, ed. Occupational cancer. In: *Epidemiology of work-related diseases*, 2nd ed. London: BMJ Books, 2000. *Excellent review of occupational cancer epidemiology and the evidence for it*
- HSE. *Health and Safety Statistics 2000/01 Part 2: Occupational ill-health statistics.* Sudbury: HSE Books, 2001. *Comprehensive summary of UK occupational cancer statistics*
- Venitt S, Harrington JM, Boffetta P, Saracci R. Occupational cancer. In: Baxter BJ, Adams PH, Aw TC, Cockcroft A, Harrington JM, eds. *Hunter's diseases of occupations*, 9th ed. London: Edward Arnold, 2000:623-88. *Definitive in depth text on occupational cancer*
- IARC. Monographs on the evaluation of carcinogenic risks to humans. Volumes 1-79. Lyons: International Agency for Research on Cancer, 1972-2001. http://monographs.iarc.fr/ *Comprehensive highly detailed studies of chemicals and processes thought to cause cancer*
- Wilson JMJ, Jungner G. Principles and practice of screening for disease. WHO Public Health Paper 1968;34
- Donaldson LJ, Donaldson RJ. *The promotion of health in essential public health*, 2nd ed. Newbury: Petroc Press, 1999. *Public health textbook*
- Peckham MJ. *Oxford textbook of oncology.* Oxford: Oxford University Press, 2002. *Up to date oncology bible*

been found in various cohorts, but at least three of these workers may have previously been exposed to asbestos.

There is sufficient evidence for the carcinogenicity of inhaled crystalline silica in the form of quartz or cristobalite. Studies show the Bradford-Hill criteria of temporality, consistency, exposure-response gradients, and convergence with experimental and clinical evidence. Measures to prevent silicosis are likely to reduce lung cancer risk.

The box showing criteria for screening is adapted from Wilson JM, Jungner G. *Principles and practice of screening for disease.* WHO Public Health Paper 1968;34. The table showing levels of prevention is adapted from Donaldson LJ and Donnaldson RJ. *The promotion of health in essential public health*, 2nd ed. Newbury: Petroc Press, 1999.

16   Occupational dermatoses

Ian R White

Skin disorders are among the most often encountered problems in the occupational health setting, and although there are many dermatoses that have occupational relevance, the overwhelming majority are dermatitic. In the United Kingdom, in the period 1998-2000, of the estimated 4540 workers each year with work related skin disease seen by specialist physicians, about 80% were diagnosed as having contact dermatitis. Occupations considered to be at greatest risk are hairdressers and barbers, grinding machine setters and operators, galvanisers, rubber process operatives, and printers.

Contact dermatitis

In current terminology the term "dermatitis" is used synonymously with "eczema" to describe inflammatory reactions in the skin with a spectrum of clinical and histopathological characteristics.

A dermatitis may be entirely endogenous (constitutional) or entirely exogenous (contact). The latter consists of irritant and allergic contact reactions. Commonly, a dermatitis has a multifactoral aetiology and may be aggravated by the presence of pathogens (for example, *Staphylococcus aureus*). Assessment of the relative importance (contribution) of the possible factors can be difficult and subjective. Atopic hand dermatitis and vesicular hand dermatitis are examples of endogenous conditions.

An occupational dermatitis is one where the inflammatory reaction is caused entirely by occupational contact factors or where such agents contribute to the reaction on a compromised skin—that is, they are partially responsible.

In most cases, an occupationally related dermatitis will affect the hands alone or there may be spread onto the forearms. Occasionally, the face may be the prime site of dermatitis (for example, with airborne agents); other sites may be affected.

Irritant contact dermatitis

This is initiated by direct chemical or physical damage to the skin. All individuals are susceptible to the development of an irritant contact dermatitis if exposure to the irritant (toxic) agent or agents is sufficient. It occurs particularly where the stratum corneum is thinnest. Hence, it is often seen in the finger webs and on the backs of the hands, rather than on the palms. Irritant contact dermatitis is of two principal types: acute and chronic. The former is caused by exposure to an agent(s) causing early impairment in stratum corneum function followed by an inflammatory reaction. The latter is caused by repeated exposure to the same or different factors, resulting in "cumulative" damage until an inflammatory reaction ensues and persists for a prolonged period, even after further exposure is stopped. Those with a history of atopic eczema, and especially atopic hand eczema, are at particular risk of developing chronic irritant contact dermatitis. Chronic irritant contact dermatitis is particularly seen in "wet work."

Wet work, solvents, detergents, soluble coolants, vegetable juices, wet cement, low relative humidity, and occlusive gloves are all examples of common irritants.

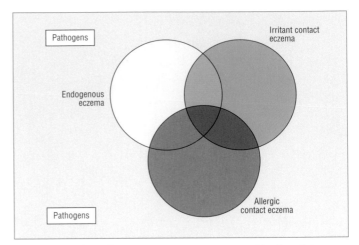

Dermatitis may be endogenous or exogenous, or a combination of these, and may be aggravated by pathogens

Indications for occupational cause of dermatitis

- A dermatitis first occurred while employed
- There is a history of aggravation by work
- There may be, at least initially, improvement (or clearance) when not at work
- There is exposure to irritant factors or potential allergens
- Work is in an "at risk" occupation

Irritant contact dermatitis

Acute
- Severity of reaction depends on "dose" of irritant agent
- "Chapping" can be considered a minor form, with a "chemical burn" (for example, cement burn) being an extreme event.
- Intermediate eczematous reactions are common; minor reactions are very common
- May occur on the face—for example, low humidity occupational dermatosis, airborne irritant vapours
- Once the irritant factor(s) has been removed, resolution is usually spontaneous without important sequelae

Chronic
- A persistent dermatitis and the most common cause of continued disability from occupational skin disease
- Problem continues for long periods even with avoidance of aggravating factors
- Re-exposure to even minor irritant factors may cause a rapid flare
- Even after apparent healing there may be an indefinitely increased susceptibility to recurrence of a dermatitis after irritant exposure

Examples of common occupational allergens

- Biocides—for example, formaldehyde, methyldibromo-glutaronitrile, methylchloroisothiazolinone
- Hairdressing chemicals—for example, *p*-phenylenediamine
- Chromate (leather, cement)
- Rubber accelerating chemicals—for example, thiurams, carbamates, mercaptobenzothiazole
- Epoxy resin monomers (plastics manufacturing, electrical manufacture)
- Plant allergens—for example, sesquiterpene lactones (horticulture)

Listing of ingredients

All cosmetic (skin care) products in Europe have full ingredient listing on the product packaging, with uniform nomenclature. Skin cleansers, barrier creams, and after work creams are legally cosmetic products. Labelling permits tracing of sources of exposure to allergens. However, there is a lack of meaningful ingredient labelling on other types of consumer and industrial products.

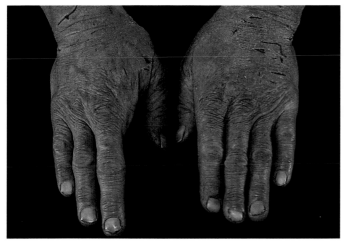

Lichenified and fissured eczema on hands of bricklayer resulting from chronic irritant dermatitis. Patch tests were negative, and he was not sensitive to chromate

Allergic contact dermatitis

This is a manifestation of a type IV (delayed) hypersensitivity reaction. An allergic contact dermatitis will develop at the site of skin contact with the allergen, but secondary spread may occur. Contaminated hands may spread the allergen to "non-exposed" sites. Trivial or occult contact with an allergen may result in the persistence of a dermatitis; some allergens are "ubiquitous."

Presentation of an allergic reaction has two phases: induction and elicitation. Even with potent experimental allergens there is a minimum period of about 10 days from the first exposure to the immunological acquisition of hypersensitivity. The probability of developing hypersensitivity depends on the sensitising capacity of the chemical and exposure to it. Exposure is assessed in terms of dose every unit area applied to the skin. Most potential allergens on the consumer and industrial market have a low intrinsic allergenic potential, but there are important exceptions, including some biocides (preservatives). Contact allergens tend to be low molecular weight (< 600) and capable of forming covalent bonds with carrier proteins in the skin. It is not possible to determine an individual's susceptibility to the development of contact allergy. Hypersensitivity is specific to a particular molecule or to molecules bearing similar allergenic sites. Although hypersensitivity may be lost over a long time, once acquired it should be considered to last indefinitely.

Management of occupational dermatitis

- An understanding of the patient's job is essential. A job title is not sufficient for this understanding: the question to be asked is not "what do you do?" but "what do you actually do and how do you do it?" The title "engineer" carries a multiple of descriptions ranging from the desk bound professional to the lathe worker exposed to soluble coolants.

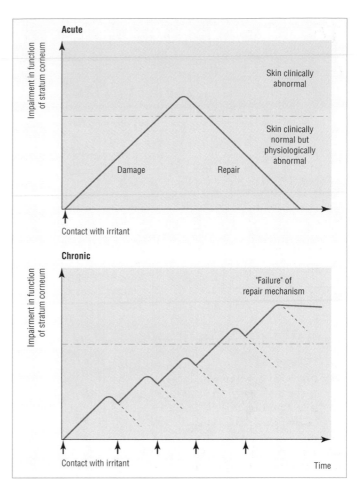

Development of acute (top) and chronic (bottom) irritant contact dermatitis

Relevance of contact allergens

- **C**urrent: exposure is causing dermatitis or is aggravating it
- **O**ld: past history of exposure but no current exposure
- **D**on't know: unknown whether there is current exposure to the allergen or whether exposure is important to the dermatitis
- **E**xposure: must have occurred but no history of it

Sheeted eczema over the dorsal aspect of the hand and up to the forearm, resulting from allergic contact dermatitis to a carbamate accelerator in protective rubber gloves

From the job description, it will be possible to estimate sources of excessive contact with potentially irritant contact factors or allergens. The provision of material safety data sheets may be helpful in this evaluation, although the information that they contain is often superficial, generic, and is that required for regulatory requirements. A site visit to watch the worker working may be necessary.

- The history and anatomical distribution of the dermatitis may provide clues as to the aetiology.
- Irritant contact dermatitis may occur as "epidemics" in a workplace if hygiene has failed. Allergic contact dermatitis is usually sporadic in a workplace.
- The evaluation of irritant factors is always subjective. Evaluation of allergic contact factors is objective and provided only by diagnostic patch test investigations. Properly performed, patch tests will show the presence or absence of relevant allergens.
- Patch testing is the only method for the objective evaluation of a dermatitis; however, there are major pitfalls in the use of this essential tool, so adequate training and experience is necessary if it is to be used properly. The ability to assess relevance of allergens is central.
- A competent assessment requires all of the above followed by recommendations on reducing or stopping exposure to the offending agent(s) and similar ones.
- The diagnosis of an occupational dermatitis should describe thoroughly the nature of the condition with due regard to any endogenous or aggravating factors. A general practitioner's entry in a medical record of "Works in a factory, contact dermatitis. 2/52" is inadequate as a description of an important disease process, and it can have profound implications on the patient's concept of his problem and employment.
- Delays in diagnosis resulting in continued exposure to relevant irritants or allergens can adversely affect the prognosis.
- Early referral to an appropriate dermatology department is necessary for a comprehensive assessment of a suspected occupational dermatitis; improper assessment can have devastating effects on future employment prospects for the individual, with important medicolegal implications. If in doubt, the patient should be referred.

Rubber latex protein sensitivity

Of continuing concern is the immediate type 1 hypersensitivity reaction to proteins present in natural rubber latex used to make gloves and other items. This should be differentiated from irritant contact dermatitis and allergic contact dermatitis, which can also be attributed to chemical agents used in latex products, particularly gloves.

Prevalence and incidence of sensitivity to rubber latex proteins remain unquantified. The prevalence in the general population is thought to be less than 1%, but is likely to be higher within certain risk groups. A prevalence of 2.8-17% has been reported in healthcare workers, and in other occupations where workers are regularly exposed to rubber latex (hairdressers, greenhouse workers, housekeeping staff, and glove factory workers) the frequency of allergy has been reported as ranging from 5-11%.

At particular risk are people with spina bifida (prevalence reported to be 18-65%), atopic individuals, and individuals with certain food allergies (for example, to avocado, chestnut or banana, and kiwi fruit).

Rubber latex protein sensitivity can result in reactions including urticaria, rhinitis, and asthma. The latter is more

The primary prevention of occupational dermatitis is aimed at providing appropriate information and protection

- Awareness by employer and employee of the potential risks of exposure
- Education on the necessity of good occupational hygiene precautions
- Adequate provision of suitable and effective means of reducing exposure
- Awareness of the limitations of personal protection devices

It is not possible to be definitive about aetiology from the distribution and morphology of a dermatitis on the hands. For example, vesicular hand dermatitis with a "classical" endogenous distribution may be mimicked by an allergic contact dermatitis to isothiazolinone biocides or chromate sensitivity. *It is a major error to rely on patterns of hand dermatitis in making a diagnosis*

Patch testing

- Properly performed requires expertise, time, and proper facilities
- Difficult to undertake adequately in the workplace. There are no short cuts
- Primarily a hospital based procedure
- Should be performed only by those with appropriate training who can prescribe an appropriately comprehensive screen, know what not to test, know what to dilute for testing, can competently read the reactions, and can give authoritative advice after interpretation of the reactions
- Anyone can patch test; few do it well. If you don't know how to do it, don't do it

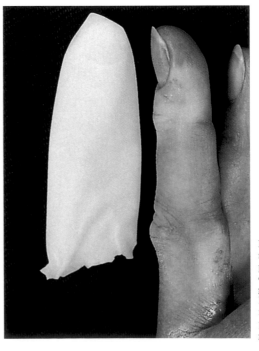

Immediate contact reaction to latex proteins in examination gloves. Type 1 hypersensitivity reactions to latex proteins are of growing concern

common when starch powdered gloves have been used. In the healthcare setting, gloves made from rubber latex are likely to be the main cause of sensitisation in staff, as well as the main cause of symptoms in those who are allergic. Therefore, prevention includes clear policy regarding the type of glove used. If latex gloves are to be used, powdered rubber latex gloves should not be used, and extractable protein levels in latex gloves must be as low as possible, as should the level of allergenic protein residues. Staff with known sensitivity should be provided with non-latex alternatives.

A definitive demonstration of hypersensitivity can be made by skin prick testing with the water soluble proteins. Commercial preparations are available; the proteins can also be eluted from a suspect rubber item. Radioallergosorbent tests are less sensitive.

Other occupational dermatoses

- Contact urticaria—type I hypersensitivity reaction—for example, natural rubber latex protein
- Chloracne (halogenacne)—acneiform eruption caused by certain halogenated aromatic hydrocarbons; a symptom of systemic absorption
- Oil folliculitis (oil acne)—irritant effect of neat petroleum oils localised to hair follicles
- Depigmentation (leukoderma)—caused by hydroquinone and phenol derivatives
- Hyperpigmentation—caused by mineral oils, halogenated hydrocarbons, photodynamic actions of psoralenes and tar products
- Skin cancer (see chapter 15)
- Skin infections (see chapter 14)

Further reading

- Beach J. The problem with material safety data sheets. *Occup Med* 2002;52:67-8
- Wakelin SH, White IR. Natural rubber latex allergy. *Clin Exp Dermatol* 1999;24:245-8
- Smith HR, Armstrong DK, Wakelin SH, Rycroft RJ, White IR, McFadden JP. Descriptive epidemiology of hand dermatitis at the St John's contact dermatitis clinic 1983-97. *Br J Dermatol* 2000;142:284-7
- Robinson MK, Gerberick GF, Ryan CA, McNamee P, White IR, Basketter DA. The importance of exposure estimation in the assessment of skin sensitization risk. *Contact Dermatitis* 2000;42:251-9
- Rycroft RJG, Menne T, Frosch PJ, Lepoittevin J-P, eds. *Textbook of contact dermatitis*, 3rd ed. Berlin: Springer-Verlag, 2001
- Kanerva L, Elsner P, Wahlberg JE, Maibach HI, eds. *Handbook of Occupational Dermatology.* Springer, 2000
- The monthly journal *Contact Dermatitis* (Blackwell Science Ltd) publishes papers and case reports on matters relevant to occupational dermatology

17 Work, genetics, and reproduction

Nicola Cherry

The sequencing of the human genome, and the intense interest that accompanied this achievement, again raised issues surrounding the interaction of genetic and environmental exposures in causing disease. Even where exposures at work and in the environment have been clearly shown to be related to specific pathologies, and preventive measures initiated, the question of genetic susceptibility remains: why do only some of those exposed develop the disease? Understanding of such susceptibility will seldom exclude workers, but it may improve understanding of the mechanisms by which disease occurs, and suggest approaches to prevention or treatment.

There is also concern that occupational or environmental exposures may affect subsequent generations through changes to stem cells; by this means an infant born to such a parent may be at greater risk of disease even if exposure of the parent ceased long before the child was conceived. Evidence from human studies of occupational exposure affecting the genetic blueprint of the next generation is sparse and controversial, but pressing questions remain about whether such exposures can cause infertility, affect the outcome of pregnancy, or influence the development of the infant in later life.

In all these areas—genetic susceptibility, genetic alteration, and reproductive health—exposures in the working population may be of particular concern because exposures tend to be greater than in the general population, a large proportion of those exposed are of reproductive age, and any exposure effects that are found are, in principle, preventable. Environmental exposures to the general public (including the very young, and pregnant or nursing mothers) through contaminants in food, water, and air may also be suspected of affecting reproductive health. For example, even trace amounts of chemicals affecting the endocrine system of pregnant women may be responsible for the increased rate of testicular cancer seen in many societies.

Work and genetics

Why should occupational health professionals be concerned with the genetic make up of people in the workforce or who seek to join it? Firstly, in some, genetic inheritance, even in the absence of a specific occupational exposure, will lead to disease that will put at risk themselves, their fellow workers, or the general public. For example, a worker genetically programmed to develop Huntington's disease, if employed as a driver of a high speed train, may put the public at risk in the early stages of the disease before a diagnosis can be made that permits redeployment or retirement on medical grounds. Secondly, some genetic conditions render a person unable to tolerate work environments that can be tolerated by other workers. For example, deep sea diving may induce a crisis in a worker carrying the gene for sickle cell disease and, as a result, the worker and others may be put at peril. Thirdly, a particular genetic variant (or polymorphism) or a combination of variants may carry a risk of ill health if a worker is exposed to a chemical that is detoxified by the enzyme produced by the gene. The case of slow acetylators is a well known example. Where such a disease is a serious threat to quality of life or life

Genetic testing

- Can identify a predisposition to illness—for example, thalassaemia, Huntington's disease, sickle cell disease
- Could be used for genetic monitoring—for example, exposure to radiation or polycyclic aromatic hydrocarbons
- Has been used for estimation of fitness to work (exclusion or protection)—for example, exclusion of those with sickle cell trait from flying, diving and compressed air work, and exclusion of those with glucose-6-phosphate dehydrogenase deficiency from work involving naphthalene or trinitrotoluene, and cultivation or processing of broad beans
- Has been proposed as a way to:
  - predict the likelihood of common diseases (diabetes, schizophrenia—for example) that might raise sickness absence rates or medical costs to employers
  - identify resistant individuals (rapid acetylators—for example) who could, in theory, be exposed without harm to higher concentrations of toxic chemicals

Genetic testing or screening in an occupational context is clearly beset with problems of ethics, effectiveness, and practicality

Genetic information

- Is a unique identifier
- Can be done on a small sample
- Can be done covertly, without consent
- Can be used for prediction
- Is of interest to employers, insurance companies, and relatives
- Has potential commercial value (patents)
- Can outlast the source
- Can define susceptible groups
- Can be used for purposes other than those for which it was collected

Statement of the Nuffield Council on Bioethics 1993

Genetic screening of employees for increased occupational risks ought only to be contemplated where:

(i) Strong evidence exists of a clear connection between the working environment and the development of the condition for which genetic testing can be conducted
(ii) The condition in question is one that seriously endangers the health of the employee or is one in which an affected employee is likely to present a serious danger to third parties
(iii) The condition is one for which the dangers cannot be eliminated or significantly reduced by reasonable measures taken by the employer to modify or respond to the environmental risks

itself, it may be tempting to consider introducing screening to monitor such workers and exclude them from exposure. The balance of opinion, however, is that such screening for genetic susceptibility is seldom, if ever, justified from either an ethical or a practical standpoint.

A further issue is whether the potential for a substance to cause mutation (and ultimately cancer) can be monitored through the formation of "adducts" when a chemical binds to DNA after exposure (for example, to polycyclic aromatic hydrocarbons) and can be measured in cells obtained from a routine blood sample. Those with the highest number of adducts may be thought to be at the greatest risk of developing cancer, either because their exposures have indeed been higher (perhaps because of poor environmental controls) or because a finding of a particularly high level of adducts may in itself be an indication of an inherent inability to detoxify a particular mutagen (or to repair damage when it occurs). Given the wide variation in adducts in the same individual measured on separate occasions and the uncertainty in interpreting such measures in assessing the risk of cancer in later years, the routine use of DNA adducts as exposure effect markers for individual workers may not be defensible. However, occupational health professionals need to understand the potential importance of such measures, as evidence of a relevant mechanism (that is, the formation of adducts) is already being used by the International Agency for Research on Cancer in the designation of chemicals as carcinogens (for example, ethylene oxide).

Genetic analysis may also have a place in the attribution of causality after disease has occurred. Mutations in the suppressor gene *p53* have been found in most types of cancer; in individual cases, it may be helpful to consider whether the mutation observed is one that occurs more often in tumours associated with one type of exposure, increasing the post facto probability that this is the exposure that was responsible. In epidemiological studies, where an excess of ill health is observed but the importance of exposure is uncertain, showing that those with a genetic susceptibility to the exposure are more likely to develop the disease may again shift the balance towards acceptance of causality.

Genetics and reproduction

The time window for genetic damage in reproductive stem cells differs markedly between men and women. In women, ova that will be available for fertilisation in adulthood go through most phases of development while the fetus is in utero. The implication is that genetic changes to the ovum that will affect children born to the woman will be caused by exposures to the grandmother while she was pregnant. In practice, there is little evidence that this does occur (at least for occupational exposures). In men, by contrast, damage to stem cells that may affect the genetic complement of the resulting child can happen at any time, from in utero exposure to the point at which production of the sperm occurs. There is then a further three month window for adverse environmental effects as the sperm that will eventually fertilise the ovum moves through its final stages of development. Although the time period of opportunity for damage is much greater for men, and the protection from external influences is less stringent than in utero, the evidence of such effects from occupational exposure in humans is sparse.

Finally, environmental exposures in utero have been suspected to cause childhood cancers, although the best evidence for this again comes from pharmaceutical products—mothers' use of diethylstilboestrol—for example,

Statement of the Human Genetics Advisory Committee 1995

(i) An individual should not be required to take a genetic test for employment purposes—an individual's "right not to know" their genetic constitution should be upheld

(ii) An individual should not be required to disclose the results of a previous genetic test unless there is clear evidence that the information it provides is needed to assess either current ability to perform a job safely or susceptibility to harm from doing a certain job

(iii) Employers should offer a genetic test (where available) if it is known that a specific working environment or practice, while meeting health and safety requirements, might pose specific risks to individuals with particular genetic variations. For certain jobs where issues of public safety arise, an employer should be able to refuse to employ a person who refuses to take a relevant genetic test

(iv) Any genetic test used for employment purposes must be subject to assured levels of accuracy and reliability, reflecting best practice. We recommend that any use of genetic testing should be evidence based and consensual. Results of any tests undertaken should always be communicated to the person tested and professional advice should be available. Information about and resulting from the taking of any test should be treated in accordance with Data Protection principles

Furthermore, test results should be carefully interpreted, taking account of how they might be affected by working conditions, and

(v) If multiple genetic tests were to be performed simultaneously, then each test should meet the standards set out in (ii), (iii), and (iv)

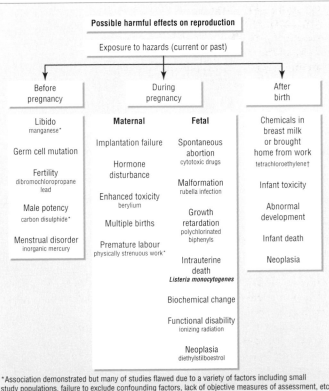

Possible harmful effects on reproduction

was responsible for vaginal cancers in female offspring as they reached adolescence and beyond. It is likely that such somatic mutations are more common than those to stem cells, which would perpetuate genetically mediated disorders through the generations.

Work and reproductive health

Although the fertility of both men and women can be adversely affected by exposure to chemical compounds (particularly certain pesticides and solvents), metals, the physical environment (heat, radiation), and other factors at work, evidence suggests that the range of exposures with such adverse reproductive effects is fairly limited. Once the fertilised ovum is implanted and begins to develop, the risk seems much greater, with exposure to chemicals, infective agents, and radiation having the capacity to interrupt fetal development during the period of organogenesis (as happened with thalidomide), to interfere with the development of the nervous system (with effects on hearing or eyesight—for example, and possibly on rates of spina bifida), or to result in retardation (not evident at birth) in the infant as it develops. Importantly, there is good epidemiological evidence that heavy physical demands at work are related to fetal death and prematurity. Few occupational cohort studies have been able to follow the offspring of workers into childhood to determine subtle effects on development that may result from exposure in utero, but if community studies of environmental exposures are correct in their interpretation, similar effects of occupational exposure would be anticipated.

Environment and reproductive health

Many of the concerns about effects on the developing infant have arisen from interpretation of community studies of the relation between exposure to lead (from flaking paint or gasoline), household pesticides (used repeatedly in poor quality housing in hot climates), and neurotoxic substances (for example, organic mercury) from diet (fish, game) or water and infant development. Of particular interest in recent years has been the suggestion that endocrine modulators from water, diet (phytoestrogens such as soya), or exposures to—for example, plasticisers such as phthalates, have effects in utero on the male fetus, leading to congenital malformations (hypospadias), low sperm count, and testicular cancer. Results of research into such effects in humans are just becoming available and are not wholly supportive of this overarching hypothesis, but the impetus arising from this elegant synthesis has pushed environmental (and occupational) reproductive health into the focus of regulators throughout the western world.

The figure showing possible harmful effects on reproduction is adapted from Barlow SM, Dayan AD, Stabile IK. Workplace exposures and reproductive effects. In: Baxter PJ, Adams PH, Aw TC, *et al.*, eds. *Hunter's diseases of occupations*. London: Edward Arnold, 2000.

Agents associated with risk to male fertility
Chemical
- Carbaryl: abnormal sperm morphology
- Carbon disulphide: oligospermia, abnormal morphology
- Chlordecone: oligospermia, reduced sperm motility, abnormal sperm morphology
- Dibromochloropropane: oligospermia/azoospermia
- Lead: oligospermia, reduced sperm motility, abnormal sperm morphology

Physical
- Heat: oligospermia
- Ionising radiation: oligospermia or azoospermia

Biological
- Mumps: oligospermia or azoospermia

Some hazards associated with adverse pregnancy outcome
Chemical
- Anaesthetic gases: spontaneous abortion, growth retardation, intrauterine death*
- Organic solvents: spontaneous abortion*
- Lead: spontaneous abortion, intrauterine death, prematurity
- Polychlorinated biphenyls (PCBs): congenital PCB syndrome

Physical
- Ionising radiation: spontaneous abortion, growth retardation, malformation of central nervous system, childhood cancer
- Heavy physical demands, shift work, extremes of temperature: spontaneous abortion, prematurity, growth retardation, intrauterine death*

Biological
- Rubella: spontaneous abortion, intrauterine death, congenital rubella syndrome
- Varicella zoster infection: neonatal infection, congenital varicella syndrome
- Parvovirus B19: hydrops fetalis, fetal loss

*The epidemiological evidence is conflicting for some of these hazards

---

Further reading
- McDonald JC, ed. *Epidemiology of work related disorders*, 2nd ed. London: BMJ Publishing 2000. *Of particular interest are chapters on work and pregnancy; occupation and infertility; and molecular assessment of exposure, effect, and effect modification*
- Rawbone RG. Future impact of genetic screening in occupational and environmental medicine. *Occup Environ Med* 1999;56:721-4
- Sharpe RM, Skakkebaek NE. Are oestrogens involved in falling sperm counts and disorders of the male reproductive tract? *Lancet* 1993;341:1392-5
- Cherry N, Mackness M, Durrington P, Povey A, Dipnall M, Smith T, et al. Paraoxonase (PON1) polymorphisms in farmers attributing ill health to sheep dip. *Lancet* 2002;359:763-4
- Information on genetic testing can be found at www.hgc.gov.uk

18 Pollution

Robert Maynard

Pollution of the air, soil, and water is a major problem in many parts of the world. In developed countries the worst excesses of industrial pollution are coming under control but have been replaced by pollutants generated by motor vehicles. In developing countries the rapid increase in industrialisation combined with the increased use of motor vehicles is producing conditions as bad, if not worse, than those seen in developed countries a century ago. Dense chemical smog is common in megacities such as Mexico City and São Paulo and is an increasing problem in many of the cities of China and India. Photochemical air pollution is a problem in the Mediterranean area; in fact, only the dense and damp smogs so characteristic of London until the 1950s seem to have disappeared. The combination of a damp, foggy climate and intensive use of soft coal in inefficient household fireplaces does not seem to have been repeated on such a scale elsewhere, although similar conditions may have occurred in Eastern European countries and in Istanbul. High concentrations of coal smoke and sulphur dioxide do occur in some Chinese cities, and forest fires have, over recent years, caused significant "haze" conditions in South East Asia.

Air pollution is not solely an outdoor problem: in many countries indoor pollution produced by the use of biomass as a fuel damages health, especially that of women and young children who may be exposed for much of a 24 hour day. The seemingly inevitable link between poverty and poor environmental conditions persists, and efforts to resolve this and instil a sense of environmental justice are only now beginning.

Air pollution is a major problem but so is pollution of water. Attention has been drawn to the contamination of drinking water with arsenic leached from soil in West Bengal. High levels of lead, nitrates, and pesticides have also been detected in drinking water in various countries. A recent problem in California has been the seepage of methyl *tert* butyl ether (MTBE) into drinking water: an ironic problem as MTBE was added to petrol as an oxygenating agent designed to reduce the production of air pollutants.

Air pollution

Air pollution is a worldwide problem. A recent publication by WHO estimated that of 17 major cities, nine had serious problems with suspended particulate matter—the WHO guideline was exceeded by more than a factor of two. The impact of air pollution on health is large: some three million deaths each year are attributed by WHO to air pollution. Of these, 2.8 million result from indoor exposure (1.9 million occurring in developing countries) and only 0.2 million occur as a result of outdoor exposure. Of these 0.2 million deaths, only 14 000 are thought to occur in developed countries. These figures are not easy to interpret. In the United Kingdom, airborne particles (PM_{10}) are thought to be associated with about 10 000 extra deaths every year. Those affected experience by far the greatest part of this exposure indoors. It is salutary to consider how much effort is put into controlling outdoor concentrations of air pollutants compared with indoor concentrations.

London street scene from 1923. The figure shows a classic London "smog"

Mixture of water vapour and smoke being emitted from an industrial site

Particulate air pollution

Until recently it was believed that airborne concentrations of particles in countries like the United Kingdom had fallen to such levels that effects on health had essentially disappeared. This is now known to be untrue.

An increase in PM_{10} of $10\,\mu g$ for every cubic metre is associated with about a 1% increase in deaths, although recent studies suggest that a lower percentage increase, perhaps 0.7%, might be more accurate. The effect on non-accidental hospital admissions is of the same degree. In a small country like the United Kingdom this leads to a large impact on health: 8100 deaths brought forward (all causes), and 10 500 hospital admissions (respiratory) either advanced in time (that is, the admission would have occurred but occurs earlier as a result of exposure to pollution) or caused de novo.

It has been argued that the extra deaths calculated in this way are merely deaths advanced by just a few days in those who are already seriously ill. This does not seem to be true, however: recent work by Schwartz has suggested that at least some of the deaths may be advanced by months. Studies in the United States have shown that living in a city with a comparatively high level of particles leads to a reduction in life expectancy.

Calculating the extent of the impact at an individual level is impossible because we do not know how many in a population are affected. If all people were affected equally, then at levels of particles found in the United Kingdom, the individual impact would be small, some days only. If, however (as is much more likely), the effect is unevenly distributed across the population, some would lose months, or even years, of life.

If this is the case in the relatively unpolluted United Kingdom then the effect in much more polluted developing countries must be large indeed. Predicting the size of the effect in developing countries is not easy as it will, in part, depend on the background prevalence of disease. Note that cardiovascular disease is increasing in some developing countries.

These calculations of the impact of particles on health have produced a revolution in thinking in inhalation toxicology. Some, being unable to understand the exact mechanism of effect, have argued that the associations are not causal. Others have, rather more usefully, set out to find the mechanism of effects, and research has flourished.

Ultrafine particles (less than 100 nm in diameter) have been suggested to play an important role. These particles contribute little to the mass concentration of the ambient aerosol but a great deal to its number concentration. The idea that the number of particles in every cubic metre of air may be more important than the mass per cubic metre has gained ground in recent years. More recently, the idea that total particle surface area per unit volume of air may be important has been discussed. If this is true then air quality standards dependent on mass measurements will need revision. The unusual and unexpected toxicological properties of ultrafine particles have been recently reviewed (see Further reading).

Photochemical air pollution

Concern about secondary pollutants generated from primary emitted pollutants by photochemical reactions began in Los Angeles in the late 1940s. Ozone is the best known photochemical air pollutant produced from nitrogen dioxide (see box) particles; other chemical species, including peroxy radicals derived from volatile organic compounds, are also important. Ozone is the classic example of a secondary air pollutant: essentially no ozone is emitted by sources of outdoor air pollution.

Ozone is a strong oxidising agent and at concentrations above 100 parts per billion $(200\,\mu g/m^3)$ produces inflammation of

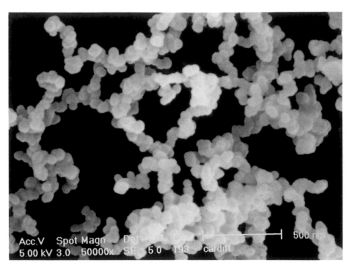

Electron micrograph of diesel particles. Individual particles are about 25 nm in diameter. Photograph kindly provided by Professor RJ Richards, Cardiff University

Modern epidemiological techniques employing time series analysis have shown that day to day variations in outdoor mass concentrations of particles are related to daily counts of events including deaths, hospital admissions, general practitioner consultations, and days of restricted activity

New trends in research on particulate air pollution

- Effects are not limited to the respiratory system; effects on the cardiovascular system are likely to be more important
- Small particles (less than 2.5 μm in diameter) are likely to play an important role
- The production of free radicals, perhaps as a result of metals acting as catalysts, is likely to be important
- Changes in the control of the heart's beat to beat interval and in the production of clotting factors may be important

Ozone production reactions

$$NO_2 + h\nu \rightarrow NO + O^{\bullet}$$
$$O^{\bullet} + O_2 \rightarrow O_3$$
$$RO_2 + NO \rightarrow NO_2 + RO$$

It will be appreciated that as long as sunlight (represented by $h\nu$), oxygen, nitrogen dioxide, and peroxy radicals (RO_2, produced from volatile organic compounds emitted by motor vehicles) are present, ozone production will continue. The reactions stop at night and levels of ozone fall, to build up again the next day. Ozone is thus a problem in cities with heavy traffic and bright sunlight: Athens, Los Angeles, and Mexico City are examples. In the United Kingdom ozone is a greater problem in rural than in urban areas, the formative reactions taking place in polluted air masses drifting from the city to the countryside

the respiratory tract. This is reflected in a reduction in the forced expiratory volume in one second and peak expiratory flow rate. Pain on deep inspiration occurs and these effects lead, unsurprisingly, to a reduction in athletic performance. Interestingly, the effect is short lived, and daily exposure studies have shown that the effect is much reduced by about the fourth or fifth day. Epidemiological studies show that daily deaths and hospital admissions for asthma and other respiratory diseases are related to daily ozone concentrations. Discussion about a possible threshold of effect remains unresolved. If no threshold is assumed, the effects in the United Kingdom are large.

Combinations of air pollutants

Chemical air pollutants never occur alone. There is always a mixture, and it is likely that effects on health are caused by the mixture and might vary with the composition of that mixture. Separating out the more important pollutants has proved to be difficult, and recent studies have shown that the effects of one pollutant may be modified by co-pollutants. This seems to be the case in co-exposures to ozone and nitrogen dioxide. Much more work is needed in this area.

Carbon monoxide (a pollutant that is well known to produce lethal effects at high concentrations) has recently been shown by epidemiological studies to be associated with heart attacks and heart failure at current outdoor concentrations—a remarkable finding. Carbon monoxide may be acting as a marker for other pollutants in the ambient mixture, or at low concentrations it may have unexpected effects in sensitive subjects. Recent studies in volunteers who had angina have shown that carboxyhaemoglobin concentrations as low as 2% are associated with a reduction in "time to pain" on exercise.

Carcinogenic air pollutants

Many well recognised human carcinogens occur in ambient air, both outdoors and, often to a greater extent, indoors. Studies in UK homes have shown—for example, that concentrations of benzene indoors may exceed those outdoors. Motor vehicles generate benzene, 1,3-butadiene, and polycyclic aromatic hydrocarbons. High levels of arsenic may occur near metal smelting works. These carcinogens are genotoxic and thus at all levels of exposure no guarantee of safety can be provided.

All estimates of increased risk of this sort are based on mathematical extrapolation from studies, in animals or man, of measured increases in risk on exposure to high concentrations. The process is unlikely to be precise and the accuracy of the predictions cannot be ascertained. This has led UK regulators to adopt a pragmatic approach and to set standards for ambient concentrations at levels at which the risk is judged to be very small and not to attempt quantification of the effects. Thus, in the case of benzene, a standard of five parts per billion ($15.6\,\mu g/m^3$) expressed as an annual average concentration has been adopted.

Indoor air pollution

All the pollutants discussed above, with the exception of ozone (which reacts rapidly with furnishings and fittings and disappears), occur indoors. Indoor concentrations are, in part, driven by outdoor sources as well as by specific indoor sources. Carbon monoxide and nitrogen dioxide may be produced by fires and by cooking—peak levels in kitchens can be higher than those commonly found outdoors. Recent work has led to concern about an association between nitrogen dioxide and respiratory infections, worsening of lung function in women with asthma, and increased sensitisation and response to allergens. Long term exposure to low levels of carbon

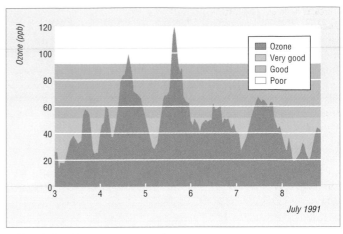

Daily variations in ozone concentrations.

Numbers of deaths and hospital admissions for respiratory diseases per year caused by ozone in both urban and rural areas of Great Britain (GB) during summer only

	GB, threshold (in parts per billion)	
	50	**0**
Deaths (all causes)	700	12 500
Hospital admissions for respiratory disease	500	9900

The WHO has published "unit risk factors" that allow the risk to be estimated (expressed as an increase in risk of getting a specified cancer as a result of lifetime exposure to a unit concentration of the carcinogen). For example, lifetime exposure to benzene of $17\,\mu g/m^3$ is estimated to be associated with an increase of risk of 1 in 10 000. The unit risk at $1\,\mu g/m^3$ is estimated as 6×10^{-6}

monoxide that produce only mild symptoms may lead to lasting neurological effects.

Regulating indoor pollutant concentrations is difficult: fewer countries have produced standards for indoor air quality than for outdoor air quality. The need for regular maintenance of devices that can produce pollutants indoors, for smoke alarms, and for constant vigilance on the part of doctors dealing with potentially poisoned patients is obvious.

Water and soil pollution

In developed countries the quality of drinking water is often accepted unthinkingly as high: we assume that the water is safe to drink. In many countries, however, such an assumption may be unwise because of microbiological and chemical contamination. The former causes more disease than the latter but will not be considered here. Accidental contamination of water supplies occurs from time to time in all countries: in the United Kingdom the accidental contamination of water with aluminium sulphate in Camelford (Cornwall) in 1988 (see chapter 20) led to widespread complaints that are still the subject of investigation. The quality of water supplies is improving in many countries, but the rate of improvement is uneven. WHO reported that in the period 1990-4 the number of people without a satisfactory water supply increased in Africa, Latin America, and the Caribbean. In some countries, including developed countries such as the United Kingdom, concern has been expressed about the possible impacts on health of so called endocrine disrupting chemicals.

Conclusion

Pollution of air, soil, and water remains a problem in nearly all parts of the world. In developed countries air pollution tends to attract the greatest attention, and considerable efforts to control outdoor sources of air pollutants have been made. In developing countries both air and water pollution remain important problems, and a large effort will be needed before these are removed.

Compounds that are of proved concerns as water and soil pollutants

Arsenic
Arsenic is found in high concentrations in many countries including Argentina, Canada, Chile, China, Japan, Mexico, the Philippines, and the United States. The recent discovery of arsenic concentrations at 70 times the national standard of 0.05 mg/l in West Bengal has highlighted this pollutant. Poisoning via water leads to evidence of chronic toxicity including melanosis, hyperkeratosis, and skin cancer. In West Bengal 200 000 people are reported to be suffering from arsenical skin lesions

Nitrates
Nitrates leached from agricultural land may enter drinking water. The use of infant food prepared with such water can lead to poisoning, methaemoglobin being produced by interaction between nitrite ions (produced from nitrate ions) and haemoglobin. The reaction is an oxidative one (ferrous iron in haemoglobin being converted to ferric iron in methaemoglobin) but the exact mechanism is unclear. In very young children cyanosis may occur. In 15 European countries 0.5-10% of the population may be exposed to nitrate levels in excess of the WHO standard of 50 mg/l

Lead
Lead can be mobilised from pipes and solder joints, especially in areas with acidic water supplies ("soft water" areas). Lead is accumulated in the body and can damage the central nervous system. A number of studies have linked lead intake and a decreased intelligence quotient. Mercury and cadmium are examples of other metals that contaminate water supplies

Fluoride
Fluoride is added to water in some countries to provide protection against tooth decay: effective protection is provided at levels of 0.5-1.0 mg/l. The margin between protective and toxic effects is unfortunately narrow, and effects ranging from dental fluorosis (mottling of enamel) to skeletal fluorosis occur in some areas. High levels of fluoride are found in parts of the Middle East, Africa, and North and South America

Based on recent work by the WHO

Further reading

- Holgate ST, Samet JM, Koren HS, Maynard RL, eds. *Air Pollution and Health*. London, New York: Academic Press, 1999. *A comprehensive review of all aspects of air pollution*
- World Health Organization. *Air Quality Guidelines for Europe*, 2nd ed. WHO Regional Publications, European Series, No 91. Copenhagen: WHO, 2000. *An update of the original 1987 edition providing guidelines for 35 air pollutants*
- World Health Organization. *Health and Environment in Sustainable Development. Five years after the Earth Summit*. Geneva: WHO, 1997. *A useful and wide ranging report*
- Maynard RL, Howard CV, eds. *Particulate matter: properties and effects upon health*. Oxford: BIOS Scientific Publishers Ltd, 1999. *Detailed collection of papers by leading research workers*
- Schwartz J. Harvesting and long term exposure effects in the relation between air pollution and mortality. *Am J Epidemiol* 2000;151:440-8. *An important paper by the leading exponent of time series studies of the effects of air pollution on health*
- Department of Health. *Committee on the medical effects of air pollutants. Non-biological particles and health*. London: HMSO, 1995. *A detailed report containing much useful information but becoming a little dated*
- Department of Health. Advisory Group on the Medical Aspects of Air Pollution Episodes. First Report. *Ozone*. London: HMSO, 1991. *A detailed report containing much useful information but now dated*
- Department of Health. Committee on the Medical Effects of Air Pollutants. *Quantification of the effects of air pollution on health in the United Kingdom*. London: HMSO, 1998. *A report providing guidance on how to estimate the effect of short term exposure to air pollutants*
- Department of Health. Committee on the Medical Effects of Air Pollutants. *Statement and Report on Long term effects of particles on mortality*. Available from http://www.doh.gov.uk/comeap/statementsreports/longtermeffects.pdf. *A report providing a novel approach to estimating the effects on life expectancy of long term exposure to air pollutants*
- Department of the Environment. Expert Panel on Air Quality Standards. *Benzene*. London: HMSO, 1994. *Provides an example of a pragmatic approach to setting standards for carcinogenic air pollutants*
- World Health Organization. *International programme on chemical safety. Guidelines for drinking-water quality*, 2nd ed. Vol. 1. *Recommendations*. Geneva: WHO, 1993
- World Health Organization. *International programme on chemical safety. Guidelines for drinking-water quality*, 2nd ed. Vol 2. *Health criteria and other supporting information*. Geneva: WHO, 1997. *These two reports contain detailed and invaluable accounts providing background material to the guidelines*
- Brunekreef B, Holgate ST. Air pollution and health. *Lancet* 2002;360:1233-42. *A comprehensive review article with extensive references*
- *Health effects of climate change*. www.doh.gov.uk/airpollution/climatechange02/index.htm. *An up-to-date and comprehensive overview of all aspects of this problem*

19   Global issues

Tony Fletcher

Environmental effects on health can be direct, as in the effect of lead pollution on the development of children, or indirect—for example, the eventual health impacts of the loss of biodiversity among plant and animal species. Many widespread and global environmental issues impact on human health. A selection of important areas follow along with some of the policy instruments that seek to mitigate these global risks.

Carrying capacity

Man's activities of production and consumption affect not only our local environment but the environment of whole regions and the entire planet. Given the large scale of such activities in an increasingly globalised world, certain polluting or resource depleting activities that the carrying capacity of the local environment used to absorb now result in overload or contamination of global proportions. One of the best recognised examples in the 20th century has been the devastating effect of acid rain on natural ecosystems whose ability to absorb and eliminate sulphuric acid was overwhelmed.

The carrying capacity amounts to some 10 hectares for every person for the richest countries compared with only 2.5 hectares per person on a global average. Thus, on this and other measures there is not enough land to support the world's population at the level of consumption enjoyed by the most industrialised countries. Of course, there is no widespread enthusiasm to reduce levels of consumption. On the contrary, there are widespread aspirations to increase industrial production and employment and to reduce, or eliminate, poverty.

Various attempts have been made to estimate how many people can comfortably and sustainably live on this planet, based on some reasonable compromise between the (low) current average standard of living and the high average in the richest countries. Realistic estimates based on food production, water usage, energy consumption, and the integrated footprints fall mostly in the range of three to five billion people. With a world population of six billion and projected increases to at least 10 billion before any prospect of levelling off, the sustainable carrying capacity of the planet is already being exceeded.

Volcanic eruption, Montserrat—pollution on a grand scale and a social disaster

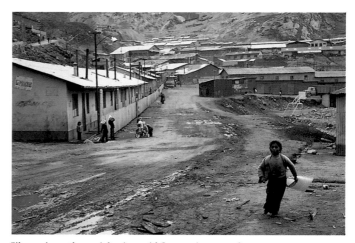

Silver mine—the social price paid for precious metal

Biodiversity

As pressure on land has increased in the past 100 years, the rate of extinction has accelerated. It is estimated that 20-50% of species present 100 years ago will have become extinct by 2100, with the rate of loss accelerating from now until then.

Many species are lost as biodiverse tropical rainforests are depleted by clearance and burning. This has practical consequences on human health by affecting food and drugs. Medicines have been identified and developed from tropical plants, and pharmacological possibilities for numerous species have not been explored. In the case of food, we have in the past relied on the cross breeding of food crops with wild strains to maintain productivity and resistance to pests, and will no doubt need to continue to do this, whatever achievements arise from genetic modification in laboratories.

> The concept of *carrying capacity* for people derives from the *ecological footprint*: "the area of productive land and water required on a continuous basis to produce all the resources consumed, and to assimilate all the wastes produced"

> The rate of loss of species is estimated to have increased from 10 000 a year in 1900 to some 50 000 a year in 2000

Arsenic in ground water

Arsenic is a widespread mineral in the Earth's crust and occurs at rather high concentrations in some ground waters that get exploited as sources of drinking water. In Europe few populations have been exposed and signs of arsenic toxicity, including melanosis and keratosis of the skin, peripheral neuropathy, and vascular and respiratory ill health, are rare. Consequently, attention has shifted to cancer risk, estimated by extrapolation from more exposed populations. Skin and internal cancers (bladder and lung in particular) have been clearly associated with higher levels of arsenic exposure and concern about risks at relatively low concentrations has prompted most countries to adopt a standard of 10 µg/l in drinking water. However, in some developing countries, most notably Bangladesh, it has recently been discovered that more than 20 million people are being exposed to over 50 µg/l and levels over 1000 µg/l have been found. Thus, many thousands of cases of arsenic poisoning have already occurred, and this is likely to be followed by many fatal cancers, especially if remediation measures are not put into place rapidly.

Global climate change

A significant upward trend in mean temperature is now in little doubt, and anthropogenic sources are substantially contributing, especially in relation to carbon dioxide. The Intergovernmental Panel on Climate Change (IPCC) in 2001 predicted an increase in 2-3°C over the course of the 21st century. The authoritative IPCC, among others, has highlighted a number of serious consequences if this were to happen. One consequence, the increase in frequency of extreme weather events, already seems to be underway. Melting of the polar ice caps, accompanied by a rise in sea levels, would lead to disastrous flooding of low lying coastal regions. Shifts in climate patterns would lead to changes in agricultural productivity and, given the time and investment it takes to adapt to such changes, most likely famine and conflict. The distribution of infectious diseases is expected to change, with malaria migrating north as temperatures rise. Other vector borne diseases threatening to spread include dengue fever, viral encephalitis, schistosomiasis, leishmaniasis, onchocerciasis, and yellow fever.

Stratospheric ozone depletion

Few have not heard of the ozone hole, with the accompanying increase in ground level exposure to ultraviolet radiation and the consequent increase of sunburn and skin cancer. Damage to the ozone layer is the result of chemical reactions between stratospheric ozone and certain chemicals, most notably the chlorofluorocarbons used as aerosol propellants and refrigerants. Although chlorofluorocarbons are inert at ground level temperatures, in the very cold stratospheric environment over the poles, sunlight breaks them down into reactive intermediates which in turn destroy the ozone present there. As the ozone is depleted, more harmful solar radiation gets through. In recognition of this problem, chlorofluorocarbons were banned under the Montreal Protocol of 1987. This was not implemented in every country, however, and in the meantime other ozone destroying chemicals have been identified. Because it takes some time for the ozone to build up again, ozone depletion is not expected to recover until the middle of the 21st century. Ground level ultraviolet light is predicted to rise by 12-15% relative to 1970s levels.

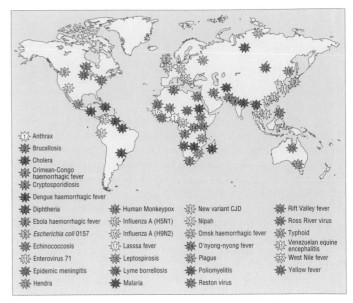

Unexpected outbreaks—examples of emerging and re-emerging infectious diseases, 1994–9

Emerging and re-emerging infectious diseases

Emerging infectious diseases are those that have been recently discovered, have increased in humans over the past two decades, or threaten to increase in the future

Re-emerging infections are infectious diseases which have increased (previously having diminished in incidence) because of ecological changes, public health decline, or development of drug resistance

Six major factors have contributed to their emergence or re-emergence:

1. Changes in human demography and behavior (for example, immunosuppression, aging population, migration, risky behaviours)
2. Advances in technology and changes in industry practices (for example, air conditioning cooling towers, changes in food processing, changes in rendering.)
3. Economic development and changes in land use patterns (encroachment on the tropical rainforests, conservation efforts, climate changes)
4. Dramatic increases in volume and speed of international travel and commerce of people, animals, and foodstuffs
5. Microbial adaptation and changes
6. Breakdown of public health capacity for infectious diseases

In most instances, the emergence of a specific agent results from a complex interaction of several factors

Examples of emerging and re-emerging infections include:

HIV
Legionnaire's disease
Hantavirus
E.Coli O157
Vancomycin resistant enterococci
Severe acute respiratory syndrome (SARS)

Lead in the environment

Lead has multiple toxic health effects—haematological, renal, and neurological—although at typical levels of exposure in the environment, neuropsychological impacts are the main concern, especially for developing children. Aside from local contamination or pollution, exposure to lead has been quite widespread from dissolution into drinking water from lead piping, use of lead in paint in old houses, and airborne exposure from leaded petrol. In addition, people have been exposed via their food from the use of lead solder for sealing cans, although this has now been completely phased out. However, the other sources still lead to exposure. Although the use of lead additive in petrol has virtually ceased, there is still much dust on roadsides from past use and this is resuspended or picked up by children; lead present in paint in older houses remains an important source as it is chipped off through normal wear and tear; again in older dwellings, lead pipes in the home or connecting with the main water supply can be a source, with solubility depending on the chemistry and pH of the water supply. Research into the effects of lead exposure on children's neurological development measures their intelligence quotient and emotional and behavioural development.

> **In children, a doubling of body lead burden 10–20 mcg/dl is associated with a deficit of 1–2 full scale IQ points**

Lead smelter—the starting point of dissemination of a toxic metal

Polychlorinated biphenyls (PCBs)

PCBs, along with dioxins and chlorinated pesticides such as DDT, exhibit a particular persistence. They are not broken down in the environment and indeed are accumulated as they are taken up by plants, herbivores, and carnivores, with concentrations increasing at each level. Mass production of PCBs started in 1929 and expanded enormously until environmental damage was recognised in the 1960s. The first evidence of adverse health effect came in 1968 with the mass poisoning of Japanese who ate rice oil contaminated with PCBs. The resulting Yusho disease (named after the place where this incident took place), entailed disfiguring pigmentation of the skin, sweating, conjunctivitis, headaches, weakness, cough, and liver damage then later an increased incidence of cancer. For pregnant women, exposure led to malformed children. The effect of bioaccumulation on wildlife was subsequently established—for example, reduced fertility in various seabirds feeding on fish with accumulated PCBs. Production and use was, after some delay, reduced, with bans being introduced in the 1970s in Western Europe and the 1980s in Eastern Europe. Environmental levels of PCBs are slowly reducing again.

Smokestack industry—global relocation to the poorest countries

Transport and health

In recent years attention has been increasingly focused on the links between transport and health. The traditional dominant concern—death and injury from collision—has been extended to embrace transport related emissions. Pollution from industry and domestic fireplaces has fallen, but as a result of the phenomenal increase in mobility and car ownership, motor vehicles are now the main source of emissions in the United Kingdom (directly or through atmospheric reactions) of particulates, oxides of nitrogen, and ozone.

Added to these more obvious health risks are other concerns relating to quality of life and health—for example, trade-offs between different psychosocial impacts. Greater mobility has the potential to increase more distant social contacts and potentially to provide protection against vulnerability to assault. Set against this is the community severance and loss of social networking and support within communities that is a consequence of busy roads passing through residential areas. Regular physical exercise is reduced if walking and cycling are cut in favour of car journeys; this has been shown dramatically in the case of children's journeys to school. Not only is this unhealthy per se, but it ingrains the habit of car dependence, leading to the cumulative effect of insufficient exercise.

Policy responses

This range of examples has been selected to illustrate the wide range of environmental impacts on health. Our choice of mode of transport has both local and global impacts. Our energy consumption has an impact via its contribution to global warming. Toxic chemicals in the environment may be local problems or bioaccumulating and thus contribute to very distant increases of risk. These may be natural as in the case of the arsenic contamination of drinking water, or manmade as in lead pollution.

In a parallel manner, the range of policy instruments for preventing adverse environmental impacts operates on various levels. At a global level international conventions play a major role, although the important and potentially expensive ones are the most difficult to get all parties to agree to and ratify. The Kyoto agreement on limiting climate change gases will remain in limbo as long as the major polluters refuse to ratify it.

Regulation at national and, for the European Union, European level is embodied in directives, regulations, and policies, such as, in the United Kingdom, NAAQS.

Local initiatives prompted by the meeting on the environment and development in Rio de Janeiro have become an important focus for both local authority initiatives and the involvement of civil society. The so-called La21, or Local Agenda 21, developed as an idea intended to catalyse local environmental initiatives.

Finally, industrial undertakings by their very size can have large environmental impacts, or make products with significant environmental impacts. Responsible corporate and product stewardship can be implemented to seek to reduce adverse environmental (or environmental health) impacts. This may be represented by adherence within the worksite to quality standards such as the Eco-Management and Audit Scheme or ISO 14 000 environmental quality schemes, or the adoption of "cradle to grave" product stewardship initiatives, ensuring that raw materials such as wood are derived from sustainable sources, recycling is maximised, and products are designed so that they can be recycled.

Toxic waste

Many of the materials we use are useful yet have an inherent toxicity, or to produce them entails generating toxic waste, which in any case needs careful disposal to avoid or at least minimise human exposure. This has frequently not been the case, with a legacy of contaminated land or poorly documented waste sites in the United Kingdom, or waste being exported to other less well regulated countries. This latter practice has been somewhat restricted through international agreements such as the Basel Convention on the Control of Transboundary Movements of Hazardous Wastes and Their Disposal (1989), although not all countries are signatories to this convention.

War pollution—burning oil wells in Kuwait

Further reading
- Fletcher T, McMichael AJ, eds. *Health at the Crossroads: Transport Policy and Urban Health.* Wiley, 1997
- Intergovernmental Panel on Climate Change. *Third assessment report.* Cambridge: Cambridge University Press, 2001
- Koppe JG, Keys J. *PCBs and the precautionary principle in late lessons from early warnings: the precautionary principle 1896-2000.* Copenhagen: European Environment Agency, 2001
- Lippmann M, ed. *Environmental toxicants: human exposures and their health effects,* 2nd ed. Wiley, 2000
- McMichael T. *Human frontiers, environments and disease; past patterns, uncertain futures.* Cambridge: Cambridge University Press, 2001
- Patz JA, Kovats RS. Hotspots in climate change and health. *BMJ* 2002;325:1094-8. *A readable account of the key issues*
- Smith AH, Lingas EO, Rahman M. Contamination of drinking water by arsenic in Bangladesh: a public health emergency. *Bulletin of the World Health Organization* 2000;78:1093-1103
- United Nations Environment Programme. www.unep.org. *Up-to-date information on world environmental issues such as POPs (persistent organic pollutants), post-conflict problems, sustainable construction, safe construction, safe technology transfer, fair trade, and disaster management, as well as the topics highlighted in this chapter*
- World Development Report 1992: Development and Environment. Oxford: Oxford University Press, 1992

The figure showing examples of emerging and re-emerging infectious diseases is adapted from the World Health organization infectious disease report (http://www.int/int/infectious-disease-report)

20   Occupational and environmental disease of uncertain aetiology

Andy Slovak

Occupational and environmental conditions, by their nature, invite and create contention. This is particularly so where causality is uncertain. The diagram seeks to explain why this might be. Individual and group beliefs, behaviours, and so on, and their social modulation seem to play as substantial a part in the experience of symptoms as does exposure to the range of putative causal agents.

The issues of causality, attitude, and perception that affect approaches to these conditions are discussed first, before discussing specific syndromes. From a practical point of view, there is an obvious dichotomy between the support it is proper to give to patients and the more detached objectivity one would wish to bring to understanding their condition scientifically. This is particularly so when, as is often the case, health professionals are invited to make a commitment to a particular belief system related to the causality of the disease under discussion. At the same time, those health professionals are all members of the public and as such are susceptible to prevalent, popular, belief systems.

The box lists a selection of medical syndromes whose nature and aetiology are at present uncertain. They are an apparently disparate grouping, but as far as broader circumstances are concerned, they tend to reflect some common themes:

* Multifactoriality (both symptoms and putative causes)
* Lack of control ("involuntary" exposure)
* Marked variation in susceptibility
* Tendency to ascribe to external causes.

As such, there are resonances between these conditions and others considered elsewhere in this book or that are beyond its scope. These conditions include non-specific upper limb disorders, regional pain syndromes, fibromyalgia, and stress.

It is also perhaps worthwhile deconstructing the nature of the multifactoriality a little. In the cases of sick building syndromes, multiple chemical sensitivity, and war syndromes, the factors implicated are truly extensive and highly varied, whereas in situational syndromes (for example, after the Braer disaster and Camelford incidents) they are defined by the event, although still difficult to pinpoint. The debates about electromagnetic fields and nuclear installations are even more unusual because they are biphasic with more or less distinct occupational and environmental modes.

Landfill sites present another situational pattern, having a wide but segmented range of attributed, putative effects (in time and space), and an even wider range of possible hazards and attendant risks. In contrast to all of the foregoing, the putative causal agents cited for conditions attributed to sheep dipping are highly specific—namely, organophosphate pesticides. Acute effects are well known and well characterised, but the controversy continues as to how they might be implicated in longer term effects.

More dramatic examples are provided by disasters and their health consequences, which may vary according to factors other than easily measurable ones. The health deficit produced by the Chernobyl incident in 1986 has been, with the exception of

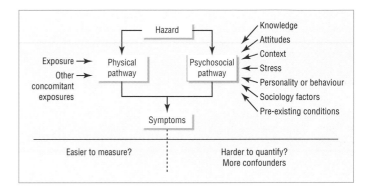

Medical syndromes with uncertain nature and aetiology

* Long term conditions claimed to be associated with proximity to electromagnetic fields (for example, power lines) and nuclear installations
* Gulf war syndromes
* Multiple chemical sensitivity
* Situational syndromes: the Braer disaster and the Camelford incident
* Sick building syndromes
* Conditions claimed to be associated with proximity to landfill sites
* Long term conditions claimed to be associated with pesticides used for sheep dipping

"Natural" disasters such as volcanic eruptions are less likely to have prolonged health effects (other than obvious immediate ones or secondary effects due to—for example, evacuation) than manmade disasters that usually last longer (food contamination), take time to come to light (bovine spongiform encephalopathy or variant Creutzfeldt-Jakob disease), can have a serious impact on Government or medical credibility, and create many cases of "illness" among the worried well

a few thousand cases of childhood thyroid cancer, wholly psychological and socioeconomic.

Electromagnetic fields and nuclear installations

Studies, mainly epidemiological, relating to power lines have been pursued for about 30 years and for nuclear installations, for about 20 years. Their conclusions are still hotly debated.

The suspect agent in the electrical sector has been electromagnetic fields. The issues of interest occupationally have been leukaemia and brain cancer in electrical workers. Environmental concerns have focused on childhood leukaemia and, to a lesser extent, other childhood cancers.

The outcomes of extensive, painstaking epidemiological work on electromagnetic fields in both the occupational and environmental sectors have been tantalising.

As an example, the table shows the amalgamated risk data from a number of recent Nordic studies of electromagnetic fields "exposure" and childhood leukaemia.

Numbers are sparse and exposure criteria poorly defined. This situation of finding difficulty in differentiating "effect from background noise" is typical of these sorts of long running debates. The rationale for continuing is nevertheless powerful because of the universality of exposure, the likelihood that exposure will increase in the future, and for reasons of risk perception. Studies on those occupationally exposed are even weaker.

With regard to nuclear installations, concerns have also centred around childhood leukaemia and other childhood cancers. In the United Kingdom the debate was initiated by a single television programme in 1983. The putative risk factor at that time was assumed to be installation discharges of radioactive materials. However, such discharges produce doses to the general public that are very small (by several orders of magnitude) when compared with those that might be expected to produce such effects according to robust scientific risk estimations.

> Studies on electromagnetic fields have struggled to develop sufficient power to dispel the tentative concerns raised by other studies

> In a letter to the *Lancet*, Ahlbom and colleagues reported: "Our results show that the three Nordic studies taken together support the hypothesis that exposure to magnetic fields of the type generated by transmission lines has some aetiological role in the development of leukaemia in children" (*Lancet* 1993;342:1295)

Amalgamated data from three principal Nordic studies concerning childhood cancer risk and proximity to power lines

Study	Leukaemia			Nervous system tumours			Lymphoma			Total		
	Cases	Relative risk	95% CI	Cases	Relative risk	95% CI	Cases	Relative risk	95% CI	Cases	Relative risk	95% CI
1	7	2.7	1.0 to 6.3	2	0.7	0.1 to 2.7	2	1.3	0.2 to 5.1	12	1.1	0.5 to 2.1
2	3	1.5	0.3 to 6.7	2	1.0	0.2 to 5.0	1	5.0	0.3 to 82.0	6	1.5	0.6 to 4.1
3	2	1.6	0.3 to 4.5	5	2.3	0.8 to 5.4	0	0.0	0.0 to 4.2	11	1.5	0.7 to 2.7
Total	13	2.1	1.1 to 4.1	9	1.5	0.7 to 3.2	3	1.0	0.3 to 3.7	29	1.3	0.9 to 2.1

* Data from Anlbom et al. *Lancet* 1993; 342: 1295.

A period of intensive research (1983-90) failed to find much support for an environmental (discharge) hypothesis, and this theory was substantively supplanted in 1990 by an occupational hypothesis based on paternal preconceptual irradiation in radiation workers. Centred on the experience of workers living in Seascale, a village near Sellafield in Cumbria, the paternal preconceptual irradiation theory did not survive when tested elsewhere in Cumbria and more generally in the United Kingdom and other countries. More recently, excess childhood leukaemia rates have been attributed to population mixing in communities that have a high proportion of incomers, raising the possibility of a viral aetiology.

Even though the scientific plausibility has subsided, these matters can still polarise scientific opinion at the extremes of construct belief.

Gulf war syndromes

In 1992, after some months of preparation, a multinational army was engaged in a brief, one sided conflict against Iraq resulting in minimal military casualties to them. Subsequently there emerged among the veterans of some nations, particularly the United States and United Kingdom, a series of symptoms now collectively known as Gulf war syndromes. These have now been extensively studied in the surprisingly large numbers of personnel involved.

A number of separate or combined entities have been suggested as possible causes, and it is easy to draw up a list of 30 or 40 factors that might plausibly come into the frame. Some of these are listed in the box.

Epidemiological studies have looked for distinct Gulf war syndromes and what exposures or experiences might be associated with them. To date, the key observations are that there is no specific syndrome, but that war theatre veterans have discernibly stronger symptoms per person than military personnel who did not serve in the Gulf. There is an association between symptom frequency and complexity of inoculation programmes (where given). Mortality, morbidity, and reproductive outcomes have been unremarkable to date, although, of course, it is early days yet. The same caution that is applied to negative data must also be applied to early positive associations now beginning to be reported (for example, amyotrophic lateral sclerosis).

Those who remember the Vietnam war recall analogous later manifestations of complaints attributed to that experience and specifically to Agent Orange, a widely deployed defoliant. Recent retrospective research suggests that increased symptom frequency may be associated with conflict experience back to the mid-19th century. This subject is set to run for some time.

Multiple chemical sensitivity

Multiple chemical sensitivity is a difficult entity to position clinically. The range of symptoms observed within the scope of the condition are protean. They include chronic fatigue type syndromes, weakness, sleep disturbance, rashes, headache, chest tightness, and oppression, but these examples are far from a complete and arguable list.

It is accepted that multiple chemical sensitivity applies to a group of patients with a disabling condition with symptomatology whose severity seems to be lessened by restriction of exposure to the everyday environment, particularly by inhalation. It is inferred, therefore, that the aetiology or precipitation of the condition is derived from that environment. Underlying immunological and neurological mechanisms have been proposed but not substantiated. Diagnostic criteria are hard to define, as are objective investigative methods.

Braer and Camelford

The Braer oil tanker ran aground in Northern Scotland, releasing a cargo of light crude oil (1992-3). At Camelford in Cornwall in 1988, a specific agent, aluminium sulphate, was inadvertently introduced into the water supply. Both incidents resulted in immediate symptoms in local residents. Those associated with the Braer were primarily acute and upper

Some of the most popular possible causes of Gulf war syndromes

- Inoculation programmes
- Prophylaxis against biological warfare agents
- Depleted uranium
- Insecticide spraying
- Pyrolysis due to military action or "scorched earth" action
- Involuntary dispersal of chemical or biological war agents due to military action

Gulf war soldiers in protective clothing

 spiratory, whereas those in Camelford were more diffuse. The former did not persist; the latter did.

The persistence of a "malaise" syndrome, as at Camelford (for example, fatigue, joint pain, depression, memory loss) is a feature of a number of the conditions described in this chapter, and the contrast offered between the Braer and Camelford events may therefore be generally instructive. Toxicologically the circumstances were different, and indeed it is possible to argue that local exposures after the Braer disaster were minimal or non-existent because of vigorous weather dispersal of pollution.

Others have argued that the difference lay in contrasting approaches to the situation by the responsible public authorities. In a perhaps oversimplistic way, it has therefore been inferred that a strong social and sociopsychological modulation of response can be obtained in situational events by authoritative communication and action.

Aspects of societal action that have been perceived as positive in these circumstances are given in the box.

Sick building syndrome

Originally seen and reported as primarily a respiratory occupational disease in the early 1980s, sick building syndrome has more recently seemed more protean and diffuse. Thus, a malaise syndrome similar to situational events was increasingly recognised in later studies; the incidence of complaint was found to be overlaid on quite high prevalence of such symptoms even in buildings not associated with sick building syndrome. Strong linkages to upper limb disorders and stress symptomatologies have also been increasingly reported. It seems likely that these different functional ways of looking at syndromes may be taking different slices out of what is part of the same cake.

Landfills

The figure shows the geographical distribution of UK landfill sites and perhaps also the futility of "nimbyism." (Nimby is an acronymic characterisation—"not in my back yard"—of resistance to the location of any undesired feature in a particular neighbourhood.)

A recent large UK study showed a small association (about 1%) between congenital abnormalities and proximity to a landfill site. It was unclear whether this finding should be seen as reassuring, given that the effect was small and "proximity" encompassed a majority of the UK population. Landfill and other "amenity" sites are particularly likely to be the subject of local symptomatic complaint and anecdotal reporting of cluster events (for example, cancers). Investigationally, the range of reported conditions and (usually) the lack of easily definable toxic exposure may result in unsatisfactory outcomes for all parties involved.

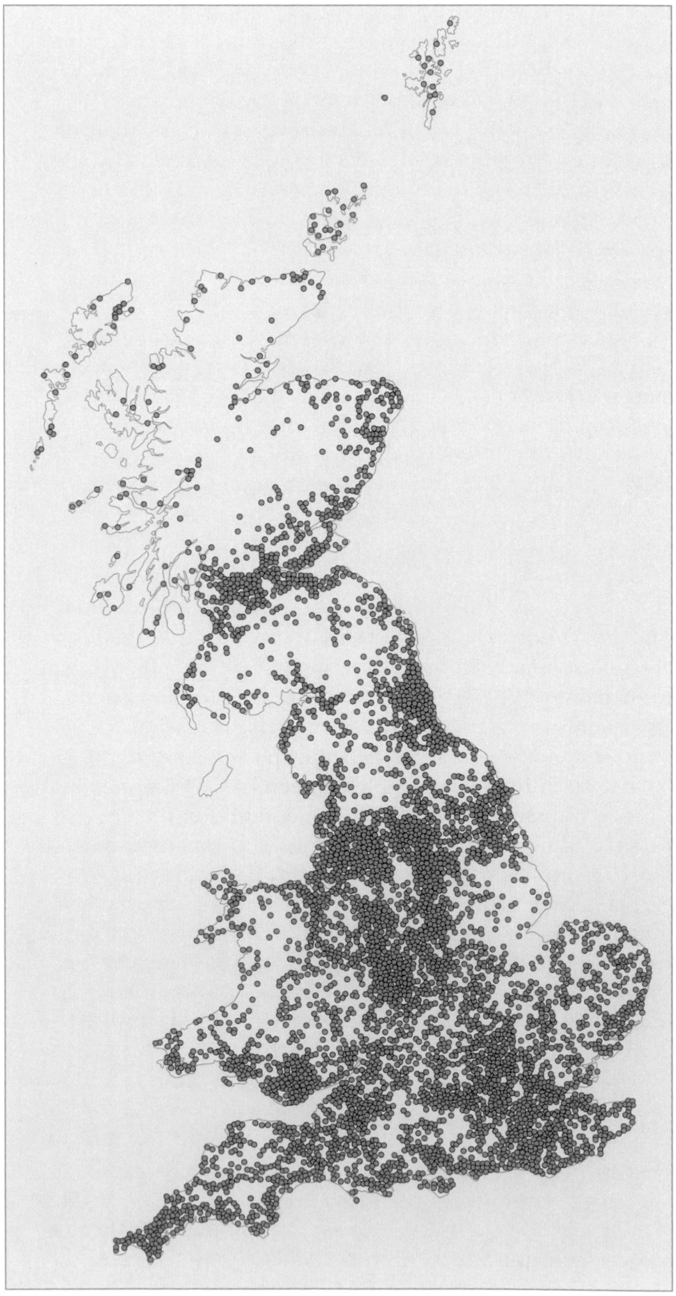

Organophosphate sheep dips

Organophosphates are well characterised neurotoxins that exert their effects acutely by inhibiting of the widespread neurotransmitter enzyme acetylcholinesterase. This toxic effect has been widely exploited in pesticide applications, as in sheep dips for parasitic infestations. The acute effects have also been widely seen in humans in occupational, domestic, and deliberate overexposures. A typical acute syndrome of stomach cramps, weakness, paralysis, and collapse is directly associated

---

Aspects of societal action perceived as positive following situational disasters such as Braer and Camelford

- Timely communication of an action plan
- Timely communication of hazard information
- Effective dialogue with the population at risk
- Feedback to the population at risk

Distribution of UK landfill sites

with measurable cholinesterase suppression in a traditional dose-response relation.

Two syndromes of longer duration have been attributed to long term effects of organophosphate exposure, mainly in sheep dippers who have high and repeated contact with these agents. One, known colloquially as "dipper's flu," is reported to come on some time after exposure, typically up to a day later. As the name indicates, the illness is described as "flu-like" in nature and duration. The other syndrome or syndrome set is reported to be truly chronic, and the syndrome range is typical of that described repeatedly in this chapter. At the anecdotal level, some preponderance of chronic fatigue and cognitive deficits is claimed.

Dipper's flu has been subjected to objective field investigations of exposure and symptoms following dipping. Little difference was observed between symptoms of dippers and unexposed controls when symptoms were grouped (for example, cognitive, visual, flu-like). When symptoms were degrouped and analysed separately, some emerged as more common in dippers but these were not those of flu. Thus, despite quite extensive research, the findings continue to be inconclusive or perverse, and there is no clear dose or dose-surrogate relation. Complaints of neuropathy are more frequent in sheep dippers, especially those handling concentrate, who are also more prone to anxiety and depression. Again, no cause and effect relation has been established, and objective signs of damage have not been in evidence.

Puzzlingly, a plausible mechanism of action has not been found for the longer term or chronic effects attributed to organophosphate exposure. The long term effects are not associated with cholinesterase inhibition, the acute toxic mechanism, in any discernible or direct way. It is possible, speculatively, to postulate some "shadow" effect of cholinesterase inhibition, or some other unknown mechanism of the agent or some contaminant, but the investigations to date have been elusive and discouraging of the existence of such mechanisms.

Conclusion

The foregoing sections describe a substantive sample of occupationally and environmentally ascribed complaints of uncertain origins. Others of no less importance are noted here but have not otherwise been selected for discussion.

To a greater or lesser extent they posit scientific problems associated with differentiating between hazard (innate adverse characteristics) and risk (the likelihood of them happening). Ill understood by society, the difference between hazard and risk is, or seems to be, being marginalised in a society where such issues are now more dominantly subject to perception and the precautionary principle (where ultimately hazard equals risk). The natural course of issues of the type discussed in this chapter is often a cycle of initial concern, resistance, disturbance, investigation, assimilation, and exhaustion. This is shown in the figures, which examine the epidemiological time course of investigations into the nuclear installations issue discussed earlier, and soft tissue sarcoma associated with herbicide application, moving from the sentinel observation towards regression to the mean.

To resolve such issues effectively in the altered perceptual framework of the society in which they flourish probably needs some fundamental reordering of current "expert" and "authoritarian" approaches. The models that have been created to "understand" these issues, while dictated by common sense

Sheep dipping

Claims that long term effects of exposure to organophosphates leading to a variety of chronic syndromes remain unsubstantiated, both epidemiologically and toxicologically

Other environmental ascribed complaints

- Oestrogenic modulators in water and food chains
- Mercury dental amalgams
- Pesticides residues in foodchains

Further reading

- National Radiological Protection Board. *Electromagnetic Fields and the Risk of Cancer*. www.nrpb.org.uk
- Committee on Medical Aspects of Radiation in the Environment (COMARE) reports, available from www.doh.gov.uk/comare/comare.htm
- Hyams KC, Wignall FS, Roswell R. War syndromes and their evaluation from the US Civil War to the Persian Gulf War. *Ann Intern Med* 1996;126:398-405
- Eberlein-Konig B, Przbilla B, Kuhnl P, Golling G, Gebefugi I, Ring I. Multiple chemical sensitivity (MCS) and others: allergological, environmental and psychological investigations in individuals with indoor related complaints. *Int J Hyg Environ Health* 2002;205:213-20
- Campbell D, Cox D, Crum J, Foster K, Riley H. Later effects of the grounding of tanker Braer on health in Shetland. *BMJ* 1994;309:773-4
- David AS. The legend of Camelford: medical consequences of a water pollution accident. *J Psychosom Res* 1995;39:1-9
- Mayon-White RT. How should another Camelford be managed? *BMJ* 1993;307(6901):398-9
- Health and Safety Executive. *Sick building syndrome: a review of the evidence on causes and solutions*. HSE Contract Report No 42/1992. Sudbury: HSE Books, 1992
- Elliott P, Briggs D, Morris S, de Hoogh C, Hurt C, Jensen TK, et al. Risk of adverse birth outcomes in populations living near landfill sites. *BMJ* 2001;323:363-8
- Health effects in relation to landfill sites. IEH report (not published in full). Dept of Health 1999 http://www.doh.gov.uk/lanl.htm
- Institute of Occupational Health. *Symptom reporting following occupational exposure to organophosphate pesticides in sheep dip*. HSE Contract Research Report 371/2001. Sudbury: HSE Books, 2001
- Spurgeon A, Gompertz D, Harrington JM. Modifiers of non-specific symptoms of occupational and environmental syndromes. *Occup Environ Med* 1996;83:361-6

and observation, are themselves authoritarian rather than consensual.

A consensual approach (that is, a process widely accepted, understood, and supported) has been attempted in the United States in dealing, practically and scientifically, with a group known as "downwinders." These were people exposed to downwind deposition of radioiodine released in north west United States in the 1940s. Features of the process are similar to those perceived to have prevented escalation of the Braer disaster but are more rigorously structured. The time, communications, and effort costs are large; the outcomes so far, imperfect.

If attribution and handling these problems in a public health context is difficult then so can be dealing with the "patients"/victims and the "worried well."

Therapeutic handling of sufferers, regardless of the putative source of their illness, usually includes accepting that there is a problem, separating out cause, symptomatology, and illness behaviour, and treating the latter by psychological techniques—an approach similar to that adopted by pain therapists.

The photograph of sheep dipping is used with permission from The University of Queensland Library, Fryer Library. Hume Family Papers. UQFLIO. Photograph album vol 8. Sheep dipping–Yandilla, (1890s). The figure showing the distribution of UK landfill sites is adapted from Eliott P, et al. *BMJ* 2001; 323:363–8. The photograph of Gulf war soldiers is reproduced with permission from Professor Simon Wessely, Academic Department of Psychological Medicine, Guy's, King's and St Thomas's School of Medicine, and Institute of Psychiatry, London.

Appendix I

Features of some important occupational zoonoses

Disease and infectious agent	Main animal reservoir	Workers at risk	Features
Brucellosis Undulant fever *Brucella abortus* *B. melitensis* *B. suis* *B. canis* **Prescribed disease** **RIDDOR reportable**	Cattle Sheep and goats Pigs Dogs	Farmers Butchers Abattoir staff Vets	**Distribution:** Worldwide, especially North and East Africa, Middle East, and Latin America **Mode of acquisition:** Direct contact with infected animals, or ingestion of contaminated milk or dairy products **Incubation period:** Variable, usually 5-60 days **Clinical features:** Acute or insidious onset with intermittent fever, fatigue, arthralgia, and localised suppurative infection of organs. Splenomegaly and lymphadenopathy occurs in about 15% of cases. Neurological symptoms may occur acutely. In the chronic form symptoms include depression, fatigue, and arthritis **Treatment:** Doxycycline with rifampicin or streptomycin Immunisation possible for cattle, but not suitable for humans
Cryptosporidiosis *Cryptosporidium parvum*	Cattle Sheep and goats	Farmers Vets	**Distribution:** Worldwide **Mode of acquisition:** Faeco-oral; ingestion of oocysts excreted in human or animal faeces **Incubation period:** 1-12 days, oocysts (the infectious stage) appear in stool at onset of symptoms, and continue to be excreted in stool for several weeks after symptoms resolve. Oocysts may remain infective for up to 6 months in a moist environment **Clinical features:** Often infection is asymptomatic. Commonest symptom is diarrhoea, often associated with abdominal cramps. Most immunocompetent people will improve within 30 days. Immunocompromised individuals may have severe and protracted illness **Treatment:** Supportive
Escherichia coli **O157** **Notifiable**	Cattle Sheep and goats Deer Horses	Farmers Healthcare staff	**Distribution:** Worldwide **Mode of acquisition:** Ingestion of contaminated food, direct contact with infected animals, direct person to person spread, and waterborne **Incubation period:** 1-9 days, haemolytic uraemic syndrome may follow after a further 5-10 days **Clinical features:** Asymptomatic, diarrhoeal illness, haemorrhagic colitis, haemolytic uraemic syndrome in up to 10% of infected patients (particularly in children), and thrombotic thrombocytopaenic purpura. Infectious dose probably < 100 organisms, and case fatality 3-17% **Treatment:** Nil specific
Erysipeloid *Erysipelothrix rhusiopathiae*	Fish Wild or domestic animals	Fishermen Butchers Fish handlers Poultry workers Vets	**Distribution:** Worldwide **Mode of acquisition:** Direct contact with infected animal **Clinical features:** Localised cutaneous skin infection/cellulitis with violaceous tinge (fishmonger's finger). Occasionally fever, articular pain, rarely septicaemia and endocarditis. Usually self-limiting **Treatment:** Penicillin, cephalosporins, erythromycin, or tetracycline
Histoplasmosis *Histoplasma capsulatum*	Chicken Bats	Poultry workers	**Distribution:** Americas, Africa, East Asia, Australia—rare in temperate climates **Mode of acquisition:** Inhalation of airborne conidia **Incubation period:** Generally within 3-17 days **Clinical features:** (a) asymptomatic, (b) acute benign respiratory, (c) acute disseminated disease, (d) chronic disseminated disease, (e) chronic pulmonary disease **Treatment:** Itraconazole or ketoconazole for immunocompetent patients with indolent non-meningeal infection. Amphoterocin for those with fulminant or severe infections
Hydatid disease (Tapeworms of genus *Echinococcosis* *E. granulosus* and *E. multilocularis*) **Prescribed disease** **RIDDOR reportable**	Dogs Sheep— intermediate host Sylvatic hosts for *E. multilocularis*	Shepherds Farmers	**Distribution:** Worldwide except Antarctica **Mode of acquisition:** Hand to mouth transfer of eggs after association with infected dogs or through contaminated food, soil, water, or fomites **Incubation period:** Months to years **Clinical features:** Usually asymptomatic until cysts cause noticeable pressure effects; symptomology will depend on size and location of cysts. Eosinophilia common **Treatment:** Surgical resection of cysts combined with albendazole Alveolar hydatid disease (caused by *E. multilocularis*) is usually fatal if not treated

continued

Appendix I   continued

Disease and infectious agent	Main animal reservoir	Workers at risk	Features
Listeriosis *Listeria monocytogenes*	Cattle, sheep, and other domestic and wild animals	Farmers Vets	**Distribution:** Worldwide **Mode of acquisition:** Mostly foodborne (soft cheeses, etc.), but also nosocomial, and direct contact with infected animals or aborted animal fetuses **Incubation period:** Variable, but 3-70 days. Infected individuals may shed organism in stool for several months **Clinical features:** General malaise or flu-like symptoms. In pregnant women infection may lead to abortion, intrauterine death, or neonatal sepsis. Immunocompromised individuals may suffer from meningoencepahlitis **Treatment:** Amoxicillin and gentamicin
Lyme disease *Borrelia burgdorferi* **RIDDOR reportable**	Wild rodents Deer	Shepherds Farmers Foresters Outdoor work	**Distribution:** United States, Canada, Europe, former Soviet Union, China, Japan **Mode of acquisition:** Tickborne—*ixodes scapularis, pacificus, ricinis,* and *persulcatus* **Incubation period:** Erythema migrans generally occurs within 7-10 days after tick bite, transmission of *B. burgdorferi* unlikely within 48 hours of tick attachment, therefore prompt removal of tick essential **Clinical features:** Initially erythema migrans (60-80%), associated lymphadenopathy, general malaise, and arthralgia. Aseptic meningitis, cranial nerve lesions, myopericarditis, AV block, cardiomegaly, and arthritis may occur up to 2 years after infection **Treatment:** Penicillin and tetracyclines Vaccine currently available in United States
Newcastle disease *Paramyxovirus*	Domesticated and wild birds	Poultry workers Pet shop staff Vets	**Distribution:** Rare in United Kingdom, occasional outbreaks in import quarantines **Mode of acquisition:** Direct contact with eyes or inhalation **Clinical features:** Mild systemic illness with conjunctivitis **Treatment:** Nil
Nipah virus *Paramyxovirus*	Natural hosts— possibly fruit bats Pigs	Pig farmers Abattoir staff	**Distribution:** South East Asia **Mode of acquisition:** Direct contact with infected blood, body fluids, or tissue **Incubation period:** 4-18 days **Clinical features:** Influenza type symptoms with severe headache, fever, respiratory symptoms, encephalitis. Death occurs in about 50% of those with symptoms **Treatment:** Supportive treatment; ribavarin has been used but effectiveness is uncertain Classified as a Hazard Group 4 agent
Orf *Parapoxvirus* **Prescribed disease**	Sheep and goats	Farm workers Abattoir staff Vets	**Distribution:** Worldwide **Mode of acquisition:** Direct contact with mucous membranes of infected animals **Incubation period:** 3-7 days **Clinical features:** Solitary maculopustular lesion surrounded by erythematous rim. Lesion dries, and crust detaches after 6-8 weeks with no persisting scar. With secondary bacterial infection, cellulitis and regional lymphadenitis occur **Treatment:** Nil
Psittacosis **Avian chlamydiosis** **Ornithosis** *Chlamydia Psittaci* **Prescribed disease** **RIDDOR reportable**	Waterfowl Pheasants Pigeons Psittacine birds	Poultry workers Pet shop staff Vets	**Distribution:** Worldwide **Mode of acquisition:** Inhalation of aerosols contaminated by infected avian faeces or fomites **Incubation period:** 1-4 weeks **Clinical features:** Fever, headache, myalgia, respiratory symptoms. (non-productive cough). Respiratory symptoms are often disproportionately mild when compared with chest *x* ray findings. Complications include encephalitis, myocarditis, and Stephens-Johnson syndrome **Treatment:** Tetracyclines or erythromycin
Ovine enzootic abortion **Prescribed disease** **RIDDOR reportable**	Sheep		Ovine strains can cause severe a septicaemic illness with intrauterine death in pregnant women. Maternal death due to disseminated intravascular coagulation may also occur. Women who are or may be pregnant should avoid exposure to sheep, particularly during lambing
Q Fever *Coxiella burnetii* **Prescribed disease** **RIDDOR reportable**	Sheep and goats Cattle Cats Dogs Wild rodents	Sheep workers Farmers Meat workers Dairy workers Abattoir staff Vets	**Distribution:** Worldwide **Mode of acquisition:** Inhalation of airborne organism, direct contact with infected animals or products **Incubation period:** 2-3 weeks **Clinical features:** Fever, retrobulbar headache, general malaise, atypical pneumonia. Occasionally, acute hepatitis. Chronic symptoms (months or years after original infection) resulting in endocarditis can occur on prosthetic or abnormal valves

continued

Appendix I   continued

Disease and infectious agent	Main animal reservoir	Workers at risk	Features
			Treatment: Tetracyclines. Endocarditis will require specialist advice with combination therapy A vaccine is available in some countries for at-risk workers
Ringworm Various species of genera *Trichophyton,* *Microsporum* *Epidermophyton*	Dogs Cattle Cats	Vets Farmers	**Distribution:** Worldwide **Mode of acquisition**: Direct skin-to-skin contact **Incubation period:** Variable but usually 3-5 days for infection to become established and 2-3 weeks for symptoms to manifest **Clinical features:** Depends on site and causative agent, but *T. verrucosum* (from cattle) may produce large pustular lesions (kerions). Lesions on trunk or legs consist of prominent red margin with scaly central area **Treatment**: Mild infection responds to topical antifungals. Oral antifungals such as griseofulvin or terbinafine may be necessary when topical therapy fails
Streptococcus suis **Prescribed disease** **RIDDOR reportable**	Pigs	Pig workers Pork processors	**Distribution:** Worldwide **Mode of acquisition:** Direct contact with infected pigs or pork **Clinical features:** Primary skin infection with surrounding erythema and associated septicaemia and meningitis. Sequelae include ataxia and deafness in those with meningitis. Case fatality is extremely high in asplenics. Arthritis, pharyngitis, and diarrhoea may also occur **Treatment:** Penicillin
Toxoplasmosis *Toxoplasma gondii*	Cats	Farm workers Vets	**Distribution:** Worldwide **Mode of acquisition:** Ingestion of undercooked infected meat, contact with contaminated soil, contact with infected animals **Incubation period:** 5-20 days **Clinical features:** Mostly asymptomatic, but some have glandular fever type symptoms. Primary infection in pregnancy may result in fetal infection, abortion, intrauterine death, chorioretinitis, hepatomegaly, hydrocephalus, and mental retardation. Cerebral toxoplasmosis may occur particularly in the immunocompromised. Reactivation of latent infection may also occur **Treatment:** Not routine for uncomplicated acute infection in healthy immunocompetent adults. For toxoplasmic encephalitis a combination of pyrimethamine and sulphadiazine or pyrimethamine with clindamycin or clarithromycin, but expert advice should be sought. Spiramycin may reduce risk of transmission of maternal infection to fetus

Appendix II

Important occupationally acquired infections from human sources

Disease and infectious agent	Features
Measles *Paramyxovirus* **Notifiable disease** **Immunisation available**	**Distribution:** Although the incidence decreased after introduction of vaccination. In the United Kingdom, due to unsubstantiated concerns regarding the combined measles, mumps, and rubella vaccine, immunisation rates have dropped and outbreaks are predicted **Mode of acquisition:** Airborne by droplet spread or direct contact with nose and throat secretions. Measles is one of the most highly communicable diseases **Incubation period**: 7-18 days. **Communicability**: 1 day before the prodromal period to 4 days after the appearance of rash **Clinical features:** Prodromal fever, conjunctivitis, coryza, and Koplik's spots on buccal mucosa. Red maculopapular facial rash starts on day 3-4, and then spreads to trunk and limbs. Complications include pneumonia and encephalitis. Subacute sclerosing panencephalitis is a rare late and fatal complication developing several years after initial infection **The decrease in vaccine uptake in the United Kingdom will mean that non-immune healthcare workers are at high risk of nosocomial infection, but currently there is no consistent screening policy to identify those at risk. In the United States, all non-immune healthcare workers are identified at pre-employment and offered immunisation if non-immune** Human normal immunoglobulin (HNIG) can be offered to those who are non-immune and have compromised immunity
Meningococcal infection *Neisseria menigitidis* **Notifiable disease** **Vaccines available against serogroups A, C, W135 and Y**	**Distribution:** Worldwide there are 13 serogroups; in Europe serogroups B and C predominate. About 10% of the population are asymptomatic carriers **Mode of acquisition:** Person-to-person through respiratory droplets and direct contact with nose and throat secretions. Infectivity is relatively low and transmission requires prolonged close contact **Incubation period:** 2-10 days. **Communicability:** Patients are generally not infectious within 24 hours of antibiotic treatment **Clinical features:** Symptoms of meningitis. The appearance of a petechial rash signifies septicaemia **Healthcare personnel are rarely at risk therefore routine immunisation not indicated. Only intimate contact with infected patients—for example, mouth-to-mouth resuscitation would warrant antibiotic prophylaxis**
Fifth disease **Erythema infectosum** *Parvovirus B19*	**Distribution:** Worldwide, common in childhood **Mode of acquisition:** Person-to person by droplet spread. Rarely by contaminated blood products. It is highly infectious **Incubation period:** 4-20 days. **Communicability:** From 7 days before the appearance of rash until onset of rash. In aplastic crises, infectivity may last for up to a week after the rash appears. In the immunosuppressed with severe anaemia, infectivity may last for months or years **Clinical features:** Initially fever that lasts until rash appears. The rash is maculopapular and generally on the limbs. The cheeks often have a "slapped cheek" appearance. Illness is mild in immunocompetent individuals, although sometimes, persistent joint pain may occur. In those with haemoglobinopathies, transient aplastic crises may occur, and in the immunosuppressed, red cell aplasia and chronic anaemia may occur. Infection in the first 20 weeks of pregnancy can cause hydrops fetalis and fetal loss **Pregnant women <21/40, immunocompromised individuals or those with heamoglobinopathies who have a significant contact with an infected healthcare worker in the 7 days before onset of rash will need further follow-up. In the case of immunocompromise the administration of intravenous immunoglobulin may be considered**
Rubella **Notifiable disease** **Immunisation available**	**Distribution:** Rare in most countries in Western Europe due to vaccination programmes **Mode of acquisition:** Direct person-to-person contact by respiratory droplets **Incubation period:** 2-3 weeks **Communicability:** 1 week before onset of rash to about 4 days later **Clinical features:** Generally a mild fever with sore throat and conjunctivitis precedes a macular rash. Persistent joint infection occasionally occurs, but complete and rapid recovery usual. The main importance clinically is the risk of congenital rubella syndrome
Scabies *Sarcoptes scabiei var. hominis*	**Distribution:** Worldwide **Mode of acquisition:** Transfer of parasites by direct contact with infested skin **Incubation period:** There may be no sign of infection for 2-4 weeks after exposure, although re-exposure may result in rash within a few days **Communicability:** Remains infectious until it is treated **Clinical features:** Rash which is variable (pimples, vesicles, and nodules), burrows may be seen in finger webs, and itching particularly at night. If there is impaired immunity, large numbers of mites may present (Norwegian Scabies) **If healthcare staff are infected they can return to work once treatment is completed**

continued

Appendix II   continued

Staphylococcus aureus	**Distribution:** Worldwide, but highest rates of resistant strains are in countries with liberal infection control policies such as Japan and Korea. It is carried as a skin commensal at any one time by about 30% of the population. Strains resistant to Penicillinase stable β-lactams are referred to as methicillin resistant *staphylococcus aureus* (MRSA). Recent additional problems include the emergence of resistance to mupirocin, the mainstay of treatment of skin or nasal carriage, and case reports of intermediate-level resistance to vancomycin (VISA) in Japan, France, and United States

Disease and infectious agent	Features
	Mode of acquisition: The significance of MRSA is that the organism colonises the skin, nose, and throat of both patients and healthcare staff, spreads readily by direct contact, and hence is an important cause of hospital acquired infections. While patients are usually responsible for spread of infection, the introduction of MRSA into unaffected areas by colonised staff is well documented, and staff hands are an important route of cross-infection **Incubation period:** 4-10 days, but disease may not occur until several months after colonisation **Clinical features:** Infection may cause both trivial and deep-seated infections; particular problems include infected bedsores or surgical wounds **Control of MRSA is therefore essential to patient care, and relies on scrupulously applied infection control programmes and stringent antibiotic policies**
Viral haemorrhagic fevers Lassa, Ebola, Marburg, and Crimean/Congo fevers Notifiable diseases	**Distribution:** Africa, South America, Middle East, and Eastern Europe **Mode of acquisition:** Main concern is that of potential secondary infection in healthcare workers as a result of accidental exposure to infected blood or body fluids **Incubation period:** 3-21 days **Clinical features:** Initial symptoms include general malaise, fever, headache, and muscle and joint pain. Obvious bleeding occurs at a later or terminal stage **In the England and Wales, the Advisory Committee on Dangerous Pathogens provides guidelines on response to a suspected case. Patients at moderate or high risk should be admitted to special isolation facilities, and strict infection control is necessary. For close contacts of high risk cases, daily surveillance for 21 days from the last possible exposure date is necessary**

Index

The complete ABC series

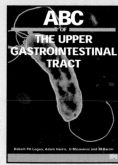

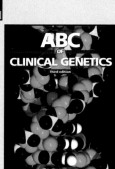

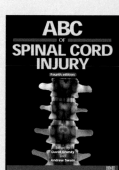